Science of Mind Archives & Library Foundation

Extension Study Course in the Science Of Mind

Volume 2: Lessons 13-24

by Ernest Holmes

Questions and Answers by Reginald C. Armor

ISBN # 978-0-9897300-4-4

Published by Science of Mind Archives & Library Foundation
573 Park Point Drive
Golden, CO 80401
http://scienceofmindarchives.org

For further information on Science of Mind®, visit Science of Mind Archives & Library Foundation at
http://scienceofmindarchives.org
573 Park Point Drive, Golden, Colorado, 80401

Contents

Law of Mind in Action

Office of the Dean

My Dear Friend,
You are now starting on the second quarter of this Course. We hope that your studies have helped you to a better understanding of your relationship with the Universe. If during these first twelve lessons you have come to believe that there is a Divine Presence in which you live and move and have your being, and a Law of Good that you can use, then you are well on the road to the discovery of the secret which has been man's quest through all the ages.

You now have completed our brief lessons on the Bible, and we trust that you have carefully read the comparative passages from other Bibles of the World. It is plain that the source of all the great religions has emanated from the One Source of all being, which is the Living Spirit. Each has told the story in his own tongue and they have told pretty much the same story.

You can find numerous books on comparative religions in any library. I particularly recommend *The Golden Bough* by Frazer for a complete exposition of the mystery religions.

But never forget that the real Bible is written in your own mind, soul, and heart, because you are an incarnation of God, the Living Spirit.

Now we must continue putting our studies more and more to the actual use of the greatest Principle of nature ever discovered, which is the Law of Mind in Action.

Sincerely,
Ernest Holmes

Lesson 13

Page 123 to *Oneness with All Law, page 127*

Our lesson states that each one maintains a personal identity in the Law. We are all individuals, each being a center of God-consciousness in the Cosmic Whole. No two are alike. Rooted in unity, we express the infinite variations of the play of Life upon Itself. In a gigantic forest each tree is rooted in a common soil, each draws from this common soil its nourishment, and each individualizes from that soil a unique variation of form. But in the case of our individuality, unlike the tree we are not rooted in one spot. We have choice, will, and imagination; we are real identities in Mind.

We cannot ponder too long or earnestly upon this marvelous unity of the whole, a unity which leaves room for every possible constructive personal self-expression. No greater gift than this could be given, no greater freedom than this could be conceived. This unity is the basic principle upon which all treatments should be given—a knowledge that God is All in All, over all, and through all, and that the Trinity includes man.

Turn now to page 638 and read our definition of *Trinity* and again you will see that through the Trinity of God-in-man there runs a self-conscious Spirit which distinguishes man from all other forms of life on this planet. We are not separated from Life but distinct entities in Life. So we are distinct entities in a Universal Wholeness.

Your personality is not an illusion; it is real. It is not something to condemn but to praise and bless. We never deny the reality of personality. We affirm that it is a part of the Eternal Reality. On page 617, *Personality* is defined as *that which constitutes distinction of person*. It is the objective evidence of individuality. Therefore our personality is the unique use we make of that Principle within us which is God, the Living Spirit Almighty.

The more completely conscious we are of the Indwelling Spirit the more dynamic our personality will become. Back of each of us stands the Whole, surging into self-expression through our thought. *To learn how to think is to learn how to live* (page 123). We do not bring good into our experience by holding thoughts, but by knowing the Truth. We must repeatedly consider this thought—there is no mental coercion whatsoever in our work. Our work is a spontaneous recognition of the spiritual universe in which we live, a recognition which automatically demonstrates.

Page 486, *God's Will for His Children*, shows that if there is but One Power, then there is nothing opposed to the Truth; that one in league with the Truth constitutes a majority. Again we see that our work is knowing the Truth and not holding thoughts. But what is the Truth we are to know? That Pure Spirit exists at the center of every physical object, animates all nature, flows through every activity, and objectifies Itself in all form, over all, in all, and through all.

It is this Spirit at the very center of your being which is the power back of your words. *He is ever inside. The outer rim of Reality is exactly at the center of Itself* (page 486). This is what the ancients meant when they spoke of the Truth as being that whose center is everywhere and whose circumference is nowhere. It is the teaching of the Macrocosm and the microcosm.

When we learn to speak from this Divine Center our words will have irresistible power because nothing opposes the Truth. It is the Father's good pleasure to give us the Kingdom. This Divine gift is forever made. Our part lies in our recognition of this Divine gift, in our willingness to comply with its laws of love and harmony and in our knowledge that we may consciously use the Law of the Lord, which is perfect. This is not a selfish concept nor is it a self-centered one. It is a legitimate concept of self-expression. Man exists to glorify God, because man is the Law of the Lord executing Itself. Man is the personality of God. Man is God incarnated. *There is none beside me . . . for I am God, and there is none else.*

Read the last paragraph on page 416 and note that it makes a great difference what we are impressing upon the Law of our being or what we are mentally entertaining as being true about ourselves. You will readily see that the entire race, through ignorance, produces the very limitation which it experiences—the civilized man after his mold and the savage after his mold.

The Law knows no purpose other than that which we give It. The Law is not a person but a Principle. We are persons. Man is a part of the Divine Person. Over and over we must tell ourselves that our thought is creative, not because we will or wish or hope or pray or long for it to be so; it is creative because that is its nature. We did not make this law; we cannot change it. Until now we have been using it in ignorance, and since ignorance of the Law excuses no one from its effects, be they good or ill, by the very law of freedom we have created bondage. But now by reversing our use of the law we create freedom. This we do by sensing the joy of the Spirit within us.

Turn to page 538 and read the Meditation at the top of the page, *Fullness of Light*, and at the bottom of the page, *Joy Has Come to Live with Me*. We must meditate upon statements similar to these until the intellect, the imagination, and the will become saturated with the realization of the Divine Presence. Then there will dawn upon us the conviction that this Presence which inhabits eternity also indwells our own souls. This will have an action on the mind similar to that physical action which takes place in our objective world when the sun rises—the darkness of night disappears and warmth and color flood the earth with a new glow. Spiritual meditations awaken a recognition of the Divine, and in our system of thought they are absolutely essential to demonstration. Turn to the Meditation, *Arise, My Spirit* at the bottom of page 536. See if this will not have a tendency to awaken within you a deeper sense of the Indwelling Christ.

On page 439 is the story of a woman who was diseased with an issue of blood for twelve years. She came up and touched the hem of Jesus' garment. Being aware of her presence, that is, sensing her mental atmosphere, Jesus turned to her and said, *Thy faith hath made thee whole*. How marvelous, how sublime, and how practical is this lesson in impersonal healing! *And the woman was made whole from that hour.*

Now what do you suppose caused her healing? Does it not seem probable that the consciousness of Jesus, at all times elevated to a comprehension of the indwelling God, was the healing power which the woman in her own faith contacted and inbreathed into her soul? Or perhaps her contact with his consciousness awakened a corresponding response in her inner thought. In any event she was made whole through a combination of belief and acceptance, and a conscious contact with Jesus' exalted idea of Reality.

Should we not all be filled with this same power? If we were, would it not follow that those who contact us would be uplifted? This, we think, is the desire of every sincere student of Truth. This is why it is necessary for people to gather together in groups, for the collective consciousness or the sum total of the belief of a group, generally rises higher than the individual consciousness, and all who contact it are helped by it. This is what Jesus meant when he said, *For where two or three are gathered together in my name, there am I in the midst of them*. Each has been furnished with a Divine torch. The wick of this torch is embedded in the oil of Spirit. Thus the Bible tells us: *The spirit of man is the candle of the Lord.*

How are we going to reconcile suffering and lack with the Goodness of God? (page 123, third paragraph). Again we are confronted with the age-long problem of evil, and we must give the only intelligent answer the world has so far received—lack and limitation are not things of themselves but rather the way in which we demonstrate our freedom. They are forms which can be changed.

Turn to page 591 under the heading, *The Fall*, and read through to the top of page 593. You will find a comprehensive explanation of the problem of evil. This is not only the explanation which the Christian Bible gives us, but the one which deeply thoughtful and spiritual-minded teachers of the ages have repeated in one way or another, using varying symbols and word pictures for the purpose of teaching this central truth—the Spirit is infinite and creates out of Itself by Self-contemplation, which means Self-knowingness. Man in his world reproduces this infinite possibility.

If you will carefully read the analysis of the variations of consciousness in the last paragraph on page 123 you will see that there is an ascending and descending scale of consciousness, from the lowest to the highest and the highest to the lowest, but that a thread of unity runs through all. This Lowell refers to as that *thread of the all-sustaining beauty which runs through all things, and doth all unite*.

Since Life Itself is infinite, Its variations must be infinite. Mind is one, but there are different levels of consciousness. To realize that when we look at discord we are creating it, and when looking into apparent discord and seeing harmony we are overcoming evil with good, is to arrive at a knowledge of the correct use of the spiritual power that is within us. It is the Law of Cause and Effect.

Turn to page 126 where you will find the statement that each of us is a result of the conscious or unconscious use we have made of this Law of Cause and Effect. This does not mean that we are dealing with duality, as though limitation were produced by a law of lack, and freedom by a law of abundance. It is the same law working two ways. There are varying gradations of consciousness in the use of the Word, therefore gradations of effect—sometimes we demonstrate what we call a little and sometimes what we call a lot, but always cause and effect remain inviolate because we have the same Life in us which is in God.

On page 475 under the heading *The Word of Power* you will note that Jesus was explaining that the life which we now have is the Life of God. Therefore in such degree as our word is spoken with a consciousness of power, it carries that very power of which it is conscious. Our whole system of demonstration is a method of self-awakening, achieving self-awareness, self-recognition, a sense of an intimate relation to the Infinite Life. This is entirely an inner act of thought; you do not go outside yourself to awaken this power which is already within you. You merely use it, and by Divine seeing, so to speak, bring harmony into existence where discord was.

The Word has power only as it is one with power (page 476). The Word is a mold, belief is a mold, faith is a mold, visualization is a mold, all thoughts are molds. The power flows into the mold, takes its form, and becomes projected into our experience. (For a complete explanation of *Visualization* turn to page 643 and read through to the top of page 645).

Words without conviction have no power. Conviction without words will never distribute or give form to the Creative Principle. We must combine faith and belief with the consciously spoken word, that is, with a definite intention. When you give a treatment you know exactly what you want to happen. It is impossible to give a scientific treatment on any other basis, for no matter how much power you generate, unless you distribute it, it will never do anything. *In treatment there should be first a realization of power, then a spoken word. One generates, the other distributes* (page 476, third paragraph).

Jesus taught his disciples that it was done unto them as they believed, not as they wished (page 127). The truth of this statement cannot be too strongly emphasized. In giving a mental and spiritual treatment you are using a power which actually takes the form of your thought. When you really believe that the power of which you think already exists, that belief creates the form. That is the meaning of the second paragraph on page 411: ... *the very law which creates bondage could as easily create freedom.* Having no intent of Its own, you give It intention. Having no direction of Its own, you direct It.

You will find this same thought expressed at the bottom of page 339: *God moves upon God*. This is the starting point of all creation. *We, as conscious Spirit, set a Universal Law in motion which makes things from ideas . . . Always, It is an obedient servant* (page 340).

Remember that we are dealing with law, and law is always neutral. Law is law in the mental and spiritual world just as it is in the physical, and we must recognize it as such. Thus it is said that each one is held accountable for the very words he speaks. *For by thy words thou shall be justified, and by thy words thou shall be condemned.*

We must see to it that our words are spoken with a deep sense of the Indwelling Spirit, and should not these words be spoken with an idea of beauty also, and with a comprehension of peace? Whatever quality we put into our thought must give birth to form, and the form must partake of the nature of the thought. Consequently the thought should be calm, peaceful, poised, and at the same time enthusiastic.

Summary

You are an individual center in the Consciousness of God. All things are rooted in the One Mind and the One Life, but each is a unique individualization of that One.

Human personality is real; it is not an illusion.

Personality is an objective evidence of the Indwelling Spirit. It is the Spirit of you back of your personality which speaks through that personality.

All words used in meditation, affirmative prayer, and treatment should be spoken from this center, with deep conviction. The Law of Mind has no purpose except the one we give It. It is like any other principle in nature. The Law is a servant; you are the master.

Each of us is surrounded by a mental atmosphere which reflects our inward consciousness of the Spirit and our activity in the Law. This atmosphere affects those around us.

One of our great desires should be that we help everyone who contacts us, and bless everything that we contact.

There is an ascending and a descending scale of consciousness, from an atom to an archangel, all in one Supreme Intelligence.

Whether we know it or not, we create our own destiny.

One of the most important things to realize is that the life we now live is God. There is only one Life, never two.

Words without conviction have no power, and conviction without words will do nothing because the conviction is not directed.

God moves upon God; nothing acts but Intelligence, and nothing reacts but Intelligence.

Questions

Brief answers to these questions should be written out by the student after studying the lesson, and the answers compared with those which will be included in next week's lesson.

1. Does our individuality imply separateness?
2. Upon what basic principle are mental treatments given?
3. Is personality evil or an illusion?
4. Is it necessary consciously to hold thoughts in mental treatment?
5. Why do we release thought instead of holding it in mental treatment?
6. What is the power back of our word?
7. What is man?
8. How can we replace bondage with freedom in our experience?
9. What do we mean by reversing our use of the Law?
10. Why will changing thought patterns change our conditions?
11. What is the efficacy of spiritual meditation in treatment?
12. What is impersonal spiritual healing?
13. What is the meaning of an ascending and descending scale of consciousness?
14. What do we mean when we say that the word, belief, faith, etc., are molds?
15. Why must faith and belief be combined with the spoken word?
16. Can one have Spiritual Power without using It?
17. What do we mean in connection with treatment when we say that God moves upon God?
18. In treatment why should our thought be calm, peaceful, poised, and at the same time enthusiastic?

Answers to Questions on Lesson 12

1. There is no explanation of why subjective mind acts creatively on our thought. It is its nature to reflect thought as form, as it is the nature of a mirror to reflect image as form.
2. By the mechanical reaction of mental law we mean that its reaction is compulsory, mechanical, and exact in its operation.
3. By *The Absolute* we mean the unconditioned Life Principle or First Cause, depending upon nothing but Itself. *The relative* is always an effect.
4. The subjective state of our thought is the cause of our conditions because it represents the sum total of ideas we are holding before the Creative Law of Mind.

5. Conscious mind entertaining new ideas changes the subjective state of our thought.
6. We do not control the Absolute; we control our use of It.
7. Our use of the Law is conditioned by our understanding of It, which means: *first*, knowledge that such a Law exists; *second*, definite operation of our word upon the Law; *third*, complete confidence and acceptance that definite results will follow.
8. The Kingdom of God will be revealed to us when our thought becomes clear enough to see it.
9. The good we desire will automatically and continuously become a part of our experience when our subjective acceptance of such good becomes automatic and continuous.
10. The Spirit of Christ means a recognition of and conscious cooperation with our own Divinity. The Spirit of Antichrist means a lack of such recognition which could lead to a negative or destructive use of the Law of God Mind.
11. No. It implies the possibility of one's choice in the use of the one Law of God Mind.
12. We dissipate evil or negation from our lives by a conscious, persistent, and positive recognition of good.
13. A certain amount of mental suggestion necessarily enters into every contact with life. However, this practice is mental explanation and spiritual re-education, and hypnotism and mesmerism do not enter into it.
14. The self-knowing mind is the conscious, discerning, spiritual faculty within us. The subconscious mind is not an entity, but is our individual use of the Law of Cause and Effect.

How to Create a Spiritual Chain Reaction

No one lives entirely by himself. We are all individual parts of humanity, and whether or not we realize it, each is influencing those around him, and each in his turn is being influenced by others. No doubt the thoughts and opinions and actions of the whole world finally are based on what everyone thinks and believes.

Since the explosion of the first atom bomb we have read a great deal about the possibility of a physical chain reaction that might destroy civilization as we understand it. Dr. Einstein and a number of leading physicists who understand these things better than we do have told us that there is such a possibility, and that consequently the nations must learn to live together in peace and harmony or face the other possibility, the very thought of which makes us shudder.

But science has also told us that this same power, if properly used, can become an instrument for the most rapid advance in civilization the world has ever known. The limitless energy that they now know how to loose could be used for the purpose of irrigating all the wastelands of the world. It might even be used in the field of medicine for the purpose of healing disease. It certainly could be used in industry everywhere. This energy might some day take the place of coal and oil and all the other natural energies that we use in modern life.

It seems almost as though nature were placing before us the possibility of the greatest blessing the world has ever had, or wrongly used, the greatest destruction. And so modern scientists are telling us that before we go any further in uncovering the energies of nature we had better stop, look, and listen, and be certain that every new advance in science is used for the betterment of humanity and not for its destruction.

We happen to know of another kind of energy which we feel is even more important than the physical energy created through the explosion of the atom. And this is the energy of faith, of affirmative prayer and spiritual meditation. There is no reason to doubt that in the field of spiritual consciousness a chain reaction could be created which would bless the whole world. And since the world finally acts the way it thinks, should a majority of people come to believe in spiritual power and the benefits that can be obtained from it, they would all have a great desire to try a new kind of experiment, one that would bless instead of curse humanity.

Did you ever notice the contagion of a happy person; one who has an enthusiastic joy in living? His spirit permeates those around him, and the contagion of his personality influences his environment to such an extent that it finally changes it. Have you ever noticed the effect that a calm and poised person has on others? How they feel safe in his presence?

We are sure you have had the experience of finding yourself more or less frustrated and confused and beginning to wonder what it is all about. Then you have had the privilege of sitting down quietly with someone whose atmosphere is permeated with peace and confidence, and gradually you have felt the rough edges of your agitation disappear until finally your own atmosphere changes, and you are filled with hope and confidence.

One of the most remarkable evidences of how this silent spiritual force works was exhibited in the life of the late Mahatma Gandhi as he sat quietly before perhaps a million people. In these great public meetings a combined atmosphere of confidence and faith was created which they called *darshan*, which means the united spiritual force of a great multitude of people. Vincent Sheean, who wrote a book about Gandhi called *Lead, Kindly Light*, said that he had felt this spiritual realization so completely that it was as though he had bathed in some refreshing stream of life.

This is an example of how spiritual reaction can work. It reaches out to all around and sets in motion a chain reaction to which there is no limit.

We know that the Power that does this is good; it is a power of life, love, truth, beauty, and peace. It is not only a power; it is the final Power in the universe because it is God. And it is God present everywhere and in all people. For just as there is an energy caught from the universe and locked in the physical atom that can be loosed, so there is a spiritual energy caught in every person's mind and locked up in the individual life waiting to be used.

Faith and conviction are the instruments through which this energy is used. And just as in physical science natural energy is hooked up to run a machine or a streetcar or to create light and heat for definite purposes, so we can use the spiritual power that is within us to heal, to bless, and to prosper those whom we think of.

It is wonderful to realize that we can sit in the quiet of our own being and consciously direct a Power greater than we are for the definite purpose of helping ourselves and someone else. This Power should be used for both purposes. For we have to get back to this simple proposition—we must use the Power to help ourselves first, in order that we may establish a realization of our ability to use It for others.

If you would bring happiness to those around you, you must first become happy yourself. But before you can become happy something has to happen to you that causes you to know that God is right where you are, that good is the final Power in the universe, and that love is an all-conquering force. You have to have confidence and self-assurance. And this kind of confidence and self-assurance comes only through having proved to yourself completely that there is a Power greater than you are, that It is a power for good, that It is available, and that you actually know how to use It. And the only proof you will ever have is what It does to you and to others.

Jesus understood this perfectly. He explained it simply. It is what he meant when he said, *As thou hast believed, so be it done unto thee*. In a certain sense he was a very scientific man in that he placed complete reliance on the Law of Good. And he was a practical man in that he said, *These signs shall follow* ... For he knew that anyone who uses the creative energy of faith will receive a direct answer or will see a sign following the use of this Power.

Jesus took the ideas of faith and prayer out of the realm of speculation and theory and put them into the realm of fact and experience. He made his religion and his spiritual conviction come alive and move through him into action. Through him it healed the sick, raised the dead, multiplied the loaves and fishes, turned water into wine, stilled the wind and wave, and above everything else it brought a consciousness of peace and security to those whom it touched.

It is this proof that we need and must have, and fortunately for us we do have this proof in an ever increasing volume. We can pray effectively if we decide to. We can build up a faith within ourselves if we have the will. We can learn to live with a sense of confidence and security if we will just get over our fears. And we can prove that love is the greatest healing power in the world.

The laboratory in which we work is our own mind, the instruments are our own thoughts, and the method is affirmative prayer and meditation. Meditation draws us close to the Divine Reality so that we sense Its atmosphere and feel Its presence. When we think about peace we become peaceful. And it is out of this feeling of peace that we speak our affirmation of power. It is from this peace that we affirm the presence of love and truth and goodness. Because our prayer of affirmation works exactly like any other law in nature, signs will follow our belief.

We need such signs. If a scientific man announced that he had discovered a new principle in nature but was never able to prove it, how would we know whether or not he was right? He might possibly be just dreaming about something that had no existence, and we should lose all confidence in him. But if he proved it to us we should know that he was right.

And so it is with the life of the Spirit. We say that God is all there is, love is an all-conquering force, faith will produce results. This is our theory. Certainly it is the most beautiful theory in the world—God, love, and faith. But now we have to prove our claim. And in so doing we shall double our capacity to use this Power.

We should use this Power in everything we do. The Power that holds a grain of sand in place is the same Power that holds the planets in their places. There is nothing big or little or hard or easy as far as the Power is concerned. It is the same Power working in and upon everything. This is the Power which we use.

Do not hesitate to use affirmative prayer for any good purpose and for all purposes that are constructive. For in so doing you will most certainly be starting a chain reaction in that particular direction. Do not think it unimportant for you to be friendly to everyone you meet, because your friendliness will start a reaction in them which will cause them to be friendly to everyone they meet and the thing will multiply and expand. It might even reach around the world. Let us, then, do everything we can to increase our own faith and conviction, and be equally certain that we are using this faith and conviction in everything we are doing.

If you want to start a chain reaction that will help those around you—realizing that it must begin at the center of your own being—suppose you take time daily to say to yourself, very simply and sincerely and perhaps repeat the process a number of times each day:

> *I know that nothing but good can go from me and nothing but good can return. It is my inward desire that everything I touch, every person I think of, shall be blessed and helped. It is my affirmative prayer, which I completely accept, that even as I pass people in the street some silent influence of good shall reach from me to them.*

If we make a practice of this we shall find something new and wonderful begin to happen, for we shall be silently broadcasting our own conviction and silently starting a chain reaction which must finally accomplish its purpose, because it is dealing with a Law of Good. We must be careful to avoid thinking that we are unimportant in the scheme of things. We are the most important persons living, as far as we are concerned.

This is not egotism, not conceit; it is a simple statement of the conviction that each one of us is rooted in the living Spirit, that we have access to the Mind of God and the love and the power and the peace of the Spirit. It is a simple conviction that no matter how humble our walk in life may appear to be, it must of necessity influence its own environment. We may not be important to men, but we certainly are necessary to God.

Placing our entire trust, our complete faith, our whole conviction in this simple thought, we should walk in confidence and speak our spiritual convictions with complete assurance, knowing that there is a Presence and a Power with us and for us and operating through us—a Presence and a Power that knows no defeat.

Meditation

Realizing that the Divine Spirit is present everywhere, and including myself in this Divine Presence, I now recognize and affirm that there is a perfect Life at the center of my own being. Every organ and action and function of my physical body is permeated with this Life. And there is a rhythm of love and peace and joy that pulsates through me. It is the harmony of God.

I now recognize that there is a Divine Intelligence that governs everything, and I affirm that this Divine Intelligence guides me into right action in everything I do and say and think.

Desiring only that which is good, for myself and for others, I affirm the Presence of Good in my own experience. I have complete confidence in It. I accept It. I know that I live and move and have my being in this Presence. And I know that everything I do shall prosper. I affirm that I am surrounded by love and friendship because only love and friendship exist in my own thinking.

It is my desire and my faith and conviction that everyone I contact shall be blessed through my recognition of the Power greater than I am and the Love that encompasses everything.

Thought, Feeling and Emotion

May I start the discussion of this subject by interjecting a personal opinion and one which I quite frankly admit may be wrong? It is for you to judge. I believe that the heart of the Universe, the essence of Reality or God, the Living Spirit, is of the essence of pure feeling. I believe that feeling is back of every creative impulse whether in God or man.

This feeling in human beings and to some degree in animals breaks down into what we call the emotions. I think that feeling is a fundamental essence in the Universe; it is a part of the nature of Reality. Our emotions are this original feeling flowing through us as the Universe individualizes Itself in us. There cannot be anything true about the individual unless it is first true about the Universe. By the same token, anything that is true about the Universe must be true about the individual, for the individual is a microcosm within a Macrocosm, or a little world within a big world, or as we state the proposition, an individualized center in the Creative Consciousness of God.

In psychiatry and psychosomatic medicine it is believed that there is a definite, fundamental, irrepressible emotion or feeling back of everything, an urge to flow through everything creatively. This has been called the libido or the emotional craving back of all things toward self-expression, the repression of which leads to psychoneurosis. Psychoneurosis means a congestion of this emotion. That there is such a feeling back of everything I do not doubt, and whether we call it the libido or the urge makes no difference. There is an emotional craving for self-expression back of everything, and when it is repressed it does lead to trouble and pretty serious trouble; perhaps to a large percentage of all of our troubles.

But even emotion and feeling are things of thought because they cannot function without consciousness, and the movement of consciousness is thought.

I realize that this proposition can be contested, and elaborate explanations written to prove it is not true and that thought itself is only the result of some kind of stimulus. This, however, has never been scientifically proved, and the whole tendency today is away from it rather than with it.

As far as we are concerned, then, we shall assume that there is a thinker, an ego, an entity, a person, and that behind him is an irresistible impulsion to express Life. In a certain sense he must live or die; he must create or perish; he must express Life, or the Life seeking expression through him will flow back inside him. There will then be a pressure from within out, and a pressure from without in. It is in this inner or between point that unconscious conflicts occur.

If we can accept the proposition that feeling and emotion are certain ways of thinking, and actually reduce them to thought or to Mind in Action, then we can see how it is that thought can change them. As a matter of fact this is what psychiatry and spiritual and mental counseling does. It may do this through having the patient talk his troubles out of himself with the kindly guidance of a wise counselor, or it may be done as in our method by the practitioner thinking back to the spiritual reality of his patient and identifying the patient with it.

The results will be the same except that in ordinary counseling the logical implications of the spiritual nature of the patient are not emphasized. But if we are rooted in this deep Reality, which we know that we must be, it follows that our thought should reach back even through the feeling and the emotion to Reality Itself.

We recognize that we cannot do this by the intellect alone. Our work has a feeling about it, a feeling of the Divine Presence and the emotion of Infinite Love. As metaphysicians, or those who believe in spiritual mind healing, we do not deny physical facts or psychic facts, nor do we hesitate to affirm that there are spiritual facts. We should put them all together. The emotions affect the physical body, and the mind can be destructive or constructive according to the way it is used. For this is the Law of Mind in Action. But back of it all is the Actor.

Wise counseling leads from the act to the actor, and brings the patient to what is called self-awareness, to a place where he sees why he acted as he did and why he can just as well act differently. It takes him back through all his emotions to the place where he was when he was an infant before all of his troubles started.

But just taking him back there is not enough, even though it does have a salutary effect. He must consciously recognize his union with the Infinite, his oneness with Life, his partnership with God.

Here is an interesting thought to speculate on. If feeling and emotion acting through the avenue of consciousness can produce such havoc, what would happen if the same feeling and emotion were constructively employed? What would happen if we could convert the energy of fear to faith, the energy of doubt and uncertainty into a feeling of belonging to the Universe and being safe in It? Would not the Original Artist Himself go forth into new creation through us?

Bibles of the World

Fragments from the spiritual history of the race
revealing fundamental UNITY of religious thought of our experience

SHINTOISM - Every little yielding to anxiety is a step away from the natural heart of man.

SIKHISM - Divine knowledge shall be revealed to him into whose heart hath entered faith in God. He shall abide free from fear, and be absorbed in Him from Whom he sprang.

TAOISM - Faith, if insufficient, is apt to become no faith at all.

ZOROASTRIANISM - The religion of the Wise One cleanses the faithful from every evil thought, word and deed, as a swift-rushing wind cleanses the plain.

BUDDHISM - Wide opened is the door of the Immortal to all who have ears to hear. Let them send forth faith to meet it.

A man full of faith, if endowed with virtue and glory, is respected whatever place he may choose.

JUDAISM and CHRISTIANITY - Be not faithless, but believing. The just shall live by faith.

Know that the Lord thy God, he is God, the faithful God, who keepeth covenant and mercy with them who love him and keep his commandments.

HINDUISM - The man of faith obtaineth wisdom if he is devoted to it, and has restrained his senses; having obtained wisdom, he speedily attains unto the peace which is supreme.

Practical Suggestion for Mental Treatment

The Practitioner Clarifies His Own Thought

Strange as it may seem, after you have listened to the negative statements of your patient in which he presents the case for materiality and produces evidence to prove that he is convicted, you as a practitioner are the first one who needs to be healed of the belief that he must necessarily remain in his prison.

The entire lack, evil, and limitation which he has described must be repudiated. You must silence his belief in your own consciousness. You must recognize that what has been operating through him is neither person, place, nor thing; it is not cause, it is not medium, it is not effect. And you should know that your word completely expels it from his consciousness.

But your word cannot expel it from his consciousness unless at the same time it expels the same condition from your own thought. Again we must reiterate the all-significant fact that the practitioner treats himself to remove the patient's false belief from his own mind.

It would be impossible for any practitioner to do this effectively unless he were first thoroughly convinced that Mind alone is the final creative factor in the universe, and that all movement takes place in consciousness.

Therefore clarify your own consciousness about your patient. And when your statement has clarified your own consciousness (healed your own thought about him), he will come to you and tell you that he is receiving benefit.

Watch this simple process as you silently practice it, and you will be amazed at the dynamic results which will follow.

Right Thought Will Always Externalize Itself

Every treatment should be a law unto itself. When you give a treatment you must know that your word is the law unto the thing which is spoken. Since we are dealing with a mental or a spiritual Principle it follows that the one using this Principle must do so mentally; his operation is a thing of thought; therefore his thought can have only as much power as he knows it to have.

Words of doubt have no affirmative power. We must know that our treatment is a good treatment, a successful treatment certain to accomplish. Every word you speak is the Presence, the Power, and the Activity of the Law within you. It is the Law unto the thing whereof you speak. It cannot and will not return unto you void, but will accomplish the purpose you have in mind. It can and will heal and demonstrate; it can and will produce the desired result.

You are not willing this to be so; you merely have a willingness that it should be so, a willingness to believe. There must be a persistent belief in the power of your own word. You must know that the Law of Good is all-powerful, and that no evil is ordained or intended. You must realize that your knowledge of the Law of Good dissipates all evil and all manifestation of evil.

You must know that right thought will always find an objective form and will always externalize itself. You must believe the will of God is always toward goodness, truth, and beauty. Goodness, truth, and beauty cannot be reversed because they have no opposites, but your knowledge of the Truth can reverse every so-called law of evil.

THE SECRET PLACE of the Most High is at the center of every man's thought; the Tabernacle of the Almighty is man's consciousness of Good. We must come to realize that all the Power there is, is God; all the Presence there is, is God; all the Law there is, is Good; and the only Mind there is, is ours right now.

> *The reservoir of Spirit is always higher than our desire, and will supply it as water in the mountain flows into the valley.*

THE CORRECT understanding that Mind in Its unformed state can be called forth into individual use is the key to all effective mental and spiritual work.

Pure Spirit exists at the center of all form.

WE ARE NOT dealing with the principle of big and little, good and bad, but with the Principle of potentiality. It can be anything to any of us. It must be to each individual what he is to It. It cannot be less, It will not be more.

> *Spirit is never bound by any form It has taken. It is never caught in any form. It is merely manifest through the form.*

MAN unconsciously creates his own destiny. In such degree as he realizes this he may re-create it consciously, subjecting himself no longer to a law of chance but to a law of certainty.

There Is nothing big and nothing little to God.

THE SUM TOTAL of race belief dominates most men's subconscious selves and controls their destiny. To rise above race suggestion is salvation. We are mesmerized by the race consciousness until we extricate ourselves from it.

> *The gift of God is made but we must accept it. As far as we are concerned, it is not made until we do accept it.*

MIND in its conscious state can change mind in its subjective state. Otherwise there would be no possibility of making conscious use of mental Law.

Meditation

I now realize that there is but One Mind, One Presence in the Universe. This Presence is God; pure, absolute, unadulterated Spirit.

This Divine Presence, being everywhere and filling all space, must be in me. It must be that which I am. I recognize It is in me and It is that which I am.

I let this recognition of my indwelling Divinity flow through my entire consciousness. I let it reach down into the very depths of my being. I rejoice in my Divinity.

Again I affirm that the Divine Presence fills all space, including myself. I am full of God; therefore I am filled with Light.

Infinite Intelligence governs every move I make. An All-wise Counselor accompanies me at all times. The Spirit of the Almighty goes before me.

As the light dispels darkness, so this Truth which I now affirm dissipates all fear. It breaks down every doubt and casts out all uncertainty. It looses all sense of bondage within my mind, stimulates my imagination with the vision of peace, of joy, and of abundance, and directs my will toward the accomplishment of my desires.

The Nature of Being

Office of the Dean

My Dear Friend,
Our lesson starts with the idea of our oneness with the Universal Mind. We want you to be sure to realize that there cannot be such a thing as your mind and God's Mind. There is God who is only and God who is all. This God is also in and through you. You use the Mind of God, but when you do this it is God using His Own Mind through you. This is what is meant by being a center of consciousness in God.

We do not put power or intelligence or action into life. We take them out, and the one who best understands this will prove it most perfectly.

You will notice that we are beginning to add practical suggestions for your practice. We are sure you will find them most helpful. They come out of years of experience, and we believe they are fundamentally right in the practice of this science.

Read carefully what we mean by going into the silence. Since there is so much confusion and even superstition about this subject, we want to be sure that you see it as it really is, a normal, natural thing.

In *The Law and the Word*, or *The Sequence of the Creative Order* in this lesson, be sure to note that the very starting point for your demonstration of using the Power of Good is in your own thought; so close to you that you cannot separate yourself from it, for it is you.

We are wishing you great success and happiness in your work.

Sincerely,
Ernest Holmes

Lesson 14

Oneness with All Law, page 127 to the top of page 133

It is our oneness with the Universal Spirit which makes our thought creative. As has been so often stated, we do not hold thoughts, nor do we mentally coerce. What we do is realize truth within our own minds. Because our minds are part of the Universal Mind, the truth which we realize becomes as effective as is the embodiment of our realization. By the embodiment of our realization we mean the actual subjective acceptance of our desire.

On page 596 you will find under *God Consciousness* the statement that *man's self-knowing mind is his Unity with the Whole*. Each one of us is a center of God Consciousness. Each one contacts the Supreme and Omnipotent Mind at the center of his own being. To understand this is one of the most subtle thoughts we can entertain in the Science of Mind, and yet it is at the center of our own being that we must provide those mental equivalents which will supply us with our daily needs.

Under the heading *Equivalent* (page 589), we read that the Divine gift is always made but it must be meted out to us through our acceptance of it. If we believe that only a little good can be ours, then we shall experience only a little good, but if we can believe in more abundant good we shall experience a more abundant good.

That which we call our subjective mind, being a point in Universal Creative Law, guarantees that we have at our disposal the use of a Law which is not only immediate, being inside us as it were, but it is also in connection with every event which transpires on this planet. There is nothing separated from it since it is the creative energy running through all things. You will find in practice that you heal yourself of the belief in the necessity of the condition with which your patient is afflicted.

If you will turn to page 500, *The Prayer of Faith*, you will see in the third paragraph: *When we pray, believing, we erase false ideas from our inner thought, then the Spirit can make the gift.* Before this can happen the prayer of faith must penetrate the subjective thought and neutralize the images of negation that are there.

Over and over again you must assure yourself that in treatment you are never trying to make things happen. You are standing aside and knowing that things are happening. The Law of Peace is at work. The Law of Abundance is finding fulfillment and meeting every legitimate desire. Your statements must be affirmative and in the present tense, since Mind as Law knows no past and no future. It is written that *today is the day of salvation.*

A belief in separation from good has a tendency to keep good away from us. It is the belief that binds us, however, and not any actual power of negation. We are bound by our false beliefs, and we shall never be permanently free until we experience a complete change of thought. This is what is meant by *The Renewing of the Mind* (first paragraph on page 494). Whatever the mind holds to and firmly believes in forms a pattern of thought within its creative mold. This pattern of thought passing from the conscious mind into a subjective state becomes a law of attraction or repulsion, drawing to us or withholding from us in accordance with the sum total of our belief.

First there is the believer, who has the possibility of spontaneous belief. Or we might say first in order of causation, relative to the individual life, there is the thinker, and next there is the thought or belief; after this everything else is a mechanical reaction. The belief is now a part of the Law of Cause and Effect and until it is changed it will operate automatically.

In the fourth paragraph on page 418 you will find the statement: *Ignorance stays with us until the day of enlightenment.* What we are now experiencing we shall cease to experience when we create a new mental image, and then by the very law which has bound us we shall be made free.

On page 404 you will find that the Law, as Law, knows no conditions. The Law depends on ideas, and conditions are the result of ideas. Mental and spiritual treatment is for the purpose of providing new impulses to the thought, new images in the mind. We neutralize fear with faith. We destroy doubt with certainty. We erase the sense of lack with the sense of abundance, and endeavor to transmute all negative thoughts into affirmative ones.

Experience has conclusively proved that our highest images of thought come from our most exalted concept of God, for in the long run man's outlook on life depends on his belief about God and his relationship to the universe of Spirit. To have a concept of the Universal Spirit as being forever available and forever ready and willing to cooperate with us is not only indicative of a healthy mind, but such an attitude will set in motion a dynamic creative power sufficient to free us from the burden of fear, lack, and limitation.

If, as our lesson suggests, man is a point of personality in limitless Mind, and if he is a thinking center in this Mind, then at the very center of his thought rests the possibility of his control of destiny. At first this seems strange and appears to contradict all the experiences of poverty, weakness, sickness, and unhappiness, and arguing from appearances we should expect these same conditions to continue. But when we stop to analyze the proposition we realize that we cannot have an Infinite which is limited. It is the nature of God to be perfect.

It is the business of the practitioner, as suggested at the top of page 621, to sense that the perfection of God is also the perfection of man; to realize that man lives in pure Spirit and *is* pure Spirit. He contradicts his negative experiences and sees them mentally dissipated, and in their place he senses spiritual perfection. The practitioner uses any words that will tend to bring about the desired mental state. Take the statement at the top of page 564: *The Spirit within me, which is God ... is Wholeness*. To dwell upon the meaning of this meditation, to repeat it in one's mind and feel it in one's imagination, is to embody it finally in one's thought, and in such degree as it is embodied it will be projected into actual experience.

Turn to the Meditation at the bottom of page 532, *Complete Confidence*. When you realize the central theme of the thought suggested by it you will be tuning in to the right mental atmosphere to use as a background for your mental work. For as practitioners we must have absolute confidence in what we are doing. We must have absolute certainty that we are working with a Law which cannot fail us, and then we can use that Law for specific purposes. We must know that we have access to a perfect Law, and that we can use this Law for ourselves or anyone who comes to us. Read the Meditation on page 520, *Within Thy Law Is Freedom*.

As stated in the third paragraph on page 128: *Everything comes from Intelligence*. Let us start right over again—if any doubt arises in our mind—realizing that everything does spring from Intelligence. We are some part of a Creative Cause and our word is creative. The most amazing thing you will ever discover in this practice is that you never seek to convince anyone but yourself. Over and over again reiterate this thought: Convince yourself, convince your own mind. Your argument is not directed toward some external appearance but to the dissolving of the belief in your own consciousness that there is any obstruction to spiritual work.

The power of right thinking is such that when you make a demand upon Mind, through belief, the thing in which you believe will appear. Over and over you must repeat this idea of Reality.

In the Summary of Part One on page 129 we learn that there is a Universal Presence which is intelligent, and a Universal Law which obeys the Will of the Spirit. You are spirit and because you are spirit and because the Law is what It is, It cannot do other than obey your word.

There is nothing in the Universe to be afraid of, but until we accept this truth the Law must present us with the images of our fear, lack, and limitation, not because the Law is limited but because we limit It in our experience. In actual experience we learn that we ourselves must accept the gift. This is the meaning of that part of the story of the Prodigal Son, page 464: *And he would fain have filled his belly with the husks that the swine did eat; and no man gave unto him.* The paragraph following says that our troubles come from an isolated sense of being; that we ourselves must decide to return to the Father's house. Certainly Jesus would never have taught this lesson unless he first knew that the return trip is possible to all.

One of the simplest and at the same time one of the most difficult things to understand is that we are unified with the Law of Cause and Effect, have complete access to It, and use It at all times. It is always reflecting back to us exactly what we reflect into It. And no matter how limited we may be, how poor, weak, sick, miserable or unhappy, there is always an intuitive perception within us that in our Father's house there is abundance. This inner intuitive perception is that which we feel but cannot explain, a sixth sense—it is God in us knowing Himself. We have known this as expressing in a belief in lack and limitation—now we must learn to know it as the consciousness of abundance.

In the third paragraph of page 405 you will find the thought expressed that we cannot contract the Absolute, but we can expand the finite. We can never break any of the laws of nature, be they physical or mental, but we can use them in a less limited way.

As suggested in the last paragraph on page 129, our evolution from now on will depend upon our conscious cooperation with the laws of nature. In making conscious use of the Science of Mind our future evolution will depend upon our conscious cooperation with the spiritual Law of our own being. This Law is that each one of us is a creative center of God-Consciousness. The very Law which binds us can free us but first we must see freedom. This seeing is a mental act. As our text says*, we live in a universe of Law through which runs a spirit of self-knowing Intelligence.*

In the Summary of the first part of the textbook, page 131, we read: *Spirit is Self-Knowing, but Law is automatic ... having no alternative other than to obey*. It was said that Jesus taught as one having authority, and of course it was his authority in the use of the Law which enabled him to perform the so-called miracles. There was never any doubt in his mind. He was certain that the Law would obey his will because he felt his will to be in harmony with the nature of Spirit. Feeling himself to be in harmony with Spirit, and knowing that the Law of his word was absolute, he used words as though they were things.

There seemed no doubt in Jesus' mind as to whether or not his word would make itself manifest. He seemed to know at all times that his word would never return to him void, and this must have been because he had such a deep, underlying sense of his unity with the Whole. As suggested on page 475, we are strong when we are in conscious unity with Good. To believe that God has absolute power over evil; to believe that evil must vanish before good; to have implicit confidence when you declare that good overcomes evil that in your specific case it will do so—this is scientific practice.

It is apparent that Jesus had such a complete conviction of his power that there never was any reaction of doubt in his mind. We will arrive at this same conviction in such degree as we convince ourselves that we are one with the Creative Mind. Since we cannot believe that the Universe is divided against Itself, we know that only by being harmonious can we arrive at a conviction of harmony. Our statements must be sincere, simple, and direct, but unless they convey a meaning to mind they will have no power.

Creation is the play of Life upon Itself. Whether we think of the action of the Spirit in the Cosmos or in our own thought, there is still but One Spirit to act. As It acts in us, It is us. When we speak the truth It is proclaiming Its own being. We need to have the conviction that this is so in order to realize that the only thing in the universe that changes is form; that time and space are created even as form is created, and that the entire manifest universe is an effect, never a cause.

We must have a clear comprehension of these truths if we are to make definite, deliberate, and scientific use of the Mind Principle. Spirit is the only active power in the universe, and man re-enacts the Divine nature. Over and over again we must ponder these few deep but simple truths until their meaning penetrates our intelligence; until finally not only our intellectual but our emotional reaction affirms our unity with Good.

Any person who can arrive at the place where his consciousness of good is greater than his belief in any particular evil has at his disposal the power with which to dissolve that particular evil, just as a light brought into a darkened room dissipates the darkness. Peace will overcome confusion when the sense of peace is greater than the fear which caused the confusion. For every negation in human experience there is a direct opposite in truth, and our access to this Divine Reality constitutes our ability to neutralize the apparent opposite of good. It is useless, however, to study this system of thought unless we consciously use it. Study without practice will never produce any beneficial results.

The desert is made to blossom as the rose only when the desert is cultivated. In the place of sage brush and cactus, rose bushes are planted. So in that garden of the soul wherein grow the forms of thought which reflect the experiences we are having, we may transplant ideas; we may uproot some and plant others, and always the Law will obey.

But sometimes it takes more than a moment to do this; hence the necessity of understanding that we are dealing with an immutable Principle in the Universe. Time, patience, and endeavor, in this as in all other things, will finally deliver to us a conscious use of the Law. And it will become second nature to use this Law for ourselves as well as for others. Let us constantly affirm our belief in our ability to do so.

Summary

Our thought is creative because we are some part of the Universal Creative Mind. It is not by will, intention, or even desire that this is true. It is true because that is its nature, and because it is true it must be accepted.

To understand this is to understand the greatest spiritual reality about ourselves. This is the Divine Gift that is eternally made, but it is of little avail unless we use it. Even the prayer of faith without it will do nothing. Your prayer or treatment does not make something happen. It merely permits things to happen.

If we believe that we are separated from good we appear to be separated from good. All states of consciousness that become subjective become automatic in their operation. The Law is the doer and you are the knower.

When you treat, all that you do is convince your own mind. This is true also of prayer or meditation, for no one could convince gravitational force to be or become gravitational force, and human ignorance cannot acquaint the Divine Mind with anything. Treat nothing but yourself, convince no one but yourself, and force nothing to happen. When you make a demand upon the Principle of Mind, the Mind Principle answers the demand on the terms of the demand.

There is nothing in the Universe to be afraid of. No matter what situation we may be in, it can be changed.

Creation is always the play of Life upon Itself. We are some part of this play of Life. Our thoughts are acted upon by a Universal Creative Medium. We act and It reacts. Anyone who can convince himself of this and act as though it were true can prove it.

Questions

Brief answers to these questions should be written out by the student after studying the lesson, and the answers compared with those which will be included in next week's lesson.

1. Where do we contact the Supreme Mind?
2. How do we turn a little good into a more abundant good?
3. How is it that we can contact all things at the center of our own thought?
4. How does one treat another?
5. Why must treatment be in the present tense?
6. What is a thought pattern?
7. How do we mentally attract or repel things and experiences in our lives?
8. What is meant by a subjective thought pattern?
9. Why is the perfection of God also the perfection of man?
10. If a person doubts his ability to heal and to help, what should he do?
11. What is one of the most amazing and important things a mental practitioner discovers in treating others?
12. Why does our further evolution depend upon our cooperation with the laws of nature?
13. What is the word of authority?
14. Why must our statements convey a meaning to our own mind?
15. Why must both our intellectual and emotional faculties affirm our unity with good?
16. When will peace overcome confusion?

17. Why will study without practice produce no beneficial results?

Answers to Questions on Lesson 13

1. Our individuality is a unique expression of the Spirit of God. Hence there is no separation, even though there is a multiplied expression of personality.
2. The basic principle upon which spiritual treatments are given is the Unity of God and man.
3. Personality is neither evil nor an illusion. It is some part of God.
4. In mental treatment we do not hold thoughts. We release thoughts into the subjective Law.
5. We release thought instead of holding it because holding thoughts implies coercion, while releasing them implies confidence, faith, and acceptance.
6. The power back of our word is the Spirit within us.
7. Man is the personality of God, or God incarnated.
8. We replace bondage with freedom in our experience by reversing our use of the Law.
9. By reversing our use of the Law we mean changing our thought patterns.
10. Changing thought patterns will change our conditions because all conditions are a result of thought patterns.
11. The efficacy of spiritual meditation, which is a recognition of our unity with Spirit, Substance, and the Law of Cause and Effect, is that it so increases our acceptance and belief that our thought patterns, thus clarified, automatically have more power.
12. Impersonal spiritual healing is that healing which takes place when one contacts, with faith, any state of consciousness greater than one's own, i.e., the case of the woman who was healed by touching Jesus' garment; also in cases where one contacts the collective consciousness of a group which is in a state of faith and expectancy.
13. An ascending and descending scale of consciousness means that the One Mind is manifest in everything from the atom to the highest form of intelligence.
14. We say that the word, belief, faith, etc., are molds because they are mental patterns through which the Creative Energy works.
15. Faith and belief must be combined with the spoken word because power undirected does nothing definite, and law unused has no purpose.
16. All people have spiritual power, but only those who recognize it, comply with its law, and consciously use it, can hope to receive definite results.
17. God moving upon God means that the Creative Spirit moves upon Itself. Since man is some part of this Spirit, when he thinks, he moves upon It. Hence the creative power of his thought in treatment.
18. In treatment our thought should be peaceful, poised, etc., because thought patterns project their own likeness.

What Do We Mean By the Silence?

In the metaphysical world you frequently hear people speak of going into the silence. Naturally, one wonders what is meant by the silence, and if there is one thing we must avoid it is confusion. To make plain the few simple facts of the Science of Mind, to deliver a simple and definite technique for its practice, and at the same time to give proper spiritual value to such practice, is your whole aim and purpose in studying one of the finest of all arts—the art of spiritual mind healing.

Very frequently people will say to you, "What is meant by the silence?" Or they might say, "I have been reading how to go into the silence," and you will need to explain to them that the very idea that it is necessary to go into some place called *The Silence* is itself confusing. With great patience you will find it necessary to point to the simple and direct approach to Principle, and particularly to the necessity of maintaining a self-conscious state at all times.

All life is in motion, or at least all manifest life is in a state of vibration. But at the very center of this vibration there appears to be something which is motionless, something which itself does not move and yet from which all motion must come. We can liken this to the Creator and His Creation, to the artist and his art, or to the thinker and his thought.

The thinker exists before his thought, the Creator exists before any particular creation, and within all action there evidently is a Principle which does not move. We might state it this way; God does not move, but movement takes place within God. Spirit does not move anywhere, but all particular *wheres* exist in Spirit.

Going into the silence does not mean that either our mental or physical reactions are obliterated, for if they were we should pass into oblivion. We are not trying to discover how to be less ourselves, but how to be more ourselves.

Jesus gave a good example of going into the silence when he told us that in prayer we should enter the closet and close the door. It is evident that he was not referring to any real objective closet. He could not have been referring to any particular physical space, walled in like a small room. His language was symbolic. Entering the closet means withdrawing into one's own mind. For it is from one's own mind that the creativeness which one possesses emanates.

The closet has been referred to as the Secret Place of the Most High, the Holy of Holies, and the Tabernacle of the Almighty, and typifies the silent processes of nature. The creative principle in plant life is silent; all processes of nature are silent. The Invisible Cause is always silent. Expansion and self-expression are always the loosing of an energy which already exists at the center of the evolving or expressing medium or vehicle.

To enter one's closet is to put aside the external confusion, the clash of will and intention, to judge not from outward appearances but from inward tranquility. The Chinese sage said that all things are possible to him who can perfectly practice inaction, which is but another way of saying, *Be still and know that I am God*. We are told that God is not in the wind nor in the earthquake, but in the Still, Small Voice.

It is evident that the closet is not a place of mental and spiritual oblivion, for a movement of consciousness still takes place. He who practices this movement of consciousness in the silence is practicing the inaction from which action flows. To *Be still and know that I am God* is to enter the sanctuary of one's own consciousness. From this center the issues of life proceed. *Keep thy heart (mind) with all diligence; for out of it are the issues of life.*

Here in our Secret Place of the Most High, the inner chamber of our own soul, are written the sacred words: *I AM*. It is from this consciousness, this *I AM*, conceived in silent recognition, that power flows.

It was said that only the high priest could enter the sacred precinct. The high priest symbolizes our own Divine Self. That which belongs to external causation must be left outside, for we shall never discover the true Creative Cause while we are limiting It to any existing effect. We do not judge righteously when we judge according to appearances only. We must enter the closet and close the door. Our mental gaze is to be upward and inward and not external, for this is the secret of the Secret Place of the Most High.

Next we are told that having entered this Secret Place, and having closed the door, and having temporarily shut out external appearances, which means all created facts and every circumstance whatsoever (and do not forget that this shutting out includes both sin and sinner, all erroneous cause and effect and any and every idea which denies the unity of good)—having entered this Secret Place, and having closed the door, we have entered into the silence. This is what the silence means. We are still alive, awake, and aware. We are still conscious and consciously conscious. We are not less but more ourselves. We have more consciously entered that place of inaction from which action proceeds. It is certain that we enter the Absolute in such degree as we withdraw from the relative, and vice versa.

The next step we are told is to *make known our requests in secret*. It is evident, then, that this Secret Place of the Most High, this Tabernacle of the Almighty, this inner chamber, is not a place where we pass into unconsciousness. Nor is it a place where our consciousness ceases to operate as an individual entity.

We are told that whatsoever things we desire, we are to make known, implying as it certainly does the highest possible degree of specialization and conscious use of the Law. We are to make known our requests in secret to *the Father which seeth in secret*. This Father, of course, represents the eternal Principle of the ever-present Mind, the Parent Mind, the originating creative intelligence in the universe.

We are to bring our petitions, our thoughts, and our desires to some place in our consciousness symbolized as the closet and as the Secret Place of the Most High, where absolute Causation exists, unconditioned by any existing fact or circumstance. Good and bad have disappeared; big and little have melted into unity. The creative Cause receives our desire at first hand, directly, completely.

We have brought no contradictions, no denials, no fears, no sense of lack or limitation into this silence. The unconditioned Cause receives the imprint of our thought exactly as we formulate it. This is the Father which seeth in secret, the secret process of nature, the silent Power projecting Itself through nature, the invisible Presence, the unseen Host whose guests we are.

Jesus nowhere implied that the Father is likely to refuse our request. In the parable of the Prodigal Son we are told that the Father saw the son afar off and advanced to meet him. So we have this beautiful symbolism of the Father turning to us as we turn to Him. The Creative Principle, which sees and receives in secret, rewards us openly. What is this but a statement of the invisible Law of Cause and Effect, the silent process of nature honoring our requests?

This does not constitute the entire teaching of Jesus, for he also said that it is useless to bring our gifts to the altar while we have anything in our consciousness against our brother. This we could interpret to mean while we have any pettiness, animosity, hate, fear or any other attitude which tends to draw the veil before the face of Reality. It is but another way of saying that love alone can beget love, that if we wish to have joy we must give it; it is a subtle pronouncement of the Law of Cause and Effect.

When we have complied with the conditions of love, harmony, and unity, whatsoever requests we make are to be honored, even the requests for happiness, health, success, and friendship. The Great Teacher never denied man the privilege of enjoying the life he lives. He affirmed that he would always enjoy it if he were always in tune with Reality. Therefore, whatsoever things we desire, the Father which seeth in secret does give us openly. That is, the silent creative process of nature, which we employ in giving a mental treatment, projects actual, tangible, visible effects, gives birth to form, and creates after the pattern and the type of the thought we entertain.

It is good for us to have these thoughts clearly in mind, and it is good for us to teach those who come to us that the silence is not some peculiar, strange place which we arrive at either by fasting or feasting. It is any moment in our experience, day or night, when the mind realizes its unity with good, its oneness with *the Father which seeth in secret*.

Sometimes we enter this silence in a momentary flash of consciousness. Sometimes we travel laboriously toward it. Sometimes we seem to miss it. But at all times we should be conscious of its existence. Nor should we ever fall into the mistaken idea that there is any secret way to Reality. All ways are good ways. But our way must be our way and not the way of someone else. The approach is direct and conscious. We need not hesitate to bring our requests, to make them known, to enumerate them.

Good is not withheld from anyone, but ignorance of the Law excuses no one from Its use or Its abuse. Anything is good to have, provided it harms no other person but helps our own self-expression. Whatsoever things we desire we are to receive.

Suppose we had a friend who never refused our petitions, who always had the power to grant our requests; someone strong, affluent and self-sufficient, who had at his disposal infinite resources so that he could honor our requests. And suppose his greatest desire was to benefit us. Should we not feel fortunate indeed?

Further, let us suppose that the only condition this friend imposes on us is that everything he gives us is to be used for constructive purposes. And suppose he promises us that if we use all these gifts for constructive purposes alone no harm should ever come to us—suppose he guarantees us absolute protection. Should we not feel him the most wonderful of all friends?

This is exactly the principle which Jesus laid before us when he said to enter into the closet of our own consciousness and make known our requests in secret to that Father which seeing in secret rewards us openly. Should we not consider this the greatest of all gifts, and should we not consider our approach to it the most fascinating of all experiments?

On the other hand, suppose our friend laid down the condition that we must come and take the gift? And that we could not take it unless we first believed that he fully intended to give it to us, and that he already had made the gift but we must receive it? Even this would not be difficult for us to understand, for we should immediately say to ourselves, "Why, of course, if my friend has made the gift I must receive it. He cannot force me to take it. The gift cannot be complete without a receiver. Someone must receive the gift." We should not hesitate to receive the gift, and this is exactly the position we are in relative to the Universal Creative Mind and Intelligence. The gift awaits our taking.

Certain natural and necessary restrictions are laid upon us. They are merely those restrictions that keep us from using the gift destructively. They are not restrictions of limitation or of bondage. They are merely such restrictions as must necessarily be consistent with a universe of law, of order, of harmony, of unity, and of love. We cannot consider them as being restrictions, since we know that peace, joy, and happiness go with the gift. Surely, if we had a friend who was such a giver we should think of him as being no less than Divine.

Now suppose we take a closer and more intimate viewpoint of this friend and think of him as being at the center of our own life, at the very center of our own thought and consciousness; think of him as being the very Presence and Intelligence by which we think, so that we do not have to go out to find him; he is always at home and his home is within our own souls. Should we not feel that we have the most wonderful companion imaginable? Should we not spend some time in daily communion with this companion? Leaving all external confusion and fear outside, should we not enter this Holy of Holies, and meditating before the Ark of the Covenant, should we not reach in, unroll the scroll and read from it the Divine message: *Before they call, I will answer; and while they are yet speaking, I will hear* (Isaiah 65:24).

The Law and the Word or the Sequence of the Creative Order

By the Law and the Word we mean the operation of our spontaneous word consciously and volitionally spoken, and the reaction of a mechanical and mathematical but intelligent and creative force which is the medium through which the Law of Mind in Action operates. The principle of the Science of Mind is exact and mathematical, while the use of it is personal.

Our Bible starts with this initial statement: *In the beginning God* . . . (refer to Lesson 1 of this series). In the beginning of all creation there is nothing but pure, absolute Intelligence. The Bible then refers to the Spirit moving upon the face of the deep, which means Absolute Intelligence thinking within Itself. This is but another way of saying that the starting point of every creation is the Word of God or the Word of a Universal Intelligence.

The Word moves upon the face of the deep, or in our language it moves upon the subjective Law of Mind which receives the impress of our thought, always tending to bring this thought into manifestation. As the starting point of creation this is what is meant by the sequence of the creative order, or an absolute Intelligence thinking, or the movement of Mind or Spirit within Itself, knowing something, realizing something, affirming something.

Next we have the face of the deep, or the waters of the Spirit, or the Creative Law set in motion by the Word. We have the Law automatically producing the situation, the condition, or the creation implied in the Word. Therefore the sequence of the creative order or the way the Law and the Word work is first of all Absolute Intelligence, next Its word or thought, following which the Law is set in motion, for the Word is the Law of Mind in Action. Then at the end of the sequence the creation or the formation of the Word in definite and specific circumstances, situations, or creations which are the logical, inevitable, mathematical and mechanical reactions of the Law to the Creative Word.

Our Bible and the original spiritual systems from which all religions have sprung assume that there is such an Infinite Intelligence; that It does create through Its word or by Its meditation; that there is a Law which reacts to It, producing the object of Its desire. In this way the Original Spirit comes into the fruition or the realization of Itself in and through what It does. Thus it has been said that creation is the meditation of God. *For he spake, and it was done*, or, *In the beginning was the Word, and the Word was with God, and the Word was God ... All things were made by him; and without him was not anything made that was made ... And the Word was made flesh, and dwelt among us.* The Centurion came to Jesus and said, *Speak the word only, and my servant shall be healed*. And in Psalm 107:20: *He sent his word, and healed them*. You will also remember that Moses said, *But the word is very nigh unto thee, in thy mouth, and in thy heart, that thou mayest do it.* Isaiah said, *So shall my word be that goeth forth out of my mouth: it shall not return unto me void, but it shall accomplish that which I please, and it shall prosper in the thing whereto I sent it.*

Throughout our Bible and all sacred books we find this same idea that the Word acting as Law produces a definite result. But right here we must remember that the Word is not something that speaks itself. There is an Intelligence that speaks the Word; therefore the initial movement of the creative sequence is Absolute Intelligence speaking a word which also becomes Absolute, because it sets an Absolute Law in motion for the purpose of producing a definite result.

Next we must remember that all these sacred writings refer to God as the Macrocosm (the Universe), and man as the microcosm (the individual), and they all teach what Jesus taught when he said, *For as the Father raiseth up the dead, and quickeneth them; even so the Son quickeneth whom he will . . . For as the Father hath life in himself; so hath he given to the Son to have life in himself*. Intelligence compels us to recognize that there must be One self-existent, self-propelling, self-perpetuating, self-energizing and self-expressing Spirit. This and this alone could be the Origin of creation.

But the Bible states, as other sacred writings do, that man reproduces this creative order on a miniature scale. Jesus said, *The Son can do nothing of himself, but what he seeth the Father do; for what things soever he doeth, these also doeth the Son likewise*. What could this mean other than that we as individuals are not separate from the Original Creative Cause? It is upon this premise (which seems rather abstract, but is simple enough if we do not become confused over the thought that it must be too profound) that the Science of Mind is based.

Let us then state it in more simple terms, after this manner: We are centers or points in a Cosmic Universal Consciousness which is the origin of all things. On the scale of our individual lives we reproduce the Divine order in its entirety. This does not mean that we are God, but we find in Psalm 82:6: *I have said, Ye are gods; and all of you are children of the most High*. The whole Divine nature is reproduced in us, but we are ignorant of the fact. Our thought is creative, but in our ignorance we use it destructively.

You will recognize this as the same idea brought out in the beginning of our Bible Lessons under the heading, *The Great Mistake, or The Great Ignorance*. Theology has called it the problem of evil. We call it a misuse of that which is good. We as individuals are centers of consciousness in a Power infinitely greater than we are, but which is placed at our command by the very nature of things. From the consequence of our use of this Power we cannot hope to escape, because It is the very Law of Life Itself.

Let us restate our proposition: We are thinking centers in a Cosmic Mind. Our lives reproduce the Original Life. Everything that happens to us must start with the movement of Intelligence within us, which is a movement of our word or contemplation or meditation within ourselves. So let us say of ourselves or to any individual: "You are a center of intelligence; you did not make it this way, you cannot change it. This is the way it is. You must accept it. You are using a creative Law from which you cannot and do not wish to escape, because It contains the possibility of all freedom when you learn how to use It. To learn to think in the right manner is to learn to create that which is good, and which gives complete expression to the self without ever containing anything destructive or negative."

The beginning of our individual word follows the same Law, the same sequence, and the same order as that of the Supreme Mind, because it is in It and of It and like It. No matter what conditions may be around us, even though they appear to be negative and unhappy, they can be changed if we retrace our mental steps and start with the proposition that our word is also the law of our lives. Everything that follows the word is an effect of the consciousness that speaks it. Therefore we start with the simple fact that we are consciousness speaking its word, thinking a thought, to which word or thought the Law of Mind reacts creatively.

If we can get this simple proposition firmly fixed in mind, simply stated and as simply believed in, we shall see that everything surrounding us is in the nature of an effect, and effects can be changed when we set new causes in motion. Therefore instead of being confused by the situations around us we should be calm, tranquil, and confident that through re-forming our word and changing our whole body of thinking, we can as easily change the existing conditions as perpetuate them.

This calls for a whole change of thinking. What we need is a complete assurance, an inner conviction, a faith, a confidence to know that we can proceed with definite, deliberate determination, and that there can be no question about the results; they will be inevitable.

It was this consciousness that enabled Jesus to perform what to those around him seemed miraculous, or the intervention of a Divine Providence on his behalf. He was consciously and definitely using a power that he knew about, the very Power of God Himself. And now it is up to us to follow in his footsteps, for as the Bible states: *If ye know these things, happy are ye if ye do them*. To know of this Principle and to understand the way It works is not enough. We must use It.

In actual practice we must be quiet and calm within ourselves and begin to think new thoughts even though they contradict everything that appears, for that which created can re-create; that which molded can remold. The Principle we are using is not limited by anything that is happening, because all external things are in the nature of effect while the Principle Itself is Absolute Creation, creating new effects whenever It receives a new impulsion.

This is what we mean by the Law and the Word, or the sequence of the Creative Order. We can initiate a new creative series by the definite and deliberate contemplation of our own minds, and out of the new thoughts will come new things, for the Law is a reflector only. While It is intelligent and creative, Its whole business is to receive the impulsion of the Word that dominates It. This is an apparent paradox, but it is true. We shall discover that the very Law that bound us will now free us; the Power that seemed to stifle us will bring emancipation. The very Power which appeared to produce evil will produce the opposite if, as, and when we change our thought patterns.

The changing of these thought patterns is more than a thing of the intellect; it is also a thing of feeling, of a deep, inner conviction. We must feel that we are one with the Eternal Reality, and that our word is spoken in complete reliance on It; therefore It cannot fail.

Gradually, as we re-form our thoughts they will become subjective; they will sink into that place in mind which is the Power within us and which must constitute the meeting place between the Absolute Cause and the relative effect which It projects.

It may take time to do this, but think of the reward, the gift, the outcome. Keeping the goal in mind, refusing to be baffled or defeated, with uplifted thought and calm but definite purpose, we cannot fail.

Bibles of the World

Fragments from the spiritual history of the race
revealing fundamental UNITY of religious thought and experience

BUDDHISM - If a man make himself as he teaches others to be, then, being himself well subdued, he may subdue others; for, one's own self is difficult to subdue.

One by one, little by little, moment by moment, a wise man frees himself from personal impurities, as a refiner blows away the dross of silver.

CONFUCIANISM - Superior men give themselves to self-adjustment.

Teaching should be directed to develop that in which the pupil excels, and correct the defects to which he is prone.

HINDUISM - He who has the understanding of a chariot-driver, a man who reins in his mind—he reaches the end of his journey, that highest place of God.

The objects that touch the senses are transitory and perishable. Endure them. The self-controlled, who is the same in pain and pleasure, is fitted for immortality.

JAINISM - A sage who walks the beaten track to liberation regards the world in a different way. Knowing the nature of acts in all regards, he does not kill. He controls himself.

Fight with yourself. Why fight with external foes! He who conquers himself through himself will obtain happiness.

CHRISTIANITY - Brethren, I count not myself to have apprehended. But this one thing I do, forgetting those things which are behind, and reaching forth unto those things which are before, I press toward the mark for the prize of the high calling of God in Christ Jesus.

For none of us liveth to himself, and no man dieth to himself. For whether we live, we live unto the Lord; and whether we die, we die unto the Lord.

Practical Suggestion for Mental Treatment

Do Not Condemn Yourself

Knowing the Truth is a spiritual treatment. To know that there is no man external to the likeness of God is a part of this treatment. The treatment must rise higher in consciousness than the condition it expects to heal. If you are treating to heal pain you must come to a conclusion of peace which is greater than the experience of pain your patient is having. In such degree as you are successful in doing this the pain will cease.

In such a case one should treat until one dissolves fear. Perfect love casts out fear. Take the thought of peace, of love, of perfection. Work with it from every angle you can imagine until there comes an inner awareness of its meaning. Peace is perfection, whereas pain is not; pain is an experience which is now eliminated, now completely reversed. Over and over reassure yourself of man's perfection.

Do not condemn yourself or the self of your patient. The Truth about man is that he is God made manifest—he is the personality of God. Your knowledge of this becomes his freedom. Your knowledge of this is more than the Way Shower, it is the Way Itself. Jesus said, *I am the way, the truth, and the life; no man cometh unto the Father but by me*, which means that we approach Reality directly through our own spiritual natures. This is the only true and real mediator between God and man—there is no other.

The Real Man and the Real Body are perfect right now. Your knowledge of this establishes its manifestation in your patient's experience at the level of your own comprehension of the meaning of the words you use.

Take Away the Stone

Our word will have power in such degree as we sense that it is the activity of the Spirit within us, and the law unto that thing spoken of. We should have a sense of the indwelling Spirit, all-present and all-powerful.

If any thought rises which tells us that we do not know, or tells us we cannot accomplish, we must silence this negative argument by using one which is directly opposed to it. We must again reassure our consciousness that there is but One Presence and One Law and One Power. This Presence, Law, and Power is ours in Its entirety.

A treatment is not complete until it knows that all the power there is, is flowing through it. There must be no sense of chance about it. When Jesus, standing at the tomb of Lazarus said, *Take ye away the stone*, he was communing with the Spirit within him and establishing the consciousness that Lazarus was not dead. Then he was able to tell Lazarus to come forth.

The practitioner is continually standing before the grave of some inactive thought, some dead hope, some apparently lost cause whose door is sealed with fear, doubt, despair, and uncertainty. Who shall roll away the stone and who shall tell the dead hope to come forth, to be resurrected, to be born again? That is the work of the practitioner who speaks with assurance and certainty.

There must be no despair or uncertainty, nor even supplication or reverence, for the tomb gives up its dead not to the dead, but to the living.

Meditation

The Household of God is the Household of Perfection. It is the Secret Place of the Most High. The inmates of this Household are all Divine Beings.

Nothing can enter the consciousness of any of these inmates which contradicts the unity of Good. Each member of this Household is at peace with all other members. It is a community of peace, understanding, fellowship, love, and unity.

In this Household of God, which is any man's household who declares it to be such, there is no bickering, no jealousy, and no avenue through which any littleness or meanness may operate.

This is not only a household of peace but a household of joy, a place of happiness and general contentment. Here is warmth, color, and beauty. It is the Secret Place of the Most High objectified as an earthly household, symbolizing the Divine Harmony of the Kingdom of Good.

No one is a stranger within this Household. Nothing is alien to it. It is protected from all fear, from every sense of loss. Nothing can enter it but joy, integrity, loyalty, and friendship.

In this Household the Host is God, the Living Spirit Almighty, and all of Its inmates are the guests of this Eternal Host.

The Practice of Religious Science

Office of the Dean

My Dear Friend,
Our lesson tells us that limitation does not belong to the Spirit or to the Law of Good, but it tells us that we are subject to the law of averages until we consciously free ourselves from the bondages of race belief.

Our lesson deals too with the idea of reward and punishment. Following the lesson you will find a commentary on *Fear and Punishment* which we hope you will carefully consider, and also the other article, *God's Will Relative to Happiness, Supply, Accomplishment, and Self-expression*. All of these things you must ponder, trying to arrive at logical as well as spiritual answers.

Of course we know that it looks as though evil were a reality, and often as though the devil had the world by the throat, but we know there is no devil. We are impelled to conclude that all evil and limitation, everything that denies the ultimate good, must be a misinterpretation of that good.

We do not say that people do not suffer or experience limitation; what we do say is that ignorance produces such suffering and limitation, and that enlightenment alone can heal the suffering and do away with the limitation. The human race is on the pathway of self-discovery, and we are all on the road of evolution.

As we look back over human history we find that many ancient evils already have disappeared. If they were a part of the Eternal Reality they would still be with us. And so it must be with the evils we experience today; tomorrow they will have vanished. While evil is a problem in human experience it is not a reality to the Divine Life.

Sincerely,
Ernest Holmes

Lesson 15

Page 133 through *page 138*

Our lesson begins with the thought that limitation is not inherent in the Law but is a certain use which we make, either consciously or unconsciously, of a Law which of Itself is limitless. The Law being an infinite medium and having no personal mind or opinion of Its own, knows about us only that which we know about ourselves. It knows about man in general only what the entire human race has believed to be true about itself and what the entire human race has believed to be true about itself is true about each one of us individually.

This is what we call the Law of Averages and most people are subject to the Law of Averages. But if we wish to specialize ourselves out of this law which says that the average man must suffer all types of limitation, we must begin to make use of the Universal Law in an individualized way; we must create a new impression about ourselves in the Law.

From this viewpoint the Law knows us only as we know ourselves. It can say about us only what we say about ourselves. It has no mind of Its own. It is a mirror reflecting back to us what we think into It. But it never initiates anything for us. It follows the pattern of thought which the whole race believes about itself, or the pattern of thought which some individual believes about himself. It will follow one pattern as quickly as another, and this accounts for the fact that some people are successful while others fail. The Law of Itself is neither good nor bad; It is merely a way of Life. Yet this subjective Law which has no purpose of Its own to execute is infinite compared to the conscious mind, that is, in Its creative power.

As stated at the top of page 487: *Mental healing is subject to the* exact *laws of Mind*...This means that a change of the pattern of thought within our own consciousness must produce a corresponding change of the pattern of thought in the Universal Mind about us, and whatever pattern is held in the Universal about us will tend to become individualized. This is what mental practice is, and this is why it is so definite and why it can be consciously used.

The last paragraph on page 410 states that *wherever the image of thought is set, there the Power to create resides*. The Power itself already exists. This Power is always creative, always receptive, always neutral, and always available, but we have come under the race belief which says that we may be lucky part of the time and unlucky part of the time, Therefore this is what happens in our experience—we are lucky part of the time and unlucky part of the time; we are sick part of the time and well part of the time; we are happy part of the time and miserable part of the time, because these are the images of thought which exist in the creative medium about us.

We must deliberately change our position in the Law, and we shall discover that as we do this a gradual betterment in circumstances will inevitably follow. It may take time and attention and perseverance, but the end is certain if we follow the principle correctly. Conditions are never things of themselves; they are always reactions and never causes.

The subjective part of us is in contact with a Limitless Medium. The second paragraph on page 394 tells us that *this Limitless Medium may be used for whatsoever purpose we will*. At first we are entirely ignorant of this, and in our ignorance bring upon us the very limitation from which we seek to free ourselves. The strange part of it is that the very law which produces this limitation is itself a law of liberty and has no intention of limiting anyone.

As you will find in the first paragraph on the following page (395), the Spirit must already have ordained perfection because, since the Spirit is perfect and since Its will must be like Its nature, It could not will anything other than perfection for anyone. To assume that It could do so would be to assume that It is self-destructive.

In our ignorance we make that which is harmonious appear to be discordant. The reason it is possible for us to do this is because we are individuals, and individuality without self-choice would not be possible, and self-choice without the necessity of experiencing the results of such choice would be impossible. As this paragraph suggests, our thought does not control the Cosmos; it controls our reaction to It.

Our thought never destroys *the* harmony; it destroys *our* harmony, and that only temporarily. Harmony exists no matter how much discord we experience. Peace still exists at the center of the Divine Being, no matter how much confusion we are in. And we must turn to harmony and peace if we wish to experience them. This is the meaning of awakening the Christ within our own natures. Each of us has this Divine nature. It was a realization of this nature which caused Jesus to become the Christ.

If you turn now to page 367 and read the last two paragraphs you will find a discussion of Jesus the man, and Christ the incarnation of God. Jesus was not different from other men, either physically, mentally, or spiritually. That is, his potential nature must have been the same since we dare not believe that heaven has any favorites. But he understood the immediate availability of good, and he had complete reliance upon the Law of Cause and Effect. We have the same access that he had to this Law, but we do not have the same reliance upon It. This reliance we must learn to acquire and though it takes time and effort, it is more than worth the effort and the time that it takes.

As stated at the top of page 477, man's life is a trinity that takes place simultaneously on three planes of existence—the spiritual, the mental, and the physical. From the Spirit he receives inspiration; in the subjective life he finds a medium for the Law of Cause and Effect; and his body, be it his physical body or the body of his affairs, is an objective manifestation of his whole nature.

All three of these planes are real, and one does not contradict the other. We do have immediate access to the Spirit; we are always using the Law; and we most certainly project a physical body and objective conditions. The question is: Shall our experiences be harmonious or discordant, happy or unhappy? Shall we live a life of want and fear, or one wherein faith and plenty join hands, and with common consent glorify the Divinity which is within us?

It is stated on page 476 that our word has power only as it is one with Power. The word of itself is a mold. The Power exists before the mold, but does not do anything for us. When we awaken our own conviction, and in true faith, expectancy, receptivity, and belief accept the greater good, then the greater good will take place in our experience. Therefore we must combine conviction with definite intention.

Just to believe is not enough. We must believe in something. This cannot be too strongly emphasized. We must use belief in a definite way if we wish a definite response. For to return to our lesson on page 133, second paragraph, there is but One Mind and One Law which we all use, There is only One Ultimate Reality, and whether we are conscious of it or not, we are using It. Every day we are using this creative Power for good or for ill. The experiences of negation so torment us that we finally awake as from a dream and again seek the Father's house.

As the following paragraph (page 133) says, the Law works automatically until we consciously change it. For as great as the Subjective Law is, Its tendency is set in motion by our conscious thought. How marvelous to realize that man has within himself the key to freedom! But of what use is this key unless we unlock the door and walk in? This is what is expressed in Hermes' statement: *Nature unaided fails*.

The Law of Mind as quickly creates one form as another (page 411), but we must supply the *pattern* for Its creation. If we wish new and better patterns of thought we may find an inspiration on page 496 under the heading, *A Pattern for Thought*. We are to think on the affirmative side of life; we are to think abundance instead of lack, joy instead of sorrow, life instead of death. God will supply all our needs. That is, God is not only a Spiritual Presence; He is also a Universal Law. Receiving inspiration from the Spiritual Presence, we consciously direct the Universal Law. The Law is the servant of the Spirit throughout the ages. The Law is our servant.

But of what use is a servant unless he is directed to do something? The desert is made to blossom as the rose only when cultivated by someone's conscious intention. As stated on page 402, second paragraph, *We attract to ourselves the objective form of our subjective embodiments*. The Law knows how to convert thoughts into things. We do not know how It does this, but we experience the result of right thinking.

When we come to have the same confidence in the laws of mind that we have in the laws of physics, which are proved to be true, we shall receive just as direct results from our mental work. For as the following paragraph on the same page (402) states, thoughts of lack, poverty, and limitation contain within themselves the conditions which will produce their physical correspondents in our experience.

It is perhaps a little difficult to understand that this Law knows us only as we know ourselves, but this is one of the most important characteristics of this science, and a thing of which we should never lose sight. We must always keep in mind that thoughts are things, and that there is a Law which propels thought patterns into objective form. Whether we know it or not, and whether we believe it or not, we are surrounded by a universal Creative Medium which receives the impress of our thought and acts upon it. All that we can say of this Medium is that It is, and we use It.

Reward and punishment (which you will find discussed on pages 382 and 383) are the results of our use of the Law. We are not rewarded *because* we are virtuous, nor punished *because* we are vicious, but *by* them we are rewarded or punished. What greater justice could we ask for? Surely the Universe is foolproof and compensation for good or for ill is inevitable.

No man gives to us but ourselves, and no man takes from us but ourselves. It is a satisfaction to think that we are our own heaven and our own hell. It is the only adequate idea of justice the human mind has ever conceived. In face of all the dogma and superstition through which the world may have gone, this thought has shone bright and clear to those who have perceived Reality.

The Universe is a spiritual system, eternal and perfect, but this spiritual system appears to each individual in the light of his own fear or faith. Put on dark glasses and everything seems clouded. Reality will always be to each of us exactly as we perceive It to be. We cannot cheat It of Its nature, but can use It in a more glorious manner.

To know that heaven and hell are but two different reactions of the Law to our thought is at last to sense the possibility of freedom. The Universe asks of us only that we have implicit confidence in Its goodness, truth, and beauty. In exchanging our thoughts of morbidity, depression, and lack of confidence for the whole armor of faith, we are making a good deal.

Turn to the bottom of page 494 and the top of page 495 for a more complete discussion of the *Armor of God*. Here we discover that the Armor of God is faith in the good, and that *the breastplate of righteousness* gives protection to those who have such faith. *The fiery darts of the wicked* referred to may be taken to mean the negative impulses which press against the thought of all of us. If our armor of faith is complete, then this negation cannot penetrate our consciousness. Since only that which can penetrate our consciousness can find expression in our experience, the fiery darts of the wicked will have no existence for us.

The sword of the Spirit, which is the Word of God, indicates that a definite statement made in mind has the ability to specifically neutralize any opposite belief. You will soon discover in your practice that thoughts really are things when it comes to applying them, and that certain states of consciousness actually do produce definite, corresponding physical manifestations.

The only way to know this is to demonstrate it. You must deliberately take a certain line of thought, and without willing it to produce anything, definitely state that it is going to do it; feel that it will do it. The text says, *The Word of God is not a battle hymn . . . but . . . a psalm . . . a song of joy*. Turn to page 533 and read the Meditation, *I Fear No Evil*. After you have read this thoughtfully several times, realizing its exact meaning, then apply it to some specific problem, knowing that the particular thing you may have feared is now completely wiped out. And you will soon discover a power which you little dreamed that you possessed.

Turn again to our lesson, page 137, Chapter 8, *The Power of Thought*. Proverbs 23:7 says: *For as he thinketh in his heart, so is he*. This does not say that man is what he thinks he is; it says he is *as* he thinks. From our viewpoint it means that as the subjective state of our consciousness is, so shall our conditions become. Jesus said, *What things soever ye desire when ye pray, believe that ye receive them, and ye shall have them*. Or according to the second paragraph on page 396, the nature of Reality is such that while the Universal Mind is unlimited, as far as we are concerned It has only the power that we give It.

The power which we give to It is through the avenue of our thinking. This is why we say thoughts are things. But as we have learned, before thought can be permanently effective to draw prosperity or right conditions into our lives it must become subjective, since the subjective state of our thought is the Law, or is our use of the Law—at least it is where we personify It. It is from this viewpoint that the Law knows about us only what we know about ourselves.

As stated at the bottom of page 137, unless we discredit all human testimony we are perfectly justified in assuming that there is such a thing as spiritual mind healing. Throughout all the ages people have been healed by prayer, and since we cannot believe that God honors one man's prayer more than another's, or that there is any deific power which honors one man's religion more than another's, we must come to the conclusion that there is a Principle underlying this whole field. And this Principle is in the belief and not in the thing believed in.

Turn to page 577 in the Glossary for a definition of *Belief*, and to page 442, *Wisdom Is Justified of Her Children*. You will find that virtue is independent of any material form which it may take, and that whatever we believe in is to us real while we believe in it. If we believe in an illusion, even the illusion is real to us, but of course it is not an eternal reality. Therefore when we come to know and believe in the Truth, that Truth which we believe in will neutralize the illusion of the false belief. The Universe is not divided against Itself. We might say that the illusion may be believed in and the Reality may be known, and that the knowing of Reality dispels the illusion, which is what Jesus meant when he said, *And ye shall know the truth, and the truth shall make you free.*

As stated in the last two paragraphs on page 338, *the Divine Ideal must be perfect,* and *we are the sons of God now*. This true sonship we but dimly perceive. Meanwhile we cover the right idea of this sonship with false beliefs, and these false beliefs produce discordant circumstances in our lives. It seems impossible to believe that disease, lack, and limitation are divinely ordained, and unthinkable to believe that the all-creative Wisdom could have designed pain and trouble.

But these negations do exist as a part of our experience, and it would be senseless to deny them. We must reconcile the fact of their existence with the experiences of negation which we all have had. Without denying the experience we affirm that the great Reality need not include this negative experience. Gradually we shall become emancipated by keeping the eye single on the Truth.

Turn to page 432, *The Single Eye*. Here we discover that all outward things are propelled by inner causes, and that *Cause* as defined on page 578 is the thing which comes first. Man is defined as a center of God-consciousness, which means a center of Causation. It is because man is a center of God-causation that his thought is creative, not because he wills it to be so. As before stated, the will is directive and not creative.

Throughout the ages prayers have healed the sick; therefore throughout the ages the indestructible Principle of Reality has continuously reaffirmed Itself, but only a few have read the significance underlying the outward symbol. Jesus stands forth as one who proclaimed the Law of Life to be a thing of belief. *As thou hast believed, so be it done unto thee*.

To learn how to use this Law is the real purpose of your study. You must begin at once to demonstrate and you must never stop until you have proved this Principle so completely that it would be absolutely impossible for anyone to cause your faith to waver. The mind in you is God, and when you exercise this God-power consciously you will demonstrate. Your treatment should be direct, simple, and meaningful.

Summary

If we believe as everyone else believes, we are bound by the law of averages, which means the total of what all have believed. Since the Law follows one pattern as quickly as another, the very law that bound us can free us. Before this can take place we must change our position in the Law. And because we are individuals we can do this.

Our thought does not change the nature of Reality; it does change our position in It. Our word is a mold in the Law, but the substance which fills the mold belongs to the Universe. Faith, expectancy, and acceptance form this substance into the image and experience of our desires.

Since we must believe in something, it follows that we are believing in good or in evil, or in both good and evil. Since the Law is our servant, what we need are new patterns of thought based on a broader concept of Reality, a higher vision of Truth, and a greater realization of Love.

Reward and punishment are but the automatic reactions of the Universal Law of Cause and Effect. We do not change the nature of this Law; we merely change the way we have been using It. It always acts like a mirror reflecting back to us the images of our own thinking. This is what Jesus meant when he said when you pray believe that you already have your desire. The Universe can give to us only through the avenue of our acceptance.

Throughout the ages prayers of faith have been answered because they have complied with the Law. The sum total of our whole thinking constitutes a continual prayer or communion with the Invisible.

Questions

Brief answers to these questions should be written out by the student after studying the lesson, and the answers compared with those which will be included in next week's lesson.

1. What is the meaning of the Law of Averages?
2. Can the Law of Mind know anything about us which we do not know about ourselves?
3. How can we overcome the limitation imposed upon us by the Law of Averages and by our own belief?
4. Why should our thought patterns be definite?
5. Is the Law which limits us good or bad?
6. Is the Will of Spirit toward our perfection or imperfection?
7. Does our thought control the Cosmos?
8. Was Jesus different from other men?
9. Do the spiritual, mental, and physical planes contradict each other?
10. In mental treatment, why should we combine conviction with definite intention?
11. What did Hermes mean by *Nature unaided fails*?
12. In what way is the Law of Mind our servant?
13. What does *the objective form of subjective embodiment* mean?
14. What is punishment and reward?
15. What is the *Armor of God*?
16. What does *the sword of the Spirit* mean?
17. How can we know that our word has power?
18. Why did Jesus teach the necessity of believing that we already have what we desire?
19. If what we believe is real to us, will our belief in an illusion make a reality of such an illusion?

20. Can we believe that limitation of any nature, or evil in any form, is divinely ordained?
21. What does the *single eye* mean?
22. Why is man's thought creative?

Answers to Questions On Lesson 14

1. We contact the Supreme Mind at the center of our own thought.
2. We turn a little good into a more abundant good by mentally accepting a greater good.
3. We can contact all things at the center of our thought because our mind is a point in the Universal Creative Law.
4. One treats another by convincing himself of the other's spiritual perfection.
5. Treatment must be given in the present tense because the mental Principle knows no past or future.
6. A thought pattern is a habitual way of thinking.
7. We mentally attract or repel things and experiences in our lives according to our subjective thought patterns.
8. A subjective thought pattern means a thought which has passed from the conscious into the subconscious, and has become completely accepted by it.
9. The perfection of God is also the perfection of man because God and man are one in Spirit and in Essence.
10. If doubt arises in a person's mind when he is treating, he should immediately turn his thought to the presence and the availability of the Spiritual Principle.
11. One of the most amazing things a practitioner discovers in treating others is that he has no one to convince but himself.
12. Our further evolution depends upon our cooperation with the laws of nature, because what nature does for us she must do through us.
13. The word of authority is one which is in harmony with the nature of Reality, and which is spoken with complete confidence, belief, and acceptance.
14. Our statements must convey a meaning to our own mind because if they do not, our mind will reject them.
15. Our intellectual faculty, as well as our emotional faculty, must affirm our unity with good because the emotional faculty is creative while the intellectual faculty is directive.
16. Peace overcomes confusion when our conviction of good is greater than our fear of evil.
17. Study without practice will produce no beneficial results. We learn about the principle, and practice the definite use of it.

Fear and Punishment

We all know what fear can do; how it can shrivel up hope and dampen the ardor for living, and how finally it can close up the avenues of self-expression. When carried to an extreme it leaves one a wreck, physically and mentally. And we have observed what faith can do. We have seen people so filled with fear that nothing in life seemed worthwhile to them and we have seen them learn to have faith in life and have watched the transformation that has taken place in their lives.

The psychologist might say that such a person has a phobia—an inferiority complex—which means that he feels unable to cope with life. Or the psychiatrist might say that he is neurotic. But we must look at him and say, "Here is a spiritually complete man who is doing nothing that he has not been trained to do. He has had the intelligence and the emotional capacity to learn these lessons of fear, and to learn them well."

If it is possible for us to learn to be afraid, we can reverse the process and learn to have faith.

In the study of mental suggestion it has been discovered that if a mother fears that her child's food will not digest, it will affect his digestive processes. If she is afraid that he will not sleep well at night, his sleep will be disturbed. If he is surrounded with thoughts of irritation and emotions of anger they will all register in him. Times without number he has listened to such warnings as "Keep away from that dog, he may bite!" or, "Don't go too close to the edge, you may fall!" or, "Be sure to wash your hands, there are germs on them."

The signposts on the road to fear are too numerous to mention, but each leaves its imprint upon the growing mind and plastic memory of the child. It is little wonder that he arrives at maturity in a state of perpetual fear. He has learned it in his home, in his school, and unfortunately, in his religious instruction. We sometimes wonder whether God is not feared more than He is loved and trusted.

It is unfortunate that the idea of a future state of punishment should have been so emphasized in our religious training. For out of it have come the most morbid fears the human mind has ever entertained. How can we believe that a good God, a God of love as well as wisdom, would seek to destroy His own creation?

This does not mean that we are not responsible for our acts. We cannot escape the logical result of our thoughts and acts. The punishment for any act flows out of the act itself. Jesus said, *Forgive, and ye shall be forgiven*. In this masterful statement we find a teaching of justice but not retribution. The moment we forgive we are forgiven. God is the eternal Forgiver.

You will remember that in Jesus' parable of the laborers, some came early in the morning to work in the vineyard, some at noon, some in the afternoon, and some did not come until the eleventh hour. But the lord of the vineyard gave them all equal pay. This parable portrays a message of great significance. What Jesus was really saying is this: No matter what happened during the day, no matter how wrong we might have been in our previous experience, when the time comes that we actually do enter into the vineyard—which means life as we live it—then the lord of the vineyard—who represents God—receives us. There is no condemnation, no judgment. We are not sent into eternal perdition or future punishment. Jesus taught that there is no sin but a mistake, and no punishment but a consequence.

Again we find Jesus forgiving the thief who was crucified with him, and saying, *Today shalt thou be with me in paradise*. He told people that when they go into the temple to pray, forgiveness should be their first act. Can we ignore that this forgiveness means forgiving ourselves, just as certainly as it means forgiving everyone else? Jesus clearly taught that God is the great Giver, and because He is the great Giver, He is also the great Forgiver.

Here is another illustration: Suppose a room has been in darkness for years and we bring in a light. What becomes of the darkness? It just is not there. It would make no difference how long the room may have been dark; when the light appears the darkness disappears.

Perhaps our ideas of being good and doing good have been based on the expectation of reward or the fear of punishment instead of on common sense. Goodness should be natural and spontaneous. Goodness is normal; evil is abnormal. We should live by faith and not by fear. But because we have had so many fears and because we have built up such an unconscious sense of guilt, we seek a release from the emotional tension of this guilt-feeling by projecting the thought that we need to be punished for our mistakes. This, no doubt, is the origin of the belief in hell.

Many believe that the Bible teaches that there is a literal hell. Nothing could be further from the truth. What the Bible teaches is the Law of Cause and Effect. It teaches it over and over again, in many different places and in many different ways.

The Bible teaches that all unkind and negative reactions must be purged from the mind. This is where we get the idea of purgatory—it means a purging of the mind. It tells us that the pain of this mental purging can be likened to the fires of Gehennah, which was a place outside the city of Jerusalem where they burned the garbage. This teaching we can accept because it is logical. If our minds are filled with hatred toward others we hate really ourselves. If we lack confidence in life it is because we first lack confidence in the self. And if we are afraid of God and of the future, it is because we are not acquainted with love and confidence.

Unfortunate as it may be, there is no question but that one of the great fundamental fears of the whole human race is the belief in hell and in future punishment. And probably more sorrow, human suffering, and morbidity have come from this one belief than all others combined. It is time for us to clarify the situation and realize that the God of love cannot hate, the God of life cannot destroy, the God of good cannot desire evil.

It is on this basis that we should create a great hope and faith. We should be willing to admit that we are punished by our mistakes, and in common sense recognize that while we continue our mistakes we must of necessity continue to suffer; but always with the certainty in mind that when light comes darkness disappears, when forgiveness comes to our own mind we are forgiven, when we are willing to give we shall receive, when we learn how to enter into heaven we shall leave everything unlike heaven behind us.

The Divine Peace is not disturbed by any hymn of hate, nor is the majesty and might of the Eternal Presence disturbed by our thoughts of discord.

There is another thought that Jesus gave us which we should not overlook. He said that the Kingdom of Heaven is at hand; it is here and now. It is not something to wait for, something that is going to happen by and by. It is at hand. The question is, are we seeing it? Are we actually beholding it as he did in the here and the now?

The reason that Jesus forgave people their sins was that he recognized the fear and morbidity that had been built up throughout the ages because people were afraid of God. They feared Him rather than loved Him. And so Jesus forgave them all these mistakes and told them to think the whole thing over again until they finally realized that God is love, God is life, God is peace, God is joy. God is givingness, God is forgivingness.

But at the same time he warned them that there is a Law of Life which reacts to a person in the way he uses It, and that while he refuses to forgive he cannot be forgiven; while he refuses to see in every person he meets the Divine image he hopes is within himself, he cannot find the Son of God at the center of his own being. Jesus taught justice without judgment, liberty without license, and showed that there is a perfect balance between our thoughts, our acts, and what is going to happen to us. And it is upon this that we should base all our beliefs and acts.

Again let us remember the story of the Prodigal Son who had lost in a far country everything he possessed. And when, sick and discouraged, he returned to his Father's house, his Father did not condemn him, but welcomed him with open arms. He did not even ask where he had been or what he had been doing, but said, "Let us rejoice together."

How wonderful is this idea of being enfolded in the everlasting arms of peace and love on the very day that we forsake our distrust, our hate, our fears and doubts. And how simple should be our salvation. All that it means is turning from wrong to right, from darkness to light, from fear to faith, from hate to love, from hell to heaven. How satisfying to know that no one can hinder us but ourselves, and except for the help of the great and the good God, no one can help us but ourselves.

Someday, as surely as we live, this is the God that will be presented to humanity—one Universal Divine Presence forevermore blessing Its creation; one infinite ocean of Love in which all are immersed; our Father which art in heaven, the one and only God, who is not a God of wrath or retribution but a God of peace and joy and wholeness. The day will come when the other God will be forgotten, and humanity will learn to live as though this earth were the Kingdom of Heaven, with God Himself the host.

God's Will

Relative to HAPPINESS, SUPPLY, ACCOMPLISHMENT, and SELF-EXPRESSION

> *Finally, brethren, whatsoever things are true, whatsoever things are honest,*
> *whatsoever things are just, whatsoever things are pure,*
> *whatsoever things are lovely, whatsoever things are of good report;*
> *if there be any virtue, and if there be any praise, think on these things.*
>
> Philippians 4:8

In the Science of Mind we are frequently asked this question: 'What is God's will? Is it God's will that I should be happy, prosperous, free, and self-expressed? Or is God trying me? Is God molding my character through trial and tribulation?" Generally speaking, these questions are sincerely asked and frequently this query is made by one whose consciousness has already suffered deeply from the limitation and unhappiness of human experience.

What is God's will? This question is as old as time, and the answer has been as varied as have been the mentalities of those who gave it. To the scientific mind the will of God is manifest in the immutable laws of the universe. To the over-zealous religionist the will of God appears to come through some special revelation giving birth to a certain spiritual system of thought which forever after is to be taken dogmatically and accepted without question, a truth and a faith once and for all delivered.

If we take a rational viewpoint of this question, shall we not be compelled to accept, as the only logical conclusion, that the will of God must ever be consistent with the nature of the Divine Being? God's will and God's nature must be identical. If the nature of God is limitation and bondage, the will of God must also be limitation and bondage.

When we use the word *God* we mean the Great Reality, the Infinite Unity, the Final Truth back of all manifest life, the Absolute or Causeless Cause, the one unconditioned, complete, and perfect Being—indivisible, changeless, and whole. All of these descriptive terms are synonymous with the word God.

If the nature of God or Reality were unhappiness, then the will of God would be toward unhappiness. But to suppose that the nature of God could be toward any form of limitation is to suppose not only an inconsistency but an impossibility. As you will notice later in a series of lessons on *Self-Evident Truths*, the Truth is limitless. The nature of God, then, is not one of limitation or bondage, but one of freedom; therefore the Scriptures tell us that we have inherited not bondage but liberty.

Our Divine Inheritance is self-sufficiency, perfection, peace, wholeness, and this must include abundance, self-expression, accomplishment, and happiness. The nature of God is wholeness; the nature of wholeness is happiness; the nature of happiness is peace; the nature of peace is harmony; and the nature of harmony is joy. So whichever way we turn the proposition, we are compelled to understand that the nature of Reality, the nature of God, is perfect; therefore the will of God, which can never be divorced from God's nature, must always be a will toward wholeness, peace, poise, power, and self-expression.

If the will of God is the will of abundance, it follows that God cannot will lack, want, or limitation. It follows that all bondage is of the human. All bondage is a result of a circumscribed viewpoint of Reality. All affliction is a result of ignorance.

Because of our psychological nature and because that which we think about tends to take place in our experience, it follows that if we believe God's will is toward unhappiness and limitation we shall experience limitation because of such belief. That is why it is so important that our consciousness be clear; that we should know what we really believe about God. Indeed we might say that in the final analysis, what a man believes about God inevitably influences his entire experience in life. It certainly follows that if we believe the supreme will of the universe is toward suffering, we cannot possibly escape the suffering imposed by such an immutable will.

But the will of God is never toward suffering. In the midst of all perplexities the cry for deliverance has ever risen. The intuition senses that deliverance is at hand, but the intellect does not comprehend the manner in which it may become manifest. Hence the intuition proclaims that which the intellect does not understand, and man must constantly reaffirm his belief in the Infinite Goodness if he expects to exclude the idea of evil from his thought.

God's will for every person is happiness, peace, and joy. God's will for all creation is self-expression since creation is an expression of this invisible Cause which we call God, nor can it be considered to be anything else. Every constructive desire toward self-expression finds its prototype in the universal need for self-expression. The ceaseless struggle for liberty manifest throughout the ages, the ever reaching out toward Reality which has inspired all people to more noble efforts, is an expression of that which is largely an unconscious sense, that hope which *springs eternal in the human breast*.

God's will is always toward life and more life. When Jesus said, *God is not the God of the dead, but of the living*, he was explaining that the will of God and the nature of God are life and not death; for how can the Principle of Life produce death? We might add: How can the Principle of Harmony produce discord? We must believe that the will of God is happiness. Then we shall have a strong spiritual and psychological background for our conviction that we too should be happy. In the quest of the soul for its greatest good, which is an inner contentment, we must know that the will of God is serenity, security, certainty.

But some may say, "That all sounds very grand, but is it not a subtle argument of the devil, trying to lead us astray? Is it not really our own lustful and willful wishing, seeking to escape the dire penalties of our rash acts?"

We must patiently, persistently, and insistently show people that the will of God cannot be toward anything other than that which is good; that the will of God and the nature of God are identical and must forever remain so; that there is nothing in the universe which opposes their good except their ignorant use of the Law, which of Itself is good. This Law must present Itself to each individual according to his belief.

God's will most certainly is toward abundance. If we enjoy life, God is that much more completely expressed; the world is to that extent a happier place in which to live. There is no God who tries men's souls or beats them over the head with a cosmic club, seeing how much they can stand. There is no sin but a mistake, and no punishment but a consequence. By the same token, virtue is its own reward. If some sincere person says to you, "Then if all this is true, I can do exactly as I please since God has no will for me," explain to him again that God's will and God's nature are one, and one part of God's nature is the immutable Law of Cause and Effect. Every man must reap as he sows.

There can be no new harvest without a new seedtime. If we have been suffering from unhappiness, thinking it to be the will of God, we must realize that our thoughts are so formulated that our unhappiness is an inevitable result. Our emotions are so directed that they must create unhappiness. In other words, we suffer from ignorance.

Now if the will of God is toward peace and joy, and if the nature of God is identical with this will, then Law at God, which is also the nature of God executing the will of God, is toward joy and happiness. Consequently, when we begin to think joy and happiness they will rush to us, claiming us as their own.

Thus it is that the Father advances to meet the son and enfolds him in His embrace. They were never really separated; the son had merely misdirected his energy. The most beautiful thought of all is that when he redirected this energy into a constructive channel, his evil experience was terminated, and a new use of the Law was put into effect. In this simple but most profound lesson did the great Wayshower teach the simple truth of our relationship to the Parent Mind.

Every moment that a man is unhappy and unexpressed he is tearing down his personality. The moment he becomes inwardly contented he begins to build it up again. The will of God is toward the more abundant life because that life expresses God. The life that is cramped, warped, timid, and fearful does not express the Divine Being so completely as the free swinging self-expression of the soul pronouncing God's work to be good, announcing through every experience the ecstasy of self-expression.

We do not honor God by being poor, weak, and unhappy, nor do we limit God by such experiences. What we do in our negative experiences is misdirect the positive energy which is already in us, for there is only one final Energy, just as there is only one final Mind. This final Mind and this final Energy are always manifesting through us at the level of our consciousness of life and our comprehension of Its meaning; hence the importance of re-educating the mind to a more direct perception of its relationship to God.

All men seek self-expression, as all men seek life, because the God in us is freedom and must be expressed. If our outlet for this self-expression, for this Divine Urge, is a constructive one, no evil results can ever follow, and through our self-expression the world will be benefited. Every form of morbid argument arises to slay this great hope within us. God is trying us, the devil is tempting us, experience is too much for us, and on and on through the limitless category of human morbidity this argument of the serpent seeks to win us from our Garden of Eden.

Through every subtlety, by every illusion, by the logic of human experience, we are led from Reality into our dream of separation. It takes resolute thought, a poised mind, and a confident spirit to overcome this. It takes calm faith and quiet confidence in the supremacy of good and in the omnipotence of the Law of good. Freedom from bondage is a thing which we must inwardly perceive. This perception is the greatest of all perceptions.

The nature of God, the will of God, and the power of God are one and the same thing. It matters not that countless millions of people through endless generations have misinterpreted this will of God, and thought that it meant limitation and suffering. The nature of God is demonstrated when it is understood. It is proved when it is known.

If the truth about God is happiness, joy, self-expression and abundance, then this is the truth we should seek to demonstrate in our own lives. This is done by knowing that every thought within us abounds with peace, partakes of the Divine Bounty, includes the idea of wholeness, and is shot through with Eternal Light.

Practical Suggestion for Mental Treatment

Our Spiritual Identity Forever Expands

In spiritual mind practice, evil is never treated as an entity, but as an operation of thought. The practitioner never deals with evil as though it were big or little, and he must be careful not to locate it anywhere, in any person, or any group of persons. It is easy enough to see that the mentality of a practitioner must be kept free from the belief in evil, which unfortunately obsesses most persons' thoughts much of the time.

Limitation is not a thing of itself; it is a way of belief. Unhappiness is a condition, but it is not something of itself. Every man has an identity in Spirit, and this idea will eternally unfold; it will never grow less but will always be more of itself. What man knows about God, the Universal Truth, constitutes his real spiritual being, constitutes his personification of the Infinite; therefore the more completely conscious he is of God, Spirit, Truth, Beauty, the more perfectly will he evolve.

Since the Truth is infinite, there is room for eternal expansion, so that man passes from glory to glory, from one plane to another, or as Jesus put it, *In my Father's house are many mansions.*

The spiritual identity itself remains individual and unique though forever expanding. We cannot now visualize what the future development may be, but it is inevitable that we shall pass from this state of being into ever-ascending states forever.

It does not seem at all necessary or advisable that we spend much time wondering what is going to happen hereafter, since our evolution will take care of all those things as we come to them. What seems most important is that we be happy, well, and prosperous here and now, and that we maintain our spiritual identity wherever we go and whatever we do.

Receiving Is as Important as Giving

We need never beseech the Law to operate for us, for if there is but One Mind in the universe our mind is some part of It, and it is Its nature to respond to Itself. Nothing can hinder the Divine from flowing into us except our own free will.

The sun may be shining even while we persist in standing in a dark basement. The manna may be falling but we refuse to gather it. Now we must come out of our basement of despair into the sunshine of truth, into the warmth and color of Divine recognition, the instantaneous awareness of the Allness of Good.

God is Life and Life gives Itself to us. It does not give some of Itself; It gives all of Itself. But the gift without a receiver cannot complete itself in individual life. Emerson tells us that we are compelled to perceive that we are beneficiaries; that we stand in the light and the light is all. Then he tells us to get our bloated nothingness out of the way of the Divine Circuit.

This getting out of our own way is what mental treatment does for us, since it declares that there is nothing in us which can keep our good away. Treatment always declares the presence of good and the operation of the law of love. It is a conscious, active recognition of spiritual presence, spiritual force, spiritual law, and spiritual order.

Meditation

The Spirit has no past, It has never been bound, It has always been free. I am Pure Spirit; therefore I know that there is no causation of limitation around me, there is no burden of race belief operating through me.

It makes no difference what happened yesterday or last year or at any time in the entire history of the human race. I am not bound by anything that has ever happened. I deal with the Power that instantly makes all things new.

I am free and unfettered. I dwell in the Secret Place of the Most High; I abide under the Shadow of the Almighty. All that is God's, is mine. Today this Divine Allness, this Universal Bounty, is making Itself manifest in everything I do, say, and think.

The doorway of opportunity is opened wider than ever before. I have a clearer vision than ever before of my unity with Good. I know that my word is power and I know that my word is inspired from on High. I know that all the power there is, is God, the Living Spirit Almighty, operating through me *now*.

Today abundance, happiness, joy, success, and friendship are increasingly made manifest in my experience. I accomplish every desired good without effort. And this Divine Life operating through me remains true to Its own nature. It is my life. There is no other.

The Basic Principle of Spiritual Healing

My Dear Friend,

We all live in one Mind. If this were not true we could not know each other, talk to each other, or communicate with each other by writing. We live only because God lives in us, because Life is living Itself in and through us.

We believe there is a Spiritual Body and that it is here and now. We do not see it, but we often feel its presence. We seem to be so immersed in the traditional beliefs of the whole race that it is difficult for us to get a mental clearance long enough for the Spirit to flow through us.

We hope you will enjoy the rather whimsical concept of *Bodies Celestial and Bodies Terrestrial* which you will find in this section. It came to me one evening after I had retired for the night, but few changes were made from the original.

In reading the section on *Spiritual Mind Healing and Mental Suggestion* we are sure you will agree that while some mental suggestion enters into everything we do, we are not practicing this art. Our word must be independent of anything suggested if it is to use the possibility of greater power. One of the chief things to remember in our science is that each one deals with First Cause alone in his own mind, because his mind is the Mind of God individualized.

One of our endeavors is to get away from all mental suggestion into self-realization. We would not consider a statement of truth as mental suggestion, but rather a mental awakening.

These are some of the things for you to think about in this lesson.

Sincerely,
Ernest Holmes

Lesson 16

Page 139 to *Inducing Thought*, page 142

Since we can talk together, or commune with each other, it follows that intelligence responds to intelligence. If intelligence responds to intelligence in the case of two individuals—and we know that it does—why should we doubt the response of the Universal Intelligence to the individual? The same principle would be involved. For the difference is not in essence but in degree.

The Meditation on page 546, *I Behold in Thee His Image*, states that the hand that gives is the Universal Hand, and the voice that speaks of love is the Voice of God. This Divinity which is resident within everyone is an incarnation of the Infinite in the finite. But that which we call the finite is the Infinite working at the level of our comprehension. As the mystic said, *The highest God and the innermost God is one God.*

This idea of unity which we are discussing is one of the most difficult problems that faces us on the pathway to the realization of our oneness with all power. It is essential that we understand and to some degree appreciate the meaning and significance of this unity, for as our text explains, the response of the Infinite to the finite must be a correspondence. The Infinite gives back to the finite the exact image presented to It, just as an object is reflected in a mirror. The Law can know us only as we know ourselves.

Since our self-knowingness is the incarnation of the Divine in us, it follows that our self-knowingness is actually God knowing Himself through us. It is because this is so that thought has power. The power is not injected into Mind but is taken out of It. We can never too clearly realize in this science that we take power out of Mind rather than put power into It. In the paragraph, *The Light of the World*, on page 477, you will find an explanation of what Jesus meant when he said, *I am the light of the world*. Of course he was not referring to his human personality but to the incarnation of the Divine Spirit within him. *I AM*, as our text explains, is both individual and Universal. Each one of us is an individual *I AM*, an individualized center of God-consciousness.

The Law of God-consciousness, which obeys the Will of the Divine, is a mathematical sequence of cause and effect. Hence the Law follows the Word, even as Intelligence precedes it. In the manifestation of creation we start with Absolute Intelligence; next the movement of Intelligence, which is the Word; then the operation of the Law, which obeys the Word; and finally the manifestation of the Law, which is a manifestation of the Word through the Law.

As we have already explained, the Word or the Divine Intelligence alone is conscious; everything that follows is automatic. Therefore the Law of Cause and Effect obeys the will of the Word and does so mathematically. This is what is meant by Principle responding by a law of correspondence or reflection. One is cause, the other is effect.

At the top of page 478 man is referred to as *an individualization of His eternity*. Not that Eternity is limited to time, but rather that time is created by Eternity. Eternity alone is changeless; time comes and goes with individual experience. We create time and space when we have any kind of experience. Any particular time and any particular space is always in relationship to such an experience. When we change an experience we change the relationship; thus time and space, as we perceive them, are increased or diminished through an act of our own imagination.

Jesus understood this when he forgave the man before he healed him. This was his great perception when he said, *I and my Father are one*. Whatever intelligence we possess must be the Intelligence of God in us; otherwise the Universe would be a duality and not a unity, which is both unthinkable and impossible. God is, God is all there is, and God is perfect. But this perfection must translate itself to us, through us. We are living in an intelligent Universe which responds to our mental states. As our text says at the bottom of page 139, *This is why we are studying the power of thought*.

The second paragraph on page 140, speaking of man as a center of Intelligence, states that every time a person thinks, he sets Creative Mind in action, and that because of the oneness of Mind It cannot know anything about us other than that which we know about ourselves. This is what Jesus meant when he said, *As thou hast believed, so be it done unto thee*. The Principle not only is the Doer and the Giver, but It can do for us and give to us only that which we first mentally take.

Again we note that Principle responds by reflection or correspondence. If you will turn to page 460 under the heading *God Turns to Us as We Turn to Him*, you will find a discussion of the reciprocal action between the Universal and the individual mind, and how it is that the Law of Cause and Effect operates automatically. *The thought is ever father to the act*. The Universe already has been delivered to each one of us. Like the principle of mathematics, all of it belongs to everyone. The mathematician is merely the one who uses what has already been given to him, and in so doing he robs no man, nor does he exhaust his principle.

We can draw forth from the Infinite as much as we can truly vision into It—no more and no less. The act of visioning is spontaneous. The Law which produces the vision is automatic. It is cause and effect. The Spirit is both Cause and Effect in that the Word of Spirit sets the Law of creation in motion, and this Law has no intention other than that which is given to It. Hence any apparent intention It has may be instantly changed. It was an understanding of this that gave Jesus his power.

On page 411, last paragraph, is the statement that the without, or our external world, is a reflection of our within. It is this interior awareness which creates all the conditions which we personally experience, or which draws us into the experience which we have. The Principle that makes can remake, the Mind that molds can remold. We are dealing with no less a Principle than this. We must consciously use this Creative Power, because until we do, we shall be using It unconsciously and chaotically (page 401, third paragraph).

We must definitely bring this Power under our conscious control and use It for specific purposes. This is what a practitioner in the Science of Mind does. The process is simple enough. It is a reversal of thought, but a conscious and persistent one. *The answer to every question is within man, because man is within Spirit, and Spirit is an Indivisible Whole* (page 365). *We should never hesitate to say that we know the Truth* (bottom of page 364), for the very claim of knowing the Truth, in such degree as it becomes a deep spiritual conviction, is in reality the Truth proclaiming Itself.

Perhaps the most subtle thing we shall ever have to realize is that the words we speak have life in such degree as we believe they have life. The words without meaning, however, would do nothing. Turn again to the second paragraph on page 140 and try to get a deep realization of the thought suggested there, that the Law of Mind cannot contradict any thought given It, but must always reflect what is put into It. It has no other choice; therefore, as suggested in the last paragraph of page 405, we must reverse thoughts of fear, transmuting them into faith.

The reversal of thought is a conscious action of the mind. We must learn to distinguish between daydreaming and real belief. You will find this discussed in the third and fourth paragraphs on page 399. We do not dream or hope or desire; we make a definite statement in Mind, which embodies our desire as though it were already a fulfilled fact in our experience. Since our individual subjective mind is our place in the Universal Creative Order and immediately connects us with limitless Power and Energy, in creating these images of thought we do not try to force them upon a reluctant power, but rather let them sink gently into our own creative consciousness. Therefore it is done unto us as we believe.

We do not coerce, we do not create the Power; we let this Power operate through us—*Let this mind be in you which was also in Christ Jesus*. This *letting* is not merely an intellectual process nor one of profundity of thought. Quite the reverse. It is simple and direct. It is natural to believe. Childlike belief and a quick acceptance is the best method. Let the acceptance be definite, let it be an acceptance of something if you wish to demonstrate in a specific way. Always remember that the Law is definite. It is definite because It must respond to your thoughts, and unless they are specific you will be tuning in, so to speak, to the vague and the uncertain.

It is one thing to sit in silent meditation and commune with the Spirit, with the idea of acquiring a greater consciousness and more illumination—this is both wise and profitable—but when you wish a definite demonstration be sure your thought is specific. State what you wish as a definite idea, and believe you have it. In the Principle with which you are dealing there is nothing but Mind and what Mind does.

Mind can operate only upon ideas. Form is idea solidified. It is the solution of Mind held in definite shape. Mind is acted upon by thought. And while we do not create the Power, but use It, it is the Power that creates for us. Anyone can practice mental healing successfully who, knowing that he can, follows his technique definitely, persistently, and consistently, and who refuses any suggestion which would deny him the privilege of using this Law.

We must always remember that we do not compel a reluctant force; we contemplate and think within ourselves and believe that what we have thought will actually take form in our lives or in the lives of those for whom we are thinking. In this way, as our text states at the top of page 141, the Power flows through us, but it is impossible for the Spirit to make the gift as long as we refuse to take it.

Now we know that the Divine Spirit is personal to each one of us because It is already personified through us. Hence there is an intimate relationship existing between the Universal and the individual. As suggested in the third paragraph on page 365, God is more than Principle; God is the Limitless Consciousness, the Indivisible Whole, in which we all live and which lives in each of us.

God is personal where He is personified. Every individual has access to the Infinite Person, while at the same time having control of his life through the limitless Law. This is a divine partnership and we have every right to use it. Thought force is described in our text as *a movement of consciousness in a field of mechanical but intelligent Law*. Now let us define consciousness as that subtle Principle within us which enables us to know anything. Therefore the movement of consciousness is an interior perception or belief, thought, idea, or image held in mind.

Let us suppose that we are surrounded by water, and that each time we think ice is formed. Let us think of all our conditions as being like these different shapes of ice, the solidification of water which is a liquid. Now let us consider our thoughts as the molds into which the liquid is poured that it may take form. Further, we know that the liquid must be poured into the mold, and because it has no choice it must take form. Thus we see that the mold is not a cause and the liquid is not a cause, but the one who pours the liquid into the mold is the cause. In this way each is the arbiter of his own fate, the creator of his own destiny through his use of the Law which governs all things—this Law is Mind in action.

It is written of Jesus that he sent out his word and healed. What a marvelous and exalted thought that we too can send out our word, or we can think within ourselves and cause a definite physical reaction in someone's physical being. This is what spiritual mind healing is—the conscious use of this Law for the purpose of helping those who are sick or in need. Thought force is a movement of consciousness in a field of Law. First the intelligence, then the word, then the movement—cause and effect again!

Since intelligence is that which forms the word, and since the word cannot help being formed, even the word is a part of the effect; for while it is the cause of the immediate action in Law, the thinker is the cause of the word. The thinker alone is ultimate and absolute. This is why it is said that God existed before the foundations of the world, and even before any particular word which He spoke—*In the beginning God* and *God spake and it was done*. Refer again to Lesson 1 to see exactly how your concept of the beginning of any creative order can work out in your own experience.

On page 142, *The Atmosphere of Our Thinking*, is the statement that *we are all immersed in the atmosphere of our own thinking*. On page 348 under the discussion of *Race-Suggestion*, the same idea is more elaborately worked out. Each individual is surrounded by race consciousness, and there is a subjective unity maintained between all people. The law of each individual's life is the sum total of all beliefs, whether they be conscious or a part of his inheritance of the race belief. There is a tendency on the part of each one of us to repeat the entire race belief.

This race suggestion governs most of us much of the time. It is a mesmeric spell, a hypnotic influence which, as a burden of human condemnation and fear, plays its role of despot in the creative imagination of our thought. Fortunately we are dealing with belief and not with real devils, for there are no such things. Belief in them is built entirely upon an illusion. And this illusion we must dissipate by knowing that God is the only Power.

We all reproduce a monotonous array of facts, of experiences, whose causes are hidden in the race memory—causes of which we are largely unconscious. We are blinded by a misconception of our true nature. That is why we are told to awake from our sleep and let Christ give us light. Jesus, understanding his true spiritual nature, spoke from his God-center rather than from the accumulated consciousness of the human race. He tore the veil from the face of Isis and revealed the fact that the creative order of the Universe is one with the word of man.

As explained on page 331, the second and third paragraphs, in treatment we should always recognize the unity of God and man. We are not separated from Life for we *are* Life. It was this concept which Jesus referred to when he spoke of his unity with the Whole. As our lesson states on page 142, second paragraph, the emphasis in spiritual healing is on our idea of God and the unity of good as ever present, ever available, both as Divine Presence and as immutable Law. To that soul which knows its own Divinity all else must gravitate.

We must dare to believe, and since belief is a mental concept it can be consciously generated. Hence we must not only dare to believe; we must have the courage and the conviction to know that we can consciously generate a right belief and thereby change any chain of cause and effect which surrounds us.

Summary

It is essential that we understand the meaning of Unity; that the God who is within, around, and above is one and the same Presence or Being. Our self-knowingness is God in us knowing Himself.

The Law which obeys the will of this Self-knowing is not a person but a Principle; hence we can use this Principle. If this were not true we would have no science to demonstrate.

Only the word is conscious that is consciously aware. The Law is subconsciously aware or subjectively aware, which means that It knows without knowing that It knows. It has no personal preference, choice, or will of Its own.

The individual creates time just as he creates experience. Time and experience are results of his self-awareness.

It is impossible for us to stop using Creative Power because we cannot stop being conscious. We cannot stop knowing something or thinking something or being conscious of something.

We get out of the Universe only what we put into It in the sense that we are individualizations of It.

The Spirit within us is both cause and effect, or the beginning and the end of any experience. We need to bring the power of Mind under control, but we cannot do it by willing or wishing or concentrating; we do it by spiritual embodiment through recognition and realization.

Since the Law has no choice, we choose for It, and we can reverse any choice we have ever made. We should commune daily with the Spirit to acquire greater consciousness, daily speak our word, and give our treatment or prayer affirmatively from the highest level of our spiritual communion.

Questions

Brief answers to these questions should be written out by the student after studying the lesson, and the answers compared with those which will be included in next week's lesson.

1. What do we mean when we say that we understand God at the level of our own consciousness?
2. Why do we believe that the Universal Mind or Intelligence responds to us?
3. Does our word put power into Mind?
4. Explain how it is that *I AM* is both individual and universal?
5. Are time and space things of themselves?
6. How much of the mental Principle can each one of us use?
7. Does our use of the Principle of Mind in any way exhaust It?
8. Why is Spirit both cause and effect?

9. Why should we consciously use the creative power of thought?
10. Explain: *Words without meaning in mental treatment will do nothing*.
11. In treating distinguish between generalized meditation and definite work.
12. Is God more than mental Principle or Law?
13. Is God as Universal Presence personal to man?
14. What is spiritual mind healing?
15. What do we mean by race suggestion?
16. In what way does race suggestion influence us?
17. Is all race belief necessarily limiting?
18. Explain the meaning of, *Awake thou that sleepest . . . and Christ shall give thee light*.
19. What and where is man's God-center?

Answers to Questions on Lesson 15

1. The Law of Averages means the impersonal Law of Mind working through the individual. It is an impersonal acceptance of what the sum total of human thought has believed to be true about all people.
2. The Law of Mind, being a mechanical but intelligent law of cause and effect, knows about the individual only what the individual knows about himself, plus the unconscious operation of the law of averages.
3. Because the mental Law is like a mirror, which never initiates anything but follows any pattern given It, we change Its tendency of limitation by reversing our thought, thus providing a new pattern.
4. Our patterns of thought should be definite because they produce a corresponding reaction in the Universal Mind.
5. The Law which limits us is neither good nor evil. It is an impersonal Law of Cause and Effect.
6. The Will of Spirit toward us must be perfection because, like the nature of Spirit, if It were not perfect It would be self-destructive.
7. Our thought never controls Reality or the Cosmos, but by changing our reaction to It, It automatically changes Its relation to us.
8. Jesus was not different from other men, but because he understood his spiritual nature he appeared to be different.
9. The spiritual, mental, and physical planes do not contradict each other. They constitute a perfect unity in which the spiritual dominates the mental, and the mental dominates the physical.
10. We should combine conviction with definite intention in treatment because we must not only have faith, but we must also consciously direct the power of that faith.
11. The saying, *Nature unaided fails*, means that because natural laws are impersonal we must introduce the personal element before they can be specialized or consciously used.
12. The subjective Law of Mind is our servant because It must follow the pattern of our thought.
13. The objective form of a subjective embodiment means that the Law of Mind projects, as objective condition, that which we mentally accept, believe, and have faith in, and deeply comprehend the meaning of.
14. Punishment and reward are but logical results of our use of the Law of Cause and Effect.

15. The *Armor of God* is faith in the good.
16. The *sword of the Spirit* means that definite statements have the power to produce corresponding physical reactions.
17. We can know that our word has power only by proving it, that is, by applying it to some definite or specific problem.
18. Jesus taught the necessity of believing that we already have what we desire, because until we have a complete acceptance of our desire we have furnished no mold of thought for the Law to fill.
19. Our belief in an illusion cannot make a reality of such an illusion, but our knowledge of Reality can dispel illusion. We can believe that which is not real, but we can know only that which is real.
20. We cannot believe that evil or limitation are divinely ordained, since they contradict the nature of Reality.
21. Having a *single eye* means looking through conditions to a perfect, unitary Cause.
22. Man's thought is creative because God's thought is creative, and man is a center of God-creativeness.

Spiritual Mind Healing and Mental Suggestion

While it is self-evident that some degree of mental suggestion enters into all human relationships, we must be careful not to confuse spiritual mind healing with the popular concept of mental suggestion. In this practice suggestion disappears and explanation takes its place.

But someone might contend that this explanation itself is a suggestion. We admit that there is some basis for this claim if by mental suggestion is meant changing one's thought through receiving instruction from another. From this viewpoint, would we say that a teacher is practicing mental suggestion when she points out to a pupil his error in working a mathematical problem, and explains to him how it should be solved? We would not consider this mental suggestion, but explanation.

It is certain that suggestion plays a subtle role in all life. If we go out into the desert we receive a suggestion of its calmness; if we look at a glorious sunset there is a suggestion of infinite peace and beauty. It is impossible to read the daily newspaper or a book without receiving some suggestion. When we read advertisements in the street cars or in magazines, the principle of suggestion is operating.

It is not so much a question of whether or not suggestion is playing this subtle role in human life; rather, it is a question of whether the dominant suggestions of human life are constructive. In this analysis it is necessary to understand whether or not we think of mental explanation as being a suggestion. For instance, if someone says two and two make five and we explain to him that two and two make four, do we consider our explanation a suggestion? If so, then every teaching of truth becomes a suggestion. Undoubtedly we should all agree that the teaching of truth is an explanation rather than a suggestion, and in drawing our line we realize that if the teaching of truth is a mental suggestion, then it is a most desirable one. The only suggestions we need to avoid are the destructive ones, those which coerce the mind.

The question might be asked, "Is faith healing mental suggestion? Does the atmosphere of a particular shrine suggest some positive conviction that can heal?" Another question almost inevitably follows, "Is this exchanging one belief for another?" Since we are finite I suppose we are generally exchanging one belief for another, but if we make a good bargain by trading lesser beliefs for greater ones, I presume we have done well.

There have been long and varied discussions on this subject, as to whether or not spiritual mind healing is based on a principle of mental suggestion. Those whose entire interest is in the field of psychology claim that this whole field is one of mental suggestion. They call it spiritual suggestion. On the other hand, the average metaphysician will disclaim any element of suggestion in his work, and tell you that he heals through the knowledge that God is All.

It is certain that in the practice of mental suggestion the one making the suggestion must be present with his patient, and the patient must be consciously receptive to his suggestion. In our field the practitioner does not have the slightest need of knowing where his patient is when he treats him. In his treatment he does not mentally address his patient. For instance, he does not say, "John Smith, you are thus and so," or, "You are going to be thus and so."

We all know that the average suggestive therapeutist must be in the room with his patient, but in our form of healing we do not care where the patient is or what he may be doing when we are giving a treatment for him. Therefore suggestion, as it is commonly practiced, would not be effective in what we call absent treatment, and we know in our field that absent treatment is just as effective as is present treatment.

In ordinary methods of mental suggestion it is considered advisable for the patient to be relaxed, receptive, acquiescent, but the practitioner in our field does not consider these points in his practice. In some cases the patient does not know that he is a patient, the reason being that in this field the practitioner does all his work within himself.

In treating he recognizes the one he is seeking to help, by saying: "This word is for John Smith or Mary Jones or Martin Andrews." He specifies the person the treatment is for, he identifies the treatment with the person. All his work is done within his own mind, in his own thought, with complete disregard of where his patient may be or what he may be doing, or what he may be thinking about at that particular time. The practitioner clears up his own consciousness. That is what spiritual practice is. Jesus did not suggest anything to the paralyzed man when he told him to get up and walk.

Of course we do not deny that much disease is the result of suggestion, whether that suggestion be self-suggestion or whether it arises spontaneously from the consensus of human opinion, which we might call collective suggestion. We do not deny that suggestion plays not only a subtle but a powerful role in human life, individually and collectively, and that in all probability it is impossible to escape some of its effect.

What we affirm is that in this form of practice one does not try to suggest anything to one's patient. He does not say, "You are getting better," even though such a statement might be salutary. The practitioner must know that he is dealing only with the spiritual man, and the spiritual man does not get better; he is already perfect.

This form of treatment is a revelation of the self to the self, and is arrived at instantly through realization, or by stages through the reversal of consciousness.

But whether we are able to recognize instantly the Truth for someone, or through the process of affirmation and denial arrive at the same conclusion, makes no difference. In neither instance do we try to suggest anything to the patient, and yet we realize that in some way the recognition which we make must operate through the patient if it is to heal him.

Just how this happens no one knows, but that it does happen without any attempt on the part of the practitioner to do anything other than arrive at a realization for his patient, is certain. Treatment contains no element of mental coercion, practices no form of conscious suggestion or mental concentration.

Treatment is a series of statements about some person, an argument in mind about some person, or a realization of what we call the Truth about some person. But whether it takes the form of a series of statements, an argument in mind, or a realization, it is effective to such degree as the practitioner becomes inwardly conscious of what we call the Truth about his patient; that the patient is now complete and perfect.

It is our belief that wherever spiritual mind healing has been successfully practiced or demonstrated, one unifying and identical principle has run through all such practice; an element of both conviction and acceptance.

Now the question might be asked, "Does faith pass into the certainty of understanding?" The answer is both *Yes* and *No*. Faith in electricity passes into the understanding that the energy which we call electricity exists, and we may use it. But even understanding that it exists is faith that it will always respond to us according to what we have discovered to be the law of its being.

All sciences ultimately resolve themselves into a series of faiths in natural laws discovered and demonstrated. Faith may pass into understanding. Applying this principle to spiritual mind healing, we announce that faith in God or Good has throughout the ages definitely demonstrated the presence of a universal Principle of God. Thus faith may pass through experiment into scientific certainty which is knowledge.

From this standpoint we would not say that faith, as exhibited throughout the ages, is merely a mental suggestion, for it is definitely more than this. It has been and it is an unconscious mental union with Reality. It would be absurd for a modern metaphysician to deny that this experience has come historically to people of varying spiritual convictions, and it would seem intelligent to recognize that the Universal Principle always works wherever, whenever, and in such degree as anyone consciously or unconsciously, in ignorance or in wisdom, in superstition or in fear, provides an avenue through which It may work.

Thus we arrive at a concept of the universality and impersonality, the changeless reality of natural principles. Faith has been the most dynamic power throughout the ages, and it should not be denounced as mere suggestion, but understanding that faith has demonstrated a Principle, we should seek to understand that Principle, and we should make every endeavor to reproduce at will the too infrequent experiences which result from an attitude of faith.

We agree that while mental suggestion plays some subtle role in spiritual mind healing, it is not the dominant factor, and as far as the practitioner is concerned, it does not enter into it at all since he makes no attempt to suggest anything to his patient at any time or under any circumstance.

If someone tells us that the practitioner of this science does his work in the field of mental explanation, we may agree with him, but we must hasten to add that this explanation operates through some universal field which needs no coercion; which is independent of time, place, and circumstance; which knows neither big nor little, hard nor easy, past nor future, but appears to exist in an eternal now and in an everlasting here. In practice this *now* and *here* are in the mind of the practitioner.

Moreover, when we apply the ordinary concept of mental suggestion to another phase of our work, which is the control of conditions through right thinking, we find it impossible to accept suggestion as an explanation. For while we might suggest to an individual that he is successful, how could this make him successful in actual objective fact unless thought also operated in a field entirely independent of the immediate environment?

For instance, to what or whom would a grocer give suggestions if he were working for prosperity? Suppose he has no customers, then there is no one to receive his suggestions. We must fall back upon the idea that his suggestions are made to sacks of potatoes or bags of beans. These inanimate objects, the commodities which he has to sell, together with the cases in which he displays his goods, are apparently the only things open to suggestion, and whoever heard of a man suggesting to a can of beans that it could sell itself or that it could go out and find a customer?

Of course we are not denying that most advertising is suggestive, or that many methods of suggestion are used in all business. We are not denying that one may, to some slight degree at least, influence others. What we are doing is affirming that this is not the method used in this form of practice. Our grocer who has no customers to receive his suggestion, must know something which will bring him customers. This he does through the activity of right ideas, realizing that the activity of right ideas is the real activity and that there is no solid fact, that all facts are fluid. He resolves things into thoughts and handles the thoughts, not the things.

Suppose one wishes to attract new friendships. He starts out by having no friends to whom he can offer suggestions of friendship. There is nothing to coerce because there is no one there to be coerced. He can influence no one because there is no one in his environment to be influenced or to influence. He starts from scratch, and unless there were a Principle which acted independently, he could not attract new friendships into his life. It is self-evident, then, that this part of his practice is not mental suggestion. It is mental realization, which brings us right back to the central theme of our whole philosophy.

If we had to energize energy, where would we go to get the energy with which to energize it? If we had to create intelligence, from what source of information would we draw our knowledge with which to inform intelligence?

We are brought back to the fundamental proposition that self-realization is based on self-existence, and self-existence, from the universal standpoint, means that the generative, productive, and projective power of the Universe is at the point of man's self-recognition, and responds to man's self-recognition.

Practical Suggestion for Mental Treatment

One Mind in Three

Man has One Mind, but for convenience we separate it into three classifications: the conscious, the subjective (or subconscious), and the Christ Consciousness. We must be careful, however, that we do not divide man into three parts, for his conscious mind is the use he is making of his spiritual faculties, while his subconscious mind is the unconscious use he is making of the Universal Law of Cause and Effect.

It is an interesting fact that we can reach the subconscious and give it direction by use of our conscious faculties. The conscious faculty is what impresses the subconscious reaction.

The subconscious of itself, being merely a law of cause and effect, may be reorganized by the conscious direction given it. This is why mental treatment is a definite act of thought and not a haphazard or chaotic arriving at confused conclusions.

The entire theory of the control of conditions through the conscious use of thought rests on the proposition that conscious thought activity may reorganize subjective reactions, and that subjective reactions will return as objective situations as directed.

Hence we see that spiritual mind treatment is definite. It always has a conscious purpose in mind. To believe this, to understand it, and to know how to use it enables us to rise above old situations and to create new ones.

You Have Dominion

With an understanding of this science fear should disappear. And with direct application of this Principle to your problems you will discover that they will begin to seem less insistent.

Begin to act as though you already had dominion over evil, as though all fear were a phantom, and as though everything you have been afraid of were unreal. Declare the Truth by saying there is nothing to be afraid of; that you no longer entertain any images of fear; that Good is the only power there is; that this Good which is the only power there is, is now operating in your affairs.

Know that good is omnipotent. Know that the Truth instantly, effectively, and permanently destroys every fear and every effect of fear. Know that you are governed by Infinite Intelligence. Know that you are directed by Divine Guidance, and that you are compelled to think and act constructively. Therefore you may know that everything you do, say, or think carries with it a Divine authority.

Freedom already exists, but your freedom is in your own thought. Hence it is not enough to say, "God is free,'" which, of course, is a true statement; but this statement must be made personal: "The freedom of God is *my* freedom, the power of God is *my* power, the Presence of God is *in me*. The Mind of God is *my* mind, the strength of God is *my* strength, and the joy of God is *my* joy."

Feeling, Organized and Directed, Is Creation

Mind must know all things, being omniscient; hence whatever is, Mind knows, and Mind is the Principle back of all treatment. Treatment is enforcement of Principle. The words, thoughts, phrases, and statements are the way in which one makes known his feeling of the Divine Allness at any particular time.

Mind comprehends everything. Mind is at the center of man's body and at the center of his affairs, and comprehends both body and affairs. We are to demonstrate that this comprehension is perfect, harmonious, whole, prosperous, happy, complete, and eternal.

When we use such words we must feel their meaning. The feeling without the words may have a meaning but no direction, and meaning without direction will produce no creation. Feeling, organized and directed, is intelligent creation.

The practitioner knows that nothing is hid, and that the ideas of Mind are perfect. He knows that Absolute Intelligence has nothing hid from It; there is nothing covered which shall not be revealed. Everything is visible to It.

The practitioner knows that his word, being the presence, power, and activity of Mind, does uncover, reveal, make known, proclaim, and manifest itself. His word is the Law of Mind unto any case. Hence if a practitioner feels that he does not know what words to use he should immediately know that he does know what words to use.

Spiritual diagnosis exposes to thought that which is eternally true and declares that this allness is *now present* and *now manifest*.

"There are also celestial bodies; and bodies terrestrial"

Know that bone and flesh and blood
Are as waters of a river
Flowing from a hidden source.
Flesh and blood and bone and sinew
Are as matter of the Spirit,
Are as form made up of Spirit,
Are as shadows cast forth from It,
From a stuff no man has seen.

How then can this subtle substance
Shape itself in form of body,

Become flesh and blood of body,
Become bony part of body,
Become sinew of the body,
Become a form that's foul or fair?

This the alchemy of Spirit,
This the secret is of Spirit,
That the food we take in body,
That the water drunk by body,
That the air diffused in body,
Should itself become a body—
This the miracle of life.

How can this of ether only,
How can this from nature taken,
Blind with thoughts we do not see;
How can yearning, feeling, striving,
How can secret thoughts of passion
Brought to us from unseen river
Be as body, form as body,
Become flesh and blood of body,
By some alchemy of the unknown,
Made of what we do not see?

Is not this the secret meaning,
Is not this the holy meaning,
Is not this the unknown meaning
Of the flesh and blood of Christ?
When of bread we take in body,
When of air we breathe in body,
When of wine we drink in body,
Is not this the Eucharist?

He, the one who knew its meaning;
He, the one who saw its meaning;
He, the one who felt its meaning,
Is the one who spread the table;
Is the one who filled the chalice,
Is the one who broke the bread.
This he did to teach the lesson;
This he did to give the reason;
This he did to show that substance

Is of Spirit formed and held,
Is by Spirit freely given,
Is by Spirit gladly given,
Is by Spirit always given
By a process nature planned.

This the secret of the ages;
This the wisdom of the wise men;
This the truth they ever sought for;
This is what they found within—
Body has a perfect pattern,
Body has an unseen substance,
Body has a complete likeness
In the life and mind of God.

But this unseen, complete likeness
Is not hidden in the heavens,
Is not far away from earth,
Is not distant from our landscape,
Is not poised in air above us,
Is not hidden under water,
Is not buried in the ground.

Where, then, is this perfect pattern;
Where, then, is this subtle body;
Where, then, is this unseen likeness
To the body that we see?
This the truth the wise discovered;
This the lesson that they taught us;
This the secret that they found—

Everything on earth has pattern;
Everything that is, has likeness;
Every form we see has mooring
In that from which all forms emerge.
In the ether, in the silence,
In the subtle Inner substance,
In the unseen cause of causes,
In the life and mind of God;
In this pattern always given,
In this pattern always held,
Is the likeness of our body,

Is the pattern of each member,
Is an image of each action.

And this body in the ether
With its members attached to us,
With its head and hands part of us,
With its eyes and feet part of us,
Is the substance of this body,
Is the likeness of this body,
Is the pattern of this body
In the life and mind of God.

This the body that the Christ knew;
This the body that he spoke of;
This the body he brought with him;
This the body he took with him
On the mount of his transition,
On the dawn of resurrection,
On the day he left behind him
Nothing that man's eye could see.
For the pattern he brought with him
Or his likeness in the world unseen
Could not die nor be destroyed.

Only image of his pattern,
Only image of his unseen,
Only image of his likeness,
Hung upon the cross of treason
Or was buried in the tomb.
But because he knew the reason,
And because he understood
That the likeness of his pattern
And the image of his pattern
Were not separate in truth,
He could raise the image fleshy
To the likeness of its pattern,
To the form forever given,
To the form forever held there,
To the body that's eternal
To its everlasting day.

This the message that he gave us:
This the lesson that he taught us;
This is what he came to earth for—
This the purpose of his life.
But the lesson would be useless
And his message without meaning
And his mission would be fruitless
Unless we in his footsteps follow.

This he told his closest followers,
And he told those nearest to him,
What he did they too could do.
And he told them when he left them
That the Spirit ever with them
Would reveal to them the meaning
Of the words he spoke unto them,
Of the lessons that he gave them
When the image of his pattern
And the likeness of his pattern
Sojourned here on earth among them,
Talked and tarried with them
'Til the day of his ascension,
'Til the dawn of his transition,
'Til the time of his departure
To the realms of the unseen.

This the lesson that he gave them,
These the words he spoke unto them—
Go, thou, too, and do thou likewise.
So the Spirit that was with them
And the life that never left them—
Perfect pattern of their image,
Perfect likeness of their image—
Caused them to awake and listen
To the voice of all creation,
To the cause of all created,
To the Father of all mankind,
To the Maker of all earthkind.
Caused them to awake and listen,
Caused them always to remember
That they, too, had unseen pattern,
That they, too, had inner likeness,

That all humankind has likeness
In the mind and life of God.
... *Ernest Holmes*

Bibles of the World

Fragments from the spiritual history of the race
revealing fundamental UNITY of religious thought and experience

CHRISTIANITY - God that made the world, and all things therein . . . giveth to all life, and breath, and all things; and hath made of one blood all nations of men, for to dwell on all the face of the earth; that they should seek the Lord, if haply they might feel after him, and find him, though he be not far from everyone of us: For in him we live, and move, and have our being.

CONFUCIANISM - Great Heaven is intelligent, clear-seeing, and is with you in all your goings.

HINDUISM - All-pervading is He, bountiful, omnipresent and kindly.

The Eternal Witness to virtue and vice dwelleth in the heart.

Verily, there is One Supreme Soul, present in all beings and in one's own soul. All beings are of the One Soul.

SIKHISM - As I behold creation, I am amazed and astonished. God is contained in the hearts of men. In my heart I hold God, who filleth every place.

Many millions search for God and find Him in their hearts.

He whom I thought without me I now find within me. When I found this secret, I recognized the Lord of the world.

JAINISM - Seeker after the highest truth! Study the Sacred Lore, in order to cause yourself and others to obtain perfection.

The Power of Thought

Office of the Dean

My Dear Friend,

Nothing is more important than that we receive Divine Guidance in everything we do. We often wonder how to commune with the Invisible so that we shall receive Divine Guidance. If this were as difficult as it seems, it would be impossible. It is its utmost simplicity which eludes us.

This is what we have tried to explain in the special article on Divine Guidance in this lesson, and we hope you will practice affirming that Divine Guidance is yours, realizing always that the Principle of Mind in Action responds to you in the terms of the demand you make on It.

Of course you do not create the Principle but you do specify just how It is to respond, in the same sense that you decide how to plant a garden or set a hen instead of a duck, or build a house instead of an automobile. One of the main difficulties in thinking of Divine Guidance is that too often we feel that in seeking such guidance we are manipulating good. But nothing could be further from the case; in fact, just the opposite is true, because in a certain sense we are permitting God to govern our actions. Divine Guidance is a definite principle in nature, and according to our article, *Let God Do It*, when we work back to that subterranean source of life it will gush up like a living fountain.

So practice Divine Guidance every day, taking a definite time for the purpose, not trying to coerce anything, but in a relaxed way affirm that you are Divinely guided, and that you do know what to do, and then let God do it through you.

Sincerely,
Ernest Holmes

Lesson 17

Inducing Thought,* page 142, to *Understanding, page 147

In this lesson we are told that what thought has done thought can undo. Unless habits of wrong thinking could be successfully neutralized there would be no use in studying the Science of Mind. But we know that thought patterns, as soon as they are created become subjective, and that a subjective state of thought, never being a thing of itself but always being a reaction, can be changed. It is upon this ability to change subjective reactions that the entire Science of Mind rests in so far as its practical application to mental healing is concerned.

But as our text states, it is not enough to abstain from wrong thinking; there must be active right thinking. It is not enough to state that God is all there is, which would be true whether or not we made such a statement; we must realize the Divine Presence as right action in our lives, and in a specific way. That is how we use all of the principles in nature. We shall never derive satisfying results from this science unless we use it as we use other principles.

One of the great weaknesses of applied metaphysics is that people refuse to use this Principle as consciously as they use other principles. Their refusal to do so rests upon superstition and mental apathy, or spiritual inertia of thought. We must arouse ourselves from this mental drowsiness and free ourselves from the suggestion that denies us the right to have freedom. We must be active in right thinking. This is what is meant by being *doers of the word*. We must speak our word consciously.

Turn to the Meditations at the bottom of page 544 and the top of page 545 and you will find a good illustration of how to prepare yourself to give a correct, scientific, and therefore an effective mental treatment. All scientific treatments are effective. It will not be sufficient to state that the power of your word is supreme; you must definitely connect your word with some specific desire. We need the spiritual experience of having our word made manifest. We need to know that we can speak our word and have it return to us laden with the fruits of our desire. Today the world needs spiritual experience as never before. Unless an ever increasing number of people seek and find the Truth and actually do have spiritual experience, the world may have to learn in a more difficult way.

Turn next to page 445, *The Need of Spiritual Experience*. We can know only that which we experience, and no matter what great men have taught or what the illumined have told us, we must get this experience first-hand. Spiritual experience is just as much a fact as any other experience. It comes from within our own souls and is a guarantee that we ourselves are both Divine and Eternal. As you will find in the third paragraph on page 414, spiritual power is released through true thinking, since the spark which burns at the center of each soul is some part of the Eternal Flame.

We already are spiritually perfect but this spiritual perfection which we inwardly are must be realized. It was a realization of his spiritual nature which enabled Jesus to perform the so-called miracles. If you turn to the third paragraph on page 363 you will find that this Christ idea, which Jesus recognized, taught, and demonstrated, is not limited to any person, nor does it appear in only one age. This Christ Principle is inherent in each one of us.

In such degree as our thought is in harmony with the indwelling Christ it has absolute power, and it is in harmony with this indwelling Christ in such degree as we are in conscious unity and cooperation with good, truth, and beauty. Over and over again we must realize that God is *all* there is—the only Power, Presence, and Law; the only Cause, Medium, and Effect. God is not only the Creative Principle; He is the Universal Presence, and because He is the Universal Presence He is at the same time the individualized man. The recognition of this is the awakening of the indwelling Christ who reveals Himself in power and might to everyone who believes in this indwelling Presence and whose life is in harmony with goodness, truth, and beauty.

As you will find in the first paragraph on page 359, Christ is a Universal Presence personified in those who believe. We must become actively conscious of good, not passively so. We definitely neutralize an old thought and as consciously create a new one. Thus our ancient Karma is wiped out. The Law of Cause and Effect is not wiped out, but Its tendency is changed and the new experience is created—not a new law but a new experience.

A mirror remains the same mirror even though it reflects the many and varied forms of a parade. As each form appears a unique representation is reflected in the mirror. We do not change the mirror but the image in front of it. The Law cannot be changed but our experience can, else we would all be bound. We must have a consciousness of that which we wish to demonstrate, and if we do have this consciousness we are making a correct use of the Law.

Turn again to the definition of *Consciousness* on page 580. Gaining this consciousness is not a thing of will power, but of the imagination; it is a feeling or an inner conviction. We should become enthusiastic over our declarations of the Truth. On page 589 consider carefully the definition of *Enthusiasm*. It indeed may well be called the fortuneteller of life, the power of consciousness at the center of our ideas. If we would use this Divine Power for mental healing we must first believe that there is something which responds to us.

On page 597, under *Healing*, you will find among other things the thought expressed that mental treatment is a direct statement and that this statement is made in Mind. Remember that it is made in your own mind, since your own mind is some part of the One and Only Mind. Mental healing is a science as well as an art. It is a thing of feeling and conviction as well as of definite statement and conscious phrasing. Your word does not speak the Power into existence, but it does speak It into form; therefore your word must contain the form you wish to see manifested.

Limitation is a condensation of the idea of want (page 403). Mind as a Creative Law accepts the idea as true and converts the idea into form in some mysterious way which we do not understand but which we may accept, since we have already proved that it is true. Mind Itself is the solution, but this solution is held in temporary form, and the form we call a condition. The use of this Creative Principle is more than faith, and yet we must have faith in It. Our faith must be put into words and set into active operation.

When you treat for physical healing, state definitely that the word which you speak is for such and such a person; then make your declaration about him as though you were telling yourself what you believe to be true about him, never with any idea of mental coercion, nor even of suggestion. It is an explanation to yourself of what you believe about his spiritual nature.

Turn to the third paragraph on page 415 where the idea of a unifying Principle existing in an all-embracing Mind is discussed. There must be a harmonious and perfect Principle which is entirely independent of our conscious action or subjective reaction. This spiritual Principle, which is the incarnation of God in us, is always perfect, so when you are making your statements about the one you are treating, start with the assumption that there is such a spiritual Principle and build your whole argument upon that. Say, "This man is perfect; not only is he perfect but he is *now* manifesting the perfection which I know him to be."

You must have a deep, abiding conviction that it is just exactly as you state. You will arrive at this conviction in such degree as you sense the Allness of God or Good, for if God is for you, He cannot be against you. Thus you see that giving a mental treatment is more than a mechanical process even though it deals with the mechanics of mind. There is a spontaneous joy in it and an exultant recognition of the supremacy of Good. The ancient thought, *I am God and there is none else*, is good, but it must be coupled with the thought that *I and my Father* are one. This is a merging of the Universal and the individual.

It certainly is necessary that we choose how we shall think. We are individuals in a mental and spiritual world just as we are in the physical world. Unless we were individuals in a mental and spiritual world we would not and could not be individualized, and the very fact that we are individualized completely proves this viewpoint to be correct. Turn to the definition of *Individuality* on page 601, and the definition of *Personality* on page 617. We are individuals and we have a perfect right to choose, but we must expect to abide by our choice. That is, we must take what goes with it.

If, as our lesson on page 144 affirms, *Thoughts are things*, then different kinds of thoughts must produce different kinds of things. We should deliberately decide to think calmly at all times, and yet we should never lose our spontaneity. We should learn to believe in happiness and in success, no matter what appears externally. We must plunge beneath the surface appearance. We must become conscious of good. If God is all there is, and if we have accepted this viewpoint, then we must not deny it. We must believe, believe, believe, and keep on believing.

We must have faith, and we must have faith in our faith, and we must keep on believing in our faith and having faith in our belief. Often, over and over again, we must point out to ourselves that we do believe. You will find this particularly true when you give treatments. For if you find when you treat someone that the desired result is not immediately forthcoming, what are you going to do? You will have to turn again to Principle and restate your treatment, and overlooking all appearances to the contrary, reaffirm your position. If you do this you will—if not immediately, at least gradually—arrive at a correct conviction and realization of the spiritual perfection of your patient. This is the right way to practice spiritual mind healing.

The only concentration that we need in this practice (bottom of page 397), is one of mental attention and acceptance. As the next paragraph suggests, what you need is *acceptance and realization*. A person may treat himself consciously for acceptance and realization by daily declaring that he is conscious of and knows the Truth. He is conscious of the power of his word, and feels it. He is conscious that his word acts as law, and understands it. He expects a result, and experiences it. He knows that he can work, and he works. The knowledge of this Presence, this Power, and this Law was what gave Jesus his apparently miraculous power. He exercised this Power and we can do the same if we have the same belief, for the Infinite is no respecter of persons. God has no favorites, and the Law knows no favorites.

As our lesson says at the top of page 145, any prolonged mental state is bound to produce a physical correspondence. The realization of the Presence of God is the most powerful healing agency in our work. Therefore all of our words should be filled with this realization. Thus the God Principle responds to Itself as we become aware of the Divine Presence, ever animating, ever stimulating, ever expressing, and always perfect.

We should learn to think calmly, peacefully, with an inner exultation, realizing the tremendous power at our disposal, and never forgetting that the highest use of this Power is released when we are in conscious union with harmony. Truth cannot and will not be divided against Itself. We must come to realize that we are one with God and that we do have the same power which Jesus had. Every spiritual genius has had this realization and has exercised this knowledge. We must use our word definitely, always. Each word has a power commensurate with the conviction back of it.

Our main endeavor is to make a practical application of this Principle in helping ourselves and others. It is natural that we should wish more life, a greater degree of happiness, success, and the joy of harmonious companionship. There is nothing wrong about any of these things. Each is a natural expression of the God desire within us. We all seek the more abundant life, since we all have a spiritual intuition that the abundant life is for us. For the first time we are coming to understand that there is a definite mental Principle, through the use of which we may expect to demonstrate this more abundant life.

We expect to bring more abundant experiences into our own lives and the lives of those for whom we work. We must not think of this as a game of chance, but the action of certainty. Whatever we can conceive we may experience. Whatever we have experienced which has been undesirable we can neutralize. Remember that the appearance and the disappearance of form is entirely effect, and that God can do for us only what He can do through us.

Next read the first paragraph on page 470, the lower section of the same page, and also the top of page 471. The Truth cannot fail, for God is Truth. We need no longer fight the old order of thought; rather we should create new images. The Spirit has made the gift, now we must learn how to accept it, and we must do this definitely, persistently, and consciously until we do demonstrate.

Know that when you speak your word for someone else, that word has power. It is Law. Work until you know that nothing can hinder it, that *you* believe it and expect it to work, and know that it is going to work. If any doubt arises in your mind turn at once and neutralize that doubt by denying that it has any power. You will soon learn that a specific denial in mind has a tendency to erase the mental image or dissipate the energy of a thought. It certainly does something to it, for it will gradually fade away.

This whole practice rests upon the theory that Principle is responsive to thought. When you treat someone believe that your word is the Law of his life and that it is going to be effective in his experience. Believe this and state it and compel yourself to recognize that, as our lesson says, *the Power is within* (page 146).

The awakening must be within our own thought. When we depend upon past or present conditions we are not making the highest use of our thought but are limiting the Creative Power of our thought to previous experiences. We must know that the Truth can mold any condition. That which makes can remake, that which molds can remold, that which creates can re-create. Instead of depending upon conditions as they now are, let us conceive a better condition. Principle makes things out of Itself by the simple act of becoming the thing that It makes.

When you give a treatment do not think of the condition as it is, or as it used to be, but think of it as being perfect. Specifically deny that which you wish to neutralize. This denial is not necessary if your affirmation is complete, but when it is not it would be correct practice to use a denial since it is a scientific use of Principle. Remember that the Prodigal Son remained a prodigal as long as he chose to be one, and when he returned to his father's house he was instantly reinstated.

Turn now to page 460, *God Turns to Us as We Turn to Him*, and read through to the end of the story at the bottom of page 470. This is a true story of the journey of the soul and the awakening of the mind to the fact that its eternal home is here and now and perfect. There is no limitation imposed upon us, and our ignorance of the Law does not excuse us. We shall never overcome the old conditions if we insist on talking about them, reading about them, and believing in them. Let us think rather of that Principle which makes all things new.

Summary

If our thought patterns could not be changed we could not use the Principle of the Law of Mind in Action because we could not change our use of the Law of Causation.

We must use this Principle as consciously as we would plant cotton.

The use of this Principle is not conscious but acts because we initiate new channels of causation.

We all need spiritual or inward experience in order to be certain of our own position in the Law of Mind. This no one can give us but ourselves, because the Christ Principle is already within us.

God is both the Universal Presence and the individual man. It was a knowledge of this that gave Jesus his power.

Mental healing is both a science and an art because it has feeling and technique.

Science and faith are not the same thing, yet faith acts as the Law of a definite Principle which works mechanically. Therefore we must have faith in faith, and faith in our ability to use faith.

In giving treatment you identify your treatment with the person you wish to help, and then give the treatment within yourself. There is no concentration in this but there is mental attention.

Your work is not a game of chance, because treatment and faith act as a law. Your word is the law and shall prosper in the thing whereto you direct it. Act, believe, and live as though this were true and it will become true to you.

Questions

Brief answers to these questions should be written out by the student after studying the lesson, and the answers compared with those which will be included in next week's lesson.

1. What do we mean by the statement: *What thought can do, thought can undo*?
2. Why is it not enough merely to say that God is all there is?
3. Why do people refuse to use the Principle of Mind as they would other natural principles?
4. Define a scientific and effective mental treatment.
5. When does our thought have absolute power?

6. What is the Christ Principle?
7. Is enthusiasm desirable in mental treatment?
8. Does our word create power, or does it give form to power?
9. (a) In treating for physical healing, what is your first assumption? (b) Does mental suggestion or coercion enter into this treatment?
10. What mental attitude gives us the greatest spiritual conviction?
11. In failing immediately to receive the desired results in treating, what should one do?
12. In what way do we use concentration in treatment?
13. What is the most powerful healing agency in our work?
14. What gives power to your word?
15. If any doubt arises as to the power of your word, what would you do?
16. Upon what main theory is this practice based?

Answers to Questions on Lesson 16

1. *We understand God at the level of our own consciousness* means that we understand God in so far as we comprehend and embody the nature of God, i.e., we can understand God as love only to the degree that we embody the nature and character of love.
2. We believe that the Universal Mind or Intelligence responds because we know that there is an intelligent response between the minds of individuals.
3. Our word does not put power into mind, but directs the power which is already there.
4. *I AM* is both individual and Universal because the Mind of God is individualized in man.
5. Time is not a thing of itself. It is an experience in a Unitary Wholeness; while space is relative to the object of such experience.
6. Each one of us has as much of the mental Principle to use as he conceives of himself as having.
7. Our use of the Principle of Mind in no way exhausts It, since It is Infinite. (Note: conservation of energy in physical science and the use of the principle of mathematics.)
8. The Spirit is both cause and effect because action as cause and reaction or effect take place within It.
9. We should consciously use the Creative Power of thought, because since we are constantly using the Creative Power, our conscious use of it will be more meaningful in our lives.
10. Words without meaning in mental treatment will do nothing, for unless they mean something to us we cannot believe in them.
11. In treatment, generalized meditation is for the purpose of imbibing the Spirit and realizing the power, while definite mental work is giving direction to the Law of Mind for specific purposes.
12. God as the Principle of Mind is the Law of Cause and Effect, just as God as electricity is a certain kind of energy. God as Spirit is the Universal Presence.
13. Because Spirit is personified in man, God as Universal Presence is personal to man.
14. Spiritual mind healing is a conscious use of the mental Law of Cause and Effect for beneficent, harmonious, and constructive purposes.
15. Race suggestion means the sum total of the consciousness of the ages.
16. Because we are subjectively unified with the thought of the ages, race suggestion tends to bind us to the limitations of race belief and experience.

17. Race belief is not necessarily limiting, since whatever idea or thought of goodness, truth, etc., it contains tends to bring about a greater expression of life.
18. *Awake thou that sleepest . . . and Christ shall give thee light* means to awake from the mesmeric spell of the fear, doubt, and uncertainty of race suggestion.
19. Man's God-center is his consciousness of his Divine Union which exists at the center of his own being.

Practical Suggestion for Mental Treatment

Direction and Intention

Nothing is more definite than mental work. Mental work is not daydreaming nor fantastic wishing. It is a deliberate act of the mind, a conscious, moving action of thought in a certain definite direction, and we should think of it from this viewpoint. The conscious mind chooses what it wishes the subjective Law to act upon. It gives direction to a Power which is infinite compared to its own conscious capacity.

But is this not true of all laws of nature? We are always using laws which of themselves do nothing for us until we consciously use them. If we would think of the laws of thought in the same practical manner as we think of other principles in nature, and if we could free ourselves from all superstition in using spiritual laws, realizing that they also are natural, we should have the power at our command which we so greatly feel the need of and which we so deeply desire to know how to use.

This is what differentiates a practical, experienced, and scientific worker in this field from one who merely hopes, wishes, or wills things to happen. A scientific worker always knows what he is doing. He always has a method of procedure. He has a definite technique and he follows this technique specifically. He uses thought, not as will power, not as concentration, not as coercion, but always with definite direction and conscious intention.

The Law a Schoolmaster or a Servant

Wherefore the law was our schoolmaster to bring us unto Christ, that we might be justified by faith. But after that faith is come, we are no longer under a schoolmaster (Galatians 3:24, 25). This means that the Law of Cause and Effect is a taskmaster while we are ignorant of Its operation, and being ignorant we use the Law destructively.

Experience teaches us what is best. We learn that good alone can be eternal and that love overcomes hate by the same Law of Cause and Effect which made hate seem real. Thus we are justified by faith and we are no longer under the schoolmaster of the Law.

This does not mean that the Law is destroyed. It means that we have reversed our use of the Law. We have brought chance into compliance with love, reason, and faith. We have caught the lightning and made it turn the wheels of industry. We have engaged the laws of nature and harnessed their energy to our purposes.

The Law which was our schoolmaster is the same Law, but now It is our obedient servant. To know this is what constitutes the difference between spiritual wisdom and spiritual ignorance. The unwise have no alternative; they are subject to the Law of Cause and Effect as a schoolmaster until they learn Its nature and until they discover that they may transcend all previous negation, and through Christ or Truth enter into a new heaven and a new earth, a different consciousness. When consciousness is changed, experience automatically changes.

The Principle of Divine Guidance

Nothing is more important than the realization that since we are surrounded by Infinite Intelligence we are immersed in Limitless Wisdom. Emerson tells us that human history is the working of the Infinite Mind on this planet.

We are, of necessity, inlets to the Divine Mind, but since we are individuals we become outlets to the degree that we permit ourselves to become. We are surrounded by Divine Wisdom, Love, and Intelligence, and still lack Divine Guidance. Not that we lack the principle of Divine Guidance, for that is the gift of God forever made and forever delivered, but that we lack the perception of this Guidance and Its operation through us.

As we frequently state in this series of lessons, principles of themselves do nothing in particular for the individual until they are specialized or used. The desert is made to blossom as the rose when man cooperates with the principle of productivity latent in the desert. Experience has taught us that this cooperation must be conscious and definite. Moreover, it has taught us that we must understand the Law with which we are going to cooperate, before we can draw upon It for special results.

We are surrounded by a Principle of Mind and Intelligence which will become Divine Guidance to us provided we permit It to do so. Our part is to realize that Divine Guidance is a principle, and to accept this principle as operating in our everyday life. The answer to every problem is in the problem itself. It is usually so self-evident that its very obviousness conceals it.

So Divine Guidance is ours for the asking, and no matter how crude that asking may be, or may have been in the history of religious evolution, there has always been an answer. God has answered every request at the level of the mentality from which the request was made. When the scientist listens, the artist imagines, the mathematician calculates, or the poet waits for the muse to guide his fancy into word pictures, all are praying for Divine Guidance. Each in his own sphere of action receives as much guidance as he is capable of perceiving.

Why not, then, consciously specialize this law of Divine Guidance, for surely this would be a practical thing to do. It is not enough to believe that Divine Guidance can guide; we must know that Divine Intelligence is guiding. We must know that there are no mistakes in the Divine Plan, and we must know that we are some part of the universal scheme of things.

According to our theory it is not enough merely to know this. For while we understand that Law is Mind in Action and that there is a Universal Law of Cause and Effect, we know that this same Law, working for us, is inhibited or accelerated in Its action through our faith and acceptance of It. Indeed this is one of the secrets of this science, and it is really no secret at all, for experience has taught us that this is true of every law in nature. We must understand a law before we can make conscious use of it.

We must specialize any law which we wish consciously to use, and the principle of Divine Guidance is no exception to this general rule. We must believe that there is a Divine Guidance, we must affirm that there is a Divine Guidance, and we must deny every tendency to disbelieve in Divine Guidance. If Law is Mind in Action, and if we specialize this Law through the activity of our thought, which we most certainly do, then we must consciously know that we are daily guided and directed into right action. We must know that there is an Intelligence which goes before us and makes our way plain and immediate.

Whenever any problem confronts you, take it into the silence of your own contemplation and declare that there is no problem; that you already know the answer. Dissolve the belief in the problem and announce the belief in the answer. Mentally act as though the problem were an argument trying to convince you that you do not know the answer, and then through the conscious activity of your thought destroy the argument either by picking it apart a bit at a time until there is nothing left, or by the complete realization that dissipates it as the sun dissipates the mist.

When you dissolve the problem and seek Divine Guidance you are announcing that there is no problem. Announce that there is a complete answer and that this answer is made known to your mind right now, today. In this way you wait upon your Indwelling Lord, the Supreme One, the Creator and the Sustainer of your destiny.

Divine Guidance is just as definite a principle in the universe as is the Law of Attraction and Repulsion. Your use of Divine Guidance must be just as conscious as an architect drawing a plan; just as certain as a mathematician solving a problem, and the answer is just as definite.

God and Company

It is evident from the foregoing conclusion, relative to the principle of Divine Guidance and our use of It, that we are in partnership with the Infinite Mind, and the name of this partnership is *God and Company*—God standing for the Supreme Intelligence, the Universal Creative Order, the Dynamic Law, and the All Perfect Presence. This is God, the senior partner. We are the company. This partnership cannot be dissolved although it may appear to be dissolved.

We must feel that we are in league with the Universe, and that this company with which we do business, having its center everywhere and its circumference nowhere, that is, being omnipresent, is localized wherever thought and consciousness function. Wherever we place our attention, there this company is doing business.

Wherever this company does business there is activity. We must learn that the activity of right ideas is not only the Father's business, but likewise the business of the Son. The individual mind and the Parent Mind are one, and to whatever point we turn our mental attention, at that point the firm of God and Company establishes a branch which is certain to be successful.

Since there is no competition God and Company has no competitors. There are no other goods so perfect as those they manufacture, there are no other patterns so attractive, there is no other machinery so perfect and efficient. God and Company therefore, never deals with competition but always with completeness, and wherever our thought is, there this Company establishes its branch. In each branch it carries an entire stock of the Divine Goods, and we need have no fear that any one person has a monopoly on any of these Divine Goods.

What mathematician would deny us the privilege of using the principle that two and two make four? Or what musician would claim that some note which he struck used up all harmony? The mathematician uses the principle of mathematics and the musician uses the principle of harmony. A principle is that which, no matter how much it is used, is neither less nor more than it was. It always refuses to be anything except that which it is, and it is what it was, and it was what it is, and when tomorrow comes it will still be that which it is. Hence, what it was it is, and what it is it will remain.

Wherever our attention is set, there God and Company is doing business, and at that point business is good because God is good. To know this is to know the Truth about one's business, to understand what is really true about one's profession, and to know what activity really means.

Who would attempt to dissolve such a Divine Partnership as this? Surely no sane person. If we have a business which has no competitors and over which there is no monopoly, and if we have a business that is always good because it is always active, and if we have the intelligence to run this business, and if this business is really the business of living, then we are indeed successful.

In actual practice we must claim this Divine Partnership; we must claim that we are members of this firm of God and Company, and we must never deny it. We must learn to counsel with this silent Partner of ours and we must state that business is good, that the business of life is active, it is happy, it is whole. Therefore we come to the other proposition, which is that of transferring the burden of life—lifting the load.

Lifting the Load

The burden of life arises from the belief that we have neither the power nor the intelligence to solve our problems. But if we realize that our Partner, the Law, makes things of Itself by Itself becoming the thing It makes, we shall know that no matter what undesirable facts may be manifesting themselves in our present experience the Law can dissolve them for us.

We transfer the problem into the Divine Ideal. If anyone should ask us how the Divine Intelligence is going to recognize our small problem, our answer would be that the Divine works through the Universal Law of Cause and Effect.

Whoever specializes this Law will find that he can transfer the burden of personal responsibility to the Law, and that the Law will work for him as an individual on the pattern of his thought, just as It works in the rest of the cosmos. It does not do this because It likes one person better than another, but because it is Its nature to do so.

Again we must remember that the Law knows neither big nor little. It knows only to do. Because the Word sets the Law in motion, and because we can speak the Word, we know we can use the Law. For as universal as this Law is, It is also particularized through us; It specializes Itself at our request and flows through our thought into performance.

In making practical use of this we must realize that our word is law. Hence our word of expansion means expansion, and our word of contraction means contraction. If we use the Law as limitation it is not the fault of the Law; it is the way in which we have used It. If we get a clear idea of how the Law of Cause and Effect works we shall see that our Word specializes the Law in a unique and individual way—in a personal manner.

We transfer the burden, passing it over, as it were, to the Law governing our Divine Partnership, and we rely upon Divine Guidance to speak the right Word into the Law. The Word of Trust executes Itself. Our acknowledgment of good becomes the good which we acknowledge. We are told that the Word of God is faithful and true. Paul speaks of the sword of the Spirit, which is the Word of God. Or we may think of the Word as protection—*His truth shall be thy shield and buckler.*

The Word of Truth is based upon the changeless Principle of Reality. We are told in Psalm 33:6: *By the word of the Lord were the heavens made*. This means the passing of the Word, through action, into form. Naturally, then, we transfer the burden of individual responsibility into the Law of right action.

We start with the proposition that the Word is the power back of the thing; that words actually produce conditions, and that the Law flows from the Word. And if the Law flows from the Word, and if Divine Guidance compels us to speak the right Word, and if our Divine Partnership can never be dissolved, then surely the load of life is lifted, and we may pursue our way in quietness and in confidence.

However, we must always be sure that this Word is in harmony with Eternal Reality, for when we transfer our burden into the Law we are setting cause and effect in motion. And if we wish to experience only that which is good, our use of the Law must be good. This is but another way of saying that the Universe is foolproof.

But how are we to know when we are speaking the Word of God? There is only one way of knowing: Is our word harmonious? If we are sure there is nothing in it which has an element of hurt, hate, fear, limitation, or destructiveness of any nature, then it is self-evident that we are speaking the Word of God, and we may rest in absolute reliance upon the outcome.

The more we study the nature of these principles the more convinced we are that they are true; that they are the statements of the great Law of Cause and Effect which the illumined of the ages have proclaimed. They are not true because the illumined have announced them, but because they were true the spiritual-minded have perceived them.

Thus our Divine Partnership with its Divine Guidance transfers the burden and lifts the load of life. Our part is to plant the right seed; to know that the Law flows from the Word; to know that the Word is the starting point of every creation; to know that ideas are things; to know that the entire physical universe is a thing of thought. And when we have transferred the burden into the Law, and when we have consigned our own soul to peace, we shall have a new interest and a fresh outlook, for we shall be entering into the spirit of life, into the livingness of life, and into the joy of that livingness.

In our individual world we have the power and the knowledge to create those individual experiences which make life worthwhile. And there is no limit to the evolution of these experiences, for one conclusion will lead to another. This is the symbolism of the octave, which means that the end of any particular creative series is but the beginning of a new creative series.

There is in each one of us the will to live, to enjoy, to express and to unfold; this will is Divine, and our will is in partnership with this Divine Will, and our mind with this Divine Mind. Thus we expect and believe that all good shall come to us.

As we transfer the load, a new meaning comes into life, a more spontaneous self-expression; sadness gives place to joy, and confusion surrenders itself to peace. Action robbed of friction moves without fatigue, and the endless drama of life presents us with inspiring scenes and ever-moving experiences. This is the New Heaven and the New Earth. And when that final transference shall take place from this world into the next, we shall exclaim, "Into Thy hands I commend my spirit."

Let God Do It

In the Colorado Rockies there is a beautiful valley from which many fountains gush forth. Each fountain is different, more water comes from some than from others, but there is only one body of water at a deep, subterranean level which flows through each one of them.

Each fountain is supplied from one body of water, and the water that gushes through each has a pressure within itself that causes it to flow upward with an irresistible force. This may be likened to our own spiritual natures. We as individuals each have our own thoughts, feelings, hopes, aspirations, and desires, and each is directly and intimately connected with the one Divine Life, Energy, and Power.

Each of us is a fountain of Life. There is a God-pressure back of each one of us, a Life-force seeking outlet through our thoughts and acts. There are many fountains, many individuals, but only one God-pressure back of all.

One of the most remarkable sayings of Jesus was that he of himself could do nothing, . . . *the Father that dwelleth in me, he doeth the works*. Could we not say of each fountain up there in the Rockies that the fountain of itself could do nothing because it is merely an outlet for the pressure back of it?

Let us personalize these fountains and give to each the power to block the flow of water through it. One fountain might say: "Well, I don't know whether there is water enough. I am not quite certain that I am an outlet for this great ocean of water. I am not even certain that I believe there is enough pressure in it to keep on flowing—perhaps it will stop tomorrow." Another fountain might say: "I am so confused over everything, I am so uncertain about everything, that I have come to the point where I really don't know what's going to happen." And another fountain might be so filled with fear and distrust that it would block its own channel. While still another might get jealous of the other fountains and gradually come to hate them.

Let us make believe that these mental attitudes of the fountains could actually stop the flow of water through them. Would that not be about the way all of us are at times? We become so frustrated with our little thoughts and fears and doubts that it makes it impossible for us to let God flow through us with the joy of life. Our problem is not with God who is the River of Life. It is not with the Divine Pressure that seeks to express itself through us. Our trouble is with ourselves.

Each one of us is an inlet to the Divine, but because we are individuals we can inhibit Its flow, we can block It or squeeze It down to a small volume or even stop it, or by opening up all the channels of faith and conviction and hope we can increase Its flow. When the natural joy of life is unblocked it will flow freely through us and we shall become whole and happy. But doubt, fear, uncertainty, anxiety, and a sense of insecurity can so congest our mental life that nothing good can get through.

We are born with a natural desire to express life. But almost from birth certain factors entered our experience which tended to congest the flow, until finally it has almost stopped. We are trying to be fountains all on our own, not realizing that each one is rooted in God; that there is a Power greater than we are, a pressure against our lives from a Divine source which is self-acting.

When Jesus said that a Power greater than he himself was operating through him, he knew exactly what he was talking about. And because he kept the passageway of his own thought clear, this Power was able to work through him.

Jesus never made any complicated statements. His words were simple and direct. He said there is a Fountain of Life from which your life is drawn, and if you will unstop everything in your mind that congests this Fountain you will be whole. This was the foundation of his teaching—clear your mind of everything that doubts the existence of God; live as though love were the great reality; bless and curse not, and then accept and let.

Let us use another illustration from nature and think of a great body of water up in the mountains. It is our desire to use this water to irrigate the valleys. We have learned that by a natural pressure within itself, which we call gravitational force, this water will flow from the high mountaintops down into the valley. But we have met with certain obstructions—there are hills and perhaps mountains in the way.

In the early days when they brought water down into Rome they built long channels around the mountainside. This was done with terrific labor. And then there came a time when someone discovered that water, by its own pressure, will reach its own level. They discovered that if they would connect a pipe with the high level they could run water down through the valleys and up over other mountains and hills, and provided they never tried to make the water go higher than its source they could deliver it anywhere and in complete volume.

But there is something else we should remember about bringing water down from the high mountaintops: no matter how large the source, the flow to any particular spot is limited to the size of the pipe through which it flows. If it is a one-inch pipe we shall have a one-inch flow of water; if it is a ten-inch pipe we shall be able to deliver a ten-inch flow wherever we want to use it. But in no instance do we force the water down. We neither push it nor pull it nor draw it. It furnishes its own pressure.

But suppose some day we go out to open the headgate through which the water flows and no water comes. What do we then do? Do we sit down and bemoan our fate? Do we lament and beat our breast and say, "Woe is me!" Do we say, "Perhaps God doesn't want us to have water today?" Or do we question whether or not the water is withholding itself from us? We do none of these things. We realize that somewhere the pipe is blocked, and so we follow it back and discover that sand has gotten into it, or mud or silt. We clean out the debris and at once the flow resumes.

The flow did not stop of itself; it was stopped because something got in its way. But we were able to remove the obstruction. We did this definitely and deliberately. We knew what we were doing and how to do it. We were complying with a natural law, and when we let the law have its way, everything was all right.

This is pretty much what happens in our lives when we are unhappy and incomplete—somewhere we have stopped the flow. The water is still up there in the mountains, the pipe is in place, but somewhere something has gotten into this pipe that does not belong there. So we turn on the faucet and nothing happens.

Well, there is no use sitting around bemoaning our fate. It is time for us to do something about it. It is time for us to follow the pipeline of our own existence back to its source, to find out what blocks it and to loose it, to free it, that the flow may resume. It is time for us to let God do it.

But before God can do it we must clear our minds of everything that hinders His doing; we must keep the pipeline open and let the water of life flow down into our living. And remembering that everything in our thinking that is unlike our highest concept of good will clog the pipes, we must look to ourselves and be honest. If we find anything in our thinking that denies Life, let us clear it away. We can stop being afraid if we want to. We can stop having resentments. We can at once stop all unkindness, winnow out every doubt, and gain faith through the simple practice of learning to believe. Here is where faith and patience and the will to try and keep on trying must be used.

One can say to oneself every day, "I am a fountain of Life, and the living waters of God flow through me." One can say to oneself, "I will express joy today. I will be happy. I will bring gladness and enthusiasm into every experience of my life. I will maintain a quiet confidence and peace and a sense of serenity. And I will be glad for the achievement of others and rejoice in their success." One can learn to love people if one wishes to.

It is this kind of thinking that irrigates the dry places of life and brings laughter and joy into everything we do. It can bring health and freedom in place of sickness and bondage. It can bring abundance and prosperity where there might have been impoverishment.

But there is one more thing that we must remember. It is not enough to know that the pipeline of our existence begins way up there in the high mountaintops into which the hand of God is pouring the eternal waters of Life, for this is our inlet to the Divine. This inlet is forever established. We have to be certain that we are an outlet to it. And it is only as the other end of the pipe is kept open that the water flows.

This is why Jesus told us that we must forgive if we would be forgiven; we must love if we would be loved; we must make others happy if we would become happy ourselves; we must give if we would receive.

Sometimes we hug our little good too closely to ourselves, not being willing to cast it on four winds of heaven lest it will not return. But Jesus said the very act of giving will at the same time bring to us a receiving—*good measure, pressed down, and shaken together, and running over,* he called it. It is the one who gives the most who gets the most. And so let us learn to draw the Divine Substance down into our own lives, and as freely as it has been given to us, let us give it to others. Thus alone shall we be made whole.

Meditation

The All-Intelligent Creative Presence is the source of all that I am. I believe in Its ability and Its willingness to sustain me.

The Kingdom and the Power and the Glory of God flows through me. I recognize myself to be a center through which the Intelligence and the Power of the Universe finds expression.

Infinite Mind operating through me now brings order and the highest good to me. The consciousness of peace and plenty is established within me.

All that is necessary to my happiness and well-being now comes into my experience. There is no belief in failure or mistake in the Divine Plan for me. There is no discouragement and no fear.

There can be neither limitation nor lack in the One Perfect Activity. It is in full operation in and for me. I am now free from any sense of bondage.

Strength and courage are my divine birthright, and I am now expressing my true self.

All that the Father hath is mine. I draw all that I need from the Spiritual treasure house.

Prayer and Treatment

Office of the Dean

My Dear Friend,
You will find many wonderful ideas to consider in this lesson, among which is the thought that prayer is its own answer, since only the prayer that is believed in can be answered; the prayer that is not believed in denies itself.

You will find an interesting explanation about drawing on your invisible sources just as everything in all nature does—the tree, the fern, the animal, the bird. We all are rooted in the invisible and it is not we who are the power; rather, the power operates through us, the power that we are already rooted in. You can draw on these invisible forces through using the dynamic power of your consciousness.

The article, *Man Against Himself*, is based on the teaching of modern psychiatry. It is an introduction to a number of other articles that are to follow, on what we call spiritual psychosomatics, or the relationship of the body-mind to the Spirit that is within us.

Body-mind relationship is a discussion of the parallel action between mind and body. There is also a relationship which psychosomatic medicine does not take into consideration, and that is the relationship of our minds to our environment. Believing as we do that the Universe is a spiritual system governed by Law, we cannot help believing that everything comes under the control of the One Mind, the One Presence, and the One Power.

Sincerely,
Ernest Holmes

Lesson 18

***Understanding*, page 147, to *Prayer Is Its Own Answer*, page 153**

The basis of our philosophy and its practical application is the Creative Power of thought. We start with the assumption that the Infinite Spirit creates through contemplation. Contemplation, as you will find on page 581, means *to know within the self*. The inner self-knowingness of the Spirit produces a manifestation of this inner knowingness according to the Law of Correspondence, a definition of which you will find on page 581. The thing contemplated corresponds to the contemplation, just as the reflection in a mirror corresponds to the image held in front of the mirror.

As we have previously stated, the reflection in a mirror is the effect of an image held in front of it, while the image itself is an effect of the one who holds it. We would say, then, that the reflection in the mirror is entirely in the nature of an effect, which is subject to its immediate cause or the image. In its turn the image which produces the reflection is an immediate effect of the cause back of it, which is the person holding it before the mirror. We would therefore speak of the image as relative causation in that, while it is the cause of the reflection, the image itself is caused by something else. It is relative first cause. The actual first cause is the intelligence that holds the image.

As Spirit is the original Contemplator, the original Knower, then the Spirit is Absolute Causation. Absolute Causation is not in relation to anything other than Itself. It depends upon Itself alone and upon nothing else. But that which the Spirit contemplates as image or idea or reflection, is an effect. In other words, even the thought of Spirit is an effect of the consciousness that produces such a thought, and the thing which is the manifestation of the thought is an effect of the thought. From this viewpoint, while we say, and rightly, that thoughts are things, we must add that there is something that comes before the thought, and that is the thinker.

In the sequence of causation we start with pure Intelligence; then the contemplation of Intelligence creating the word or the idea, which in its turn reflects its form into the mirror of matter. This in turn produces experience. Or if we wish to put it another way: a gardener takes a seed and plants it. The plant is a result of the seed. It is a product of evolution, the unfoldment of that which was involved within the seed. But the seed itself was placed in the creative fertility of soil by the gardener. From this viewpoint the gardener is the absolute first cause; the seed is the relative first cause; the plant is entirely an effect, for while the plant depends upon the seed, the seed depends upon the gardener.

Read again the definition of *Involution* on page 603, and of *Evolution* on page 590. Involution is spiritual self-awareness, an act of the conscious thought. Evolution is merely a mechanical reaction— intelligent but non-volitional. It is the Life Principle Itself acting as Law.

If you will turn to page 472, *The Son of Man*, and read through to the top of page 475, you will find a complete discussion of how this Life Principle works, and what the result of Its actions may be or become in our experience.

Each one of us may use the Principle of unity as though it were a duality. The Creative Power of thought may bring upon us experiences which we call good and experiences which we call evil. As our text states in the second paragraph on page 148, undesirable conditions are themselves proof that we have injured ourselves by using the law of freedom in a limited way. We must now reverse our thinking, and for every negative thought we must supply an affirmative one. This is not as difficult as it seems to be, but calls for imagination and decision, not as will, but as willingness. We must affirm the Truth until we arrive at a state of consciousness which accepts our own affirmations. (See page 575 for the definition of *Affirmation*).

On page 576 read the definition of *Appearance*. You will see that your affirmation must often contradict objective appearances, but we should never forget that these objective appearances are but the reflections in the mirror and may be changed. If it were not possible to change these images of thought, spiritual healing would be impossible.

On page 611 *Mental Treatment* is defined as *the act, the art and science of inducing thought in Mind*. Hence there is a definite technique for right treatment and this technique includes the affirmation of the eternal good and the negation of the temporary evil. This is what is meant by the statement in the third paragraph on page 148, . . . *our world created by our consciousness, and our consciousness taking its color from the perception of our relation to the Infinite*.

Read page 483. Our world is created by our consciousness, but we are largely ignorant of this fact. Spiritual mind healing changes the consciousness and in turn the consciousness automatically reflects the new images of thought into our world of experience. Thus by the very law that binds us we are made free. What a marvelous conception is this! We do not have to struggle or fight; we need to know. And what is it we need to know? That God is all there is, beside which there is none other.

As man's consciousness is elevated to a more complete understanding of his inherent perfection, the freer does he become from those experiences which have been called evil. The Divine Transmutation of form into essence and essence into a new form proclaims the presence of that hidden Spirit which says, *Behold, I make all things new*. Thus, as our text states (page 148), we should strive toward a perfect understanding by practicing the expansion of thought, a sense of a deeper union with life, a more complete at-one-ment with God.

On page 420 we state that *Cosmic Consciousness* means *one's consciousness of his unity with the Whole*. There is one Life pouring Itself into numberless forms, and operating through innumerable personalities It projects a limitless variety of self-unfoldment and fulfillment.

Now this Power, which we think of as God, the Living Spirit Almighty, is the Presence at the very center of our own being. It is not something else, but identical with and is the essence of the one and only Power there is. This has been the mystical perception of the ages. In the experience of Jesus this realization has been referred to as Christ.

On pages 369 and 370, *The Triumphant Christ*, is a description of the experience which has come to those who have sensed the eternal principle of Reality at the center of their own souls. In the third paragraph on page 336 you will discover that the practical application of this spiritual evolution is a conscious recognition on the part of the practitioner of the *I AM*-ness which pervades all being. As the paragraph states: *Thus our recognition of It becomes Its recognition of us at the level of our recognition of It*. To understand the meaning of this short sentence is to uncover the spiritual secret of the ages, of the saints and the sages of every country who have always proclaimed this identical truth—that the Highest God and the Innermost God is One God, not two; and that the power and intelligence by which we contemplate the Infinite *is* the Infinite operating at the level of our comprehension. Thus Jesus exclaimed in the exaltation of his spiritual awareness, *The Father that dwelleth in me, he doeth the works.*

On page 472, under the heading *Heaven* you will find another one of those hidden ideas which Jesus, greatest of all the spiritual mystics, sought to disclose to his followers. We are already in heaven but do not know it. Heaven is not a far-off place, but a state of interior awareness. Thus it is *that the pure in heart shall see God* (page 429). *The Spirit of man is the candle of the Lord*. When this Light dissipates the superstition, fear, and uncertainty of the mind, then the perfect, the complete, and the everlasting are revealed. (Turn to page 535 for the Meditation, *My Soul Reflects Thy Life*).

We come now to a discussion of the meaning of prayer and treatment (page 149). Frequently people will ask you if prayers and treatments are the same thing. We think you will all agree that the ordinary conception of prayer should not be confused with the scientific application of spiritual mind healing, where we specifically use a definite science with a conscious technique. However, if the prayer is a conscious recognition of the Oneness of God, and if this conscious recognition is directly applied to the solution of some problem, then this prayer may be considered in the nature of effective mental treatment.

On page 455, *Fasting and Prayer*, you will find a more complete discussion of this thought. Certainly there is no God who desires that we refrain from putting butter on our bread or gravy on our potatoes. Since the Eternal Mind has created all things, all things must be for use. This Jesus understood. When they accused him of breaking the Sabbath, how marvelous was his reply! *The Son of man is Lord also of the Sabbath*. He told them plainly that God had not made man for the Sabbath, but the Sabbath for man. Jesus' whole system of thought indicates his belief that the proper use of things is never wrong; but a misuse of eternal principles is that which creates the thing we call evil and causes us to experience it until the lesson is learned. Through suffering (which is the negative approach) we learn what to avoid.

How terrible it would be, as our text on page 149 suggests, if one had to believe that God is a being of moods, or that the Divine Being favors one person above another. To think of God as the Infinite Person, now personified in oneself, and through all, and at the same time to think of the Universe as a system of order, regulated by immutable laws of cause and effect, is indeed the essence of intelligence, and the recognition of such a Universe speeds progress.

God operates through law and God is an impartial giver (page 150). If God ever answers prayer, He always does. But even God cannot answer a prayer which denies His own bounty, other than by answering it in the terms of its own negation. What do we mean by this? If we can believe only a little, then only a little can be done, for the answer to our prayer is a reflection of the petition in the terms of our own conscious or subjective acceptance. Thus Jesus tells us that when we pray we must believe that we have already received.

We must praise that for which we pray, as is indicated on page 621. Thus to praise is to increase our spiritual recognition, and through an increase of our spiritual recognition to elevate the image of our thought and automatically reflect newer and better situations. Instinctively we all believe in prayer. By intuition we have a sense that the Universe honors our requests. This intuition is correct, *for he (God) hath left not himself without witness.*

Turn once more to the definition of *Intuition* on page 603. We instinctively believe in the power of prayer and we are right. Without changing this instinctive conviction we must learn to convert our learning into affirmation and acceptance, to dissolve all negative beliefs, and to re-present them in a higher form to the Creative Law.

We are told that when we pray aright it shall be done unto us (see page 150), and that whatsoever we ask, if we ask in the name of Truth we shall receive (page 151). *In His name* means like His Nature, that is, our prayer must be an affirmation and not a negation, since God cannot argue.

On page 461 you will find a discussion of the thought that God cannot argue, for to suppose that God could argue would be to presuppose duality and not unity. Thus in this story of the Prodigal Son, Jesus presents to us the two approaches which we may make to the Universe. He shows us that the cup of every man's acceptance is filled unless the cup is turned upside down. Here even the Divine Bounty cannot force Its good upon us. *Behold, I stand at the door, and knock*. In His name means in the nature of goodness, truth, and beauty, in which we must believe. If we can believe in but a little good, then only a little good will be ours. We should learn how to increase our belief. We should awake to the greater possibility.

On page 413, the second paragraph, you will find some ideas which will be helpful in learning how to become conscious of the Presence of God. We must become conscious that the Kingdom of Heaven is within us, for the secret of spiritual power and mental treatment is in our recognition of the Principle flowing into our word and taking form through our thought, always acting as Law. In His name means such a harmony of consciousness that limitation is transmuted into freedom, that the serpent becomes the savior, that Adam is transformed into Christ.

As suggested in the third paragraph of page 151, since God does not manifest Himself alike in every man, being unique in each person, no man need feel out of place in the universe in which he lives. There is a right something for each one to do. Each is a unique institution in a Cosmic Wholeness. Each has his place in the Divine Order, a place of which no one can rob him. Each has the right to be happy and to be whole, and in such degree as we abide *in His name* we shall be made whole. But *in His name* is an interior awareness and not an exterior act.

Turn to page 529 under the heading, *Power to Live*, and realize that this Power is already within you. If, then, we would demonstrate love we must embody harmony. There is a place within each one of us which lies open to the Infinite and already this Divine Unity is forever established. Perhaps the most difficult thing we shall ever have to do in our work is to realize that the Spirit has already made the gift of life; our work is to embody a mental acceptance of it. It is written that *but as many as received him, to them gave he power* . . . and we must believe that we have the Power if we wish to use it.

Prayer, as an act of communion of the soul with the Over-Soul, is essential to our physical and mental well-being. Of course our spiritual well-being is already complete, since it is some part of God. We do not need salvation for the soul, which is never lost; we do need a salvation for the thought, for certainly it is bogged down, to say the least.

If we know God as an indwelling Presence, then prayer becomes an act of communion with this indwelling Spirit. From this viewpoint prayer should be a mental elevation, a spiritual exaltation. When we commune with the real in each other, or the Spiritual Principle back of its physical manifestation, then we are praying to the Spirit in each to come forth, and we are instructing the mind that is to be made whole.

Always in practicing spiritual mind healing we start with a recognition of man's spiritual perfection, and we endeavor to bring our mental statements to a place in thought where we recognize this spiritual perfection.

Summary

All that we can ever know must be within the self. The self reflects action into the Law of Mind, which Law reflects it back to the self. This is like the action of a mirror.

We cannot change the mirror nor the Law of Mind, but we can change our thinking, which makes it look as though we had changed both the mirror and Mind.

What we have done is change our action, permitting the mirror to change its reaction.

Our personal causation is in our own minds and nowhere else, because our minds are in Spirit and Spirit depends upon nothing but Itself. It is both Cause and Effect.

Spiritual Mind Healing changes consciousness, a change of consciousness produces a change of mental images, the new mental images create a new reflection, and in this way the mirror of life reflects back to us what we think.

It is because of this that we can make all of our experiences new. Nothing is more important than that we remember that our recognition of the Law, or our recognition in the Law of Mind, produces a corresponding recognition about us as this Law reflects our images into our experiences. This is one of the great secrets of the ages.

We must think of God as an Infinite Person, personal to us and personified in us, and the Universe as a system of immutable Law.

If any prayer is answered all prayers must be answered, but each according to its own type.

Questions

Brief answers to these questions should be written out by the student after studying the lesson, and the answers compared with those which will be included in next week's lesson.

1. How does the Spirit create?
2. What is meant by contemplation in mental treatment?
3. Why is the act of contemplation likened to an object held before a mirror?
4. What is the difference between relative first cause and actual first cause?
5. Distinguish between the Life Principle as essence and the Life Principle as law.
6. What do we mean by using the imagination, not as will but as willingness?
7. What do we mean by our consciousness?
8. What do we mean by changing our consciousness through mental treatment?
9. From the standpoint of mental healing, what is a spiritual consciousness?
10. Why is a spiritual consciousness necessary in mental healing?
11. What is Cosmic Consciousness?
12. Why is the highest God and the innermost God one?
13. Explain the difference between the generally accepted idea of prayer and mental treatment.

14. Why is God an impartial giver?
15. In what degree will our prayers be answered?
16. How may we transmute limitation into freedom?
17. Why is it that each person has a unique destiny?
18. Why is it written, *But as many as received him, to them gave he power . . .*?
19. From what do we need salvation?

Answers to Questions on Lesson 17

1. By thought undoing what thought has done, we mean that subjective thought patterns can be changed through a conscious reversal of thought.
2. It is not enough merely to say, "God is all there is," because this is a statement of Principle. To be effective it must be consciously recognized and definitely used.
3. People refuse to use the Principle of Mind as they would other natural principles because they fail to realize that the Principle of Mind actually is and that It does really respond to their thought.
4. In scientific and effective treatment, one not only recognizes the Principle of Mind and the power of his word, but he also realizes that he must definitely use this word.
5. Our thought has absolute power when it is in harmony with the Christ Principle.
6. The Christ Principle is *God in man, as man*.
7. Enthusiasm is desirable in mental treatment since, being a mental attitude of recognition, acceptance, and joy, it stimulates feeling into imagination and converts desire into acceptance.
8. Our word does not create power; it gives form to a Power which already exists.
9. (a) Your first assumption, in treating for physical healing, is that your patient is already spiritually perfect. (b) Mental suggestion or coercion need not enter into this treatment since the practitioner is thinking *within* himself *about* his patient.
10. We arrive at the greatest spiritual conviction through the mental attitude that God is all there is.
11. When one fails to receive the immediate desired result in treatment, one should start all over again.
12. We use concentration in treatment, not with a sense of coercion or compulsion, nor even in a sense of concentrating the energy of Mind and Spirit, but only for the purpose of giving definite mental attention and arriving at mental acceptance and spiritual realization.
13. The most powerful healing agency in our work is a mental recognition and a spiritual realization of the Presence of God.
14. Mental and spiritual conviction gives power to our word.
15. When doubt arises as to the power of your word, you should immediately deny such doubt and follow with an affirmation of its opposite.
16. This practice is based upon the theory that there is a Creative Mind Principle, or Mental Law, which responds to our thought.

Man Against Himself

Nature made a chemical laboratory within us to take care of our health. In a sense we might say that there are little intelligences within us acting as though they were little people, whose business it is to digest our food and assimilate it, to circulate the blood, and get rid of its impurities. There are millions of these little people inside our bodies whose purpose it is to keep us physically fit. But there also are other little people who are not so kindly minded and they try to tear things down and disrupt the work of the good little people.

Every doctor knows that when he can get the good people inside working with him, things are going to come out all right. We break a bone and when it is set nature gets busy, and all the good little people begin to knit the bone together again, and all the time they are causing the blood to circulate so there will be no infection. But we are learning that we can interfere with these little people inside us because they are subject to a greater intelligence than theirs, which is the person himself.

One of the most popular psychologists in America told me he once suffered from indigestion, and the thought came to him that he could talk to these little people inside him and tell them that it was their business to take care of his digestion. So he talked to them for a few moments every day and told them how wonderful they were and how much he appreciated what they were doing, and that he would not interfere with them any more. He was going to be happy and he knew they would take care of everything for him. He praised them and blessed them and in a few weeks his whole physical condition cleared up.

Well, this is a body-mind relationship. It is reducing psychosomatics to its simplest common denominator. There is an intelligence hid at the center of everything, and we are intelligent, and the lower form of intelligence responds to the higher form. The intelligence in the physical body is a subconscious intelligence. It works creatively, but within certain fixed limitations. It is like a man sent on an errand and told what to do and knowing only to do what he is told.

All the little people inside us are supposed to be working for us and with us, but we can so disturb them that we almost hypnotize them and cause them to work destructively instead of constructively.

This can be carried to such an extent that the wrong direction given to these little people produces a large part of our physical diseases. But right direction can reverse this process and produce physical well-being instead of disease. And we now know that while hate, animosity, and confusion can produce discord, love can heal it.

It is from simple but far-reaching facts like these that we learn some of the greatest lessons of life. And the first lesson we should learn is that Life, which is God, intends us to be well, happy, and successful. When it comes to body-mind relationships, it is helpful to imagine and feel that all the little people inside are working for us and with us, and to feel that they are connected with the Divine Intelligence which directs them—the very Power that created them. This brings us back to the need we all have for a faith, a calm assurance, and an inward sense of well-being.

Surely that which had the intelligence to create has both the will and the ability to sustain. And if in our ignorance we have misused the creative power within us, all we have to do is reverse the process and cooperate with it. In doing this one of the first lessons we learn is to bless everything, to be grateful for everything, to gladly acknowledge the Divine Presence—not as something far away but as something close and intimate.

Not only is there an Intelligence directing the activities of our physical bodies, but this same Intelligence is also directing everything we do. Not only does man operate against himself, physically, but he does so in every activity of life. How many of us really expect to be happy tomorrow? How many of us, when we lie down at night, relax and let the bed hold us up? How many of us have confidence enough in God to sleep in peace, wake in joy, and look forward to the coming day with gladness?

What we need is a conscious cooperation, and a glad one, between ourselves and the Power which, if we would let It, would rightly govern everything. But man is so used to operating against himself, so used to thinking of himself as detached and separate, so completely taking the whole burden of life on his own shoulders, that he has almost lost the ability to cooperate with that Divine Presence which seeks to be a partner to all of us. In our ignorance we have not only operated against ourselves, but have contradicted the supremacy of God. We have denied ourselves the privilege of working with rather than against the Power that put us here.

You and I know that we did not set the stars in their courses. We did not cause the sun to shine or the rain to come. But we can cooperate with this Power back of and in and through all people.

We cannot unify and cooperate with something we do not believe in. So the starting point, the very beginning of the re-education of our minds, must be a deep conviction, a firm faith. And since, in a sense, life is a stage on which each plays a part, there is no reason why we should not dramatize our relationship with the Infinite.

Just think of all these little people working inside us. God put them there. Why not hook them up in our imagination with the living Spirit, recognize their presence, praise and bless them, and even tell them what we want them to do. Each day we should think how wonderful it is to be cooperating with God. Surely this is the greatest drama of all. We do not strut across the stage of human experience as separated and isolated characters, but rather, as actors in the great play of life, the drama of human existence.

But we must not forget the Director of the play, the One who knows how to make each separate line and act become part of the whole piece, until something complete is produced. God is the Great Producer and Director even though He is invisible. We do not see the little people inside us, but they are there, and in our imagination we can feel them. We do not see the law of gravitational force which holds everything in place, and we do not see the Divine Intelligence that causes the rose to bloom or a chicken to come out of an egg.

Let us stop acting against ourselves, each other, and the world, for we know that our thoughts make impressions on our environments and on the people we meet, and silently mold conditions. Here again the imagination can be combined with the will, and each can think of himself as playing a part in the game of life, and a good one. In the theater when a man plays a part that convinces us, he must himself first believe in the part he is playing. I recently asked a director what he thought of a certain play which we had both seen, and he replied, "I didn't think much of it. I didn't care for it." And when I asked, "What was the trouble?" he answered, "The people who read the lines didn't believe them."

If our words are of the intellect only, and not spoken from the heart, the audience will not respond. This is the way it is with life. And this is why in all of his teachings Jesus laid such stress on the simple, childlike ability to believe, to feel, to accept, and to act as though the great Giver of life were still giving; as though the great Creator were still creating in us and through us.

We have wondered so much about the life of Jesus and the wonderful things he did—how he healed the sick and raised the dead and turned water into wine. But has it come to us that perhaps Jesus was the only person in history who never denied the Divine Presence; who always expected It to respond to him? And because we have set Jesus apart, as different from others, we have accepted him without accepting his teaching.

And yet he was the one who said that what he did we could do also. And he told us how to do it—stop acting against yourself; stop acting against anything, and learn to cooperate with what is best, always sensing the Presence of the Divine—and then *let the play go on*.

Meditation

I have within myself, as I sit here, the sense that though my body is real, tangible, with definite form and outline, it is at the same time somehow made of a Living Stuff which is saturated with God-Life.

I know that whatever my body consists of, though it is called material, it must be made of the One Stuff and Essence of which all things are made. Therefore I sense within the very cells and tissues of my body an eternality.

As I relax my body, consciously and definitely—which I am able to do by mentally relaxing and dropping all strain—I feel flowing through me a vital energy, a dynamic force, a great surge of living power.

The Spirit within me refreshes me daily. Right here and now I feel myself saturated with the Life Essence Itself. And I feel the same Life Essence flowing in and through me.

I feel immersed in and saturated by a vital Essence of Perfection which brings me into tune with Life. I feel myself to be a perfect instrument in Life's divine symphony, in tune with its harmony and perfection.

My body is an instrument in, through, and upon which Life plays a divine and perfect harmony.

Drawing On Your Invisible Forces

It is said that the average man draws on only about ten percent of his real capacity; the other ninety percent is mostly submerged and unused. Well, you and I would think it wonderful if we could multiply our talents many times. I have no doubt we can do this if we try.

So let us take a simple lesson from nature. Perhaps from where you are sitting you can see a tree in full bloom. If so remember that the roots through which the tree draws its life are entirely invisible. And unless the tree drew on this invisible source it would never flourish.

Our roots are in the Mind of God. Our individuality, everything that we are and do, is an effect of our invisible forces—forces which continually draw on the Infinite. But in our ignorance we limit the flow of Divine Power into our lives.

Of course this is not intentional, for we all want to make good in life; we want people to like us, and we desire to be worthwhile. But too often when we make an inventory of our assets we depend only upon the circumstances that surround us. We say, "How can I better myself? I haven't the personality," or, "I haven't the natural attractiveness which is necessary to making good in life."

Right here is where our faith in the Power greater than we are must be brought into play. For we as individuals are rooted in this Power. It was his great claim on a Power greater than he was that enabled Jesus to become a Divine Man while still living on earth. Did he not say, *Of mine own self I can do nothing . . . the Father that dwelleth in me, he doeth the works*?

Yes, we must come to believe that the Father does dwell within us, and that the same creative Spirit that is back of all things flows through us. Jesus said, *Consider the lilies of the field, how they grow; they toil not, neither do they spin: And yet I say unto you, that even Solomon in all his glory was not arrayed like one of these.*

God has need of us or He wouldn't have put us here. The Divine wishes to express through you and through me or we would have no existence. We have no existence of ourselves alone. It is only because we live in God that we live at all. If we think of ourselves as rooted in God, and expect Divine Power to flow through us, our every thought and act will be animated by the same life and power and beauty that clothes the lily of the field.

We once knew one of the country's leading cartoonists. The nature of his work was such that he had to produce new ideas daily and make pictures of them for a newspaper syndicate for millions of people to read. I asked him how he accomplished so much and he told me that he had a room with four blank walls and the only furniture in his room was a table and a chair; that when he needed ideas he would go into this room, sit down and become quiet.

He said that sometimes he would sit there for two or three hours and nothing would happen. Then all at once something would begin to flow up from within him, a new thought, a new idea, and he would take a pencil and write his impressions. What he wrote and what he drew was like the bloom of a plant as it draws upon the soil.

The creative artist and the inventor do this. And why should not we do the same? We have to start with the proposition that all things are possible to God; that God makes everything out of Himself by the simple process of becoming the thing He makes, just as the tree grows out of the ground and the invisible forces of its life turn into foliage, into blossom and into fruit, all through a silent process of nature.

Did you ever ask yourself this question: *How is it that I can eat mince pie and ham sandwiches and maybe a salad, and have it turn into flesh and blood and hair and fingernails?* Here is the miracle of life, the invisible becoming visible. We are so used to the process that we never question it; we take it for granted. Why should we not take it for granted that God will give us ideas, that the Spirit within us, as Jesus said, knows what we have need of even before we ask?

Let us get back to the tree again. Suppose every time it thought of putting forth a new branch it would say, "How am I going to do it? I have only a certain number of branches. I don't know how to make a new branch, anyway." Now just for the fun of it, let us suppose this tree is a person, and it is bemoaning its fate because it would so greatly like to have a few more branches, but it doesn't know how to make them.

And thinking of the tree as a person, let us assume that every time it says, "I don't know how to make a new branch," it is blocking off the possibility of drawing its life from the soil. If this should happen, the tree would never make any more branches; it would begin to die from that very moment.

But the tree is not a person. All it does is to depend on nature. All it knows is to grow. So it never short-circuits the Divine Energy that gives it life. But we are people and we can short-circuit the Divine Energy that ought to be flowing through us. We short-circuit it when we deny that it is there. And the reason we deny it is because we do not see this energy, and therefore we do not believe in it.

If we believe that the Father is within us, and if we believe that all things are possible to God, then we should no longer deny that God knows what to do with His own creation, and we should include ourselves in that creation.

All right, then, let us see what would happen to us if we should include ourselves in God's creation. Right at the start we should learn to have a little better opinion of ourselves. I am not talking about a conceited opinion, for we have learned that we can do nothing of ourselves—we live because we are drawing on the invisible source of all life. The only way that God can work for us is by working through us, and God cannot give us anything unless we take it. He has made the gift of life or we would not be here. Only God can give life, as only God can make a tree. But we are not living like the tree, because we deny the very power by which we live.

And now we want to change all this. We wish to draw on these invisible forces, to let our roots run deep into that Life which already is perfect and complete, and we want to live happily and without fear. For fear short-circuits this Divine Energy, while confusion and uncertainty cause it to produce bondage instead of freedom.

If we want to change this, let us start by accepting ourselves for better or for worse. But in this instance let us be sure that we accept ourselves for better, because we are thinking of that deep, hidden self which the Bible tells us is hid with Christ in God.

Here is where prayer and meditation make possible the miracle of life. Remember we are talking about affirmative prayer, for there should be nothing negative in our communion with God. It should always be affirmative. We should never say God cannot or will not, but always God can and will and does. And having cleared all doubt from our consciousness we must learn to affirm that all the power and all the presence and all the life that there is, is for us and with us and in us.

And there is one more thing we certainly should not forget to add: The higher forces of life always work constructively. When we use them constructively there seems no limit to their possibility. But the moment we begin to use them destructively, they appear to block themselves.

This seems to be the only condition that the Divine has laid down which might be considered limiting, but which is not. We could not expect to use the power of good for evil purposes, nor could we expect through hate to generate love, nor could we hope for God to give us that which we refuse to pass on to others. These are the only conditions Jesus laid down when he told us that we would always receive if we would pray aright.

Let us take a simple illustration to demonstrate this. We can love without limit—we can love everyone and everything and feel kindly disposed toward people and circumstances and situations—and this attitude toward life will never hurt us, nor will it block the flow of life through us. Rather it will tend to accelerate it. But the moment we begin to hate we block the passage of life, and gradually this negative attitude stifles us; it short-circuits the flow of energy from the roots of our being into the things we are doing.

When we are on the right track there is no limit, but when we get on the wrong track we go on to where the trail runs out and stops. It would seem as though God had imparted His own life to us, placing no limitation or condition that would restrict us other than this: Life must be lived constructively, in unity and love and sympathy with everything around us if we expect to live it to the full.

There is no other condition imposed on us from the Divine. Everyone is born to be creative and to live to the fullest and to enjoy life, to be happy and glad and prosperous and whole. We do not believe that God is a failure. God never makes any mistakes. We are the ones who err.

If we are certain that our lives are constructive, and if our whole desire is to live in such a way as to harm no one but to bless all, then we should place no limit on the possibility of our future. This great gift of Life is to be accepted, even as the lilies of the field and the birds of the air.

Let us try this simple experiment, daily saying to ourselves:

> *All that the Father hath is mine. There is nothing in me that can deny His presence, His power, His wisdom, His guidance, and His protecting love. Today and every day I shall live life to the full; I shall sing and dance and be glad. And always within me there is the Power and the Presence and the Life of God. And unto this Presence be glory and honor, dominion and power, both now and forever. Amen.*

Practical Suggestion for Mental Treatment

Because God Knows, I Know

The mind which states a problem is the mind which knows the answer. Throw the problem into mind for solution and the answer will rise to consciousness.

In actual practice one does this by stating that he already knows the answer to his problem. The Intelligence within him knows and this Intelligence within him which knows causes him to consciously know. It is not enough merely to state that Intelligence knows. We must combine our statement that there is an Intelligence which knows, with a conscious acceptance that this Intelligence is now functioning in our conscious thought, causing us to know.

It is scientific to say, "I know. I know because I know that God knows and because God knows, I know." Use any statement which will convince you that you really know. We are directed not by a blind force, but by an Infinite Intelligence which is not only willing, but whose very nature compels It to give us guidance.

All the prayers which men have uttered, no matter under what religious or spiritual banner they may have marched, have been effective not because of the peculiarity of their theology or religious belief, but because through this individual approach they used a Principle that exists at the center of every man's being.

Naturally, and humanly, they have told us that they received results because of their particular belief. But we know it was because they contacted an impersonal Principle. We know there is such a Principle involved, and we know how to make conscious use of that Principle.

God's Bounty Can Be Short-circuited but Never Depleted

Stand fast therefore in the liberty wherewith Christ hath made us free, and be not entangled again with the yoke of bondage. This is a direct statement that through a right use of the Law we may become free, but through a wrong use of It we may again we entangled in bondage. No plainer statement of the Law of Cause and Effect could be given than this. We may wire the building, turn on the electricity and have light. But if the wire is short-circuited something will go wrong and we shall again be entangled with darkness.

The darkness was never a thing of itself; it was merely a confused state. The source of our supply was not really cut off; it stopped at our place of confusion and no longer functioned for us. This is a perfect statement of the mental Law of Cause and Effect and it again warns us that we must be aware of the use we are making of the Law; we must keep our thought straight.

It is not always easy to do this, but the Law of Cause and Effect being no respecter of persons and always working automatically and mechanically and with mathematical precision, must flow through each one of us in the terms of our own acceptance. When we become confused and short-circuit this acceptance we are cutting ourselves off from its supply, but we do not destroy the supply; it is still there.

It is a wonderful thought to realize that the eternal bounty can be short-circuited only as far as we are concerned; it cannot be either exhausted or depleted. We shall never be disappointed, for the Law is always operating.

Make Each Treatment Complete

Always feel that the first treatment you give will meet the case, while at the same time never taking *No* for an answer even in a series of treatments.

Each time a treatment is given the practitioner should feel that it is complete and perfect; that it is finished and done. His treatment is not complete until he has reached this sense of finality in his own thought, until his own consciousness accepts the verdict as final and perfect.

In actual experience the practitioner may have to do this day after day over a period of time, but he must be careful to avoid the feeling that the performance must go on forever.

He must be equally careful that he knows that right thought continually poured into consciousness will heal. So what he does in practice is to make each treatment complete; to draw a final conclusion in each treatment, and then be willing to keep on until the case is met.

Vital and Effective Faith

Office of the Dean

My Dear Friend,

You are a spiritual broadcasting system, and we want you to consider this fact carefully as you study the lesson. What are you broadcasting? We are sure it is love and truth, beauty, peace, and joy, and since these thoughts are established in your mind you are blessing everything you touch. We are sure this is your desire, as it is the desire of all of us who believe in the things you are studying.

Practicing the particular suggestions for treatment in this lesson should be of great help to you.

We believe in every healing agency, whether it be a doctor, a psychiatrist, someone who prays for us, or someone of our own faith to talk with us. As our lesson states, all of these healing agencies should converge, and we think they will, and sooner than the average person realizes. Let us help this day forward by criticizing no one and blessing all, for the biggest life includes all.

We hope you will pay particular attention to *The Doctor, the Psychologist, and the Metaphysician*, because we are living in a new world with new ideas and new methods of procedure. We do have a physical body which needs to be properly cared for, a mind which should be straightened out, and we are a spirit. It is the putting of the whole man together that we are interested in.

Sincerely,
Ernest Holmes

Lesson 19

***Prayer Is Its Own Answer*, page 153 through page 158**

Under the heading *Prayer Is Its Own Answer*, page 153, occurs this statement: *Cause and effect are but two sides of thought*. Read on page 578 the definition of *Cause* as we use the word, and on page 588 the definition of *Effect* as used in this course of lessons. You will see that effect is that which does not make itself but is rather a mechanical and mathematical sequence or something which follows a cause, and which follows it inevitably. It is something projected, something experienced, which implies that there must be a projector and one who has the experience. Cause is that from which everything comes, that which comes first, and from our viewpoint Cause is the invisible but dynamic Life Principle at the center of everything.

Spirit, being all, is both Cause and Effect. On page 406, third paragraph, are the words: *The Absolute is in relationship to Itself alone*. This means that cause and effect are but two ends of the same thing, so that prayer may be said to be its own answer; that is, prayer deals with the Principle which we discussed in our previous lesson, and it deals with It in a specific way.

If you will turn to *The Prayer Of Faith* on page 500 and again carefully consider its meaning, and also to the passage, *Ask in Faith, Believing*, page 498, you will see how true it is that God can give us only what we take, how the taking is a mental act, and why it is that we must believe that we already have even before we receive. This is one of the great mysteries of life and is based on the teaching of Jesus in which he said that we must believe that we have before we really do have, or before there is any physical manifestation of our having.

It is not always easy to do this; hence we must resort to a definite technique which as we have explained, is a method for inducing thought in the subjective state. Now just what do we mean by inducing thought? Turn to our definition of *Thought* at the top of page 638, the definitions of *Induce* and *Inductive Reasoning* on page 634, in order that you may clearly understand what is meant by inducing thought or creating a subjective state of mental acceptance.

In dealing with Mind we are dealing with a force which we cannot fool. We are dealing with an immutable Law of Cause and Effect. This Law is set in motion by the conscious thought. Read pages 390-392 inclusive for a more complete summary of this idea. Study these paragraphs carefully, and think them over until it is clear to you how we consciously induce thought within Mind, and how the Mind Principle within us, reacting to the images of thought which we have involved in It, creates an object which is in exact correspondence to such images.

At the expense of seeming to be repetitious, may we assure you that it is of paramount importance that everyone who wishes to be a successful practitioner should realize that he is dealing with a definite Principle, and he should know that he can deal with It consciously. Under the heading, *Streams of Consciousness*, page 352, we stress the thought that each individual is known in Mind by the name he bears, and that according to the principle of the unity of Mind, that which is known in one place is known everywhere. Forms of themselves are but effects of Mind, and since they are effects they can be transmuted into other forms. (Our definition of *Transmutation* is found on page 638).

Prayer is its own answer. In such degree as the one praying believes that he either has received or is certain to receive a direct answer, he will receive it. Since a belief cannot be automatically effective until it becomes subjective, and since the subjective state of thought is an effect and not a cause, a person can alter conditions in his life by changing the subjective state of his thought. Thus the conscious thought can change an entire sequence of cause and effect. In this way God answers our prayer when we change our thought patterns. All good is ours because we are in God and God is in us, as us. There is nothing outside of or external to God, the Universal Creative Spirit.

On pages 641 and 642, under *Universal Spirit*, you will find this statement: *Things come from one Source through one common Law,* and, *The Complete Nature of God is reflected in man*. You will also find the idea expressed that the medium of our thought action is the Universal Law through which our Word operates, and that the Word alone is conscious.

In dealing with Mind we are dealing with a force which we cannot fool. It is impossible to think one way and act another, and expect to get the desired result. Moreover, to think affirmatively one day and negatively the next is to neutralize our own effort. This does not mean that we can neutralize the Law, but we certainly do neutralize our own vibration in It. The Apostle was right when he said that if we wish to receive anything from the Lord we must ask in faith, not wavering. He likened the one who wavers to the surge of the sea, whirled and tossed by the wind, and said, "*For let not that man think he shall receive anything of the Lord.*" Here the word *Lord* is used as Law. It is impossible for us to cheat the Law, which of course is the meaning of that saying, *I will work, and who shall let (hinder) it?*

We feel sure that you now see how it is that prayer is its own answer, and that the Truth known actually demonstrates. Perhaps it is somewhat difficult to realize that there is something, the very knowing of which produces a corresponding physical manifestation, but this is the basic Principle which we are studying; the Principle of Causation directly used by the mind of man. The reason the mind of man can directly contact Causation is that the mind of man is some part of this Causation. (Re-read pages 390, 391 and 392).

Before turning to a consideration of faith (page 155), read again the definition of *Faith* on page 591. The Universe is a Spiritual System and our comprehension of this system is a thing of thought. Prayer, faith, and belief are closely related, since they constitute our mental approach to Reality or God. We all know that some prayers are more effective than others. As suggested in a recent lesson, the reason for this is that some prayers embody more faith than others. By faith we mean a conscious attitude of thought which is no longer subjectively denied. The prayer of faith is in the conscious self-knowing mind, but if there are subjective states which deny what the conscious thought has affirmed they will neutralize its effects. They will, as it were, cancel the vibration or faith.

These subjective states do not change the Law; they merely change our tendency in It. It is written that *the Law of the Lord is perfect*. That is true of every law in nature. We never change the laws of nature nor destroy them. We do not neutralize them; we merely transcend certain limited uses of them. All laws are infinite in their capacity to produce. The limitation is not in the Law but in our use of It.

So it is with faith, belief, and prayer. They deal with a definite Principle. As a matter of fact they *are* a definite Principle, and just because they are a definite Principle, only that which is really believed can come into manifestation. To believe, even when we have not yet seen the objective manifestation of our belief, is to have faith. And to have faith is to demonstrate.

Throughout the ages faith has been recognized as a thing of tremendous power. There are different types or kinds of faith, but a sense of unity with the Infinite marks the highest form of faith known to the mind of man. The reason this is so is that this type of faith is a direct intuition. It is one of those things we know without having to reason it out, something we feel even before we analyze it.

We all live by faith, although we do not know it. Those who have great faith have great power; no matter what that thing may be in which they place their faith. All successful people have faith in success, just as all unsuccessful people have faith in failure.

God does not answer one man's prayer while refusing another's. The result of all prayer is in accord with a definite Law of Cause and Effect. As our lesson suggests, our fear of lack is a denial of the abundance of God. We all have had this fear at times just as we have had fear of other great negations, whether it be the fear of lack, of death, of physical pain, or loss of friends. All these fears, which constitute the great negations of life, are basically denials of the omnipresence of Good and the ever-availability of Spirit as the God-power that is within all of us.

What is fear but faith misplaced? Certainly fear is also a positive attitude. It is an attitude of faith in the thing feared. It will help us if we realize that all attitudes more or less result in one attitude, that is, faith and fear are the same thing used in two different ways. This conception will help us, since it will cause us to see that in using faith we are not fighting fear; we are merely transmuting it.

We do not have to fight the attitude that hinders in order to attain the attitude that helps. This is our perception of unity, without which we could not proceed. The Universe would be divided against Itself if this were not true, and that is why it is written, *If God be for us, who can be against us?*

Fear must be converted into faith and faith into understanding. To convert faith into understanding means to appreciate exactly what we have been discussing in the last few paragraphs, that we are not dealing with two powers but with One Power which must forever present Itself in the terms of our mental acceptance of It. This is a basic Principle of our science. There is nothing but Life and what It does; nothing but Intelligence and Its movement. This movement is always upon Itself. So our faith is a movement upon Life, upon Intelligence, upon the Universal Law.

We understand that an affirmative statement about anything actually has the power to produce an affirmative manifestation relative to the thing mentioned. For instance, when you treat someone you say, "This word is for that person," then you make your statements about him. He may be afraid, but you are not. You, acting as practitioner, understand that your word will neutralize his fear, cast out all doubt and transmute his negative state into an affirmative one through the Law of Cause and Effect, which is that for every action there is an equal reaction, perfectly balancing it.

The *As thou hast believed, so be it done unto thee* of Jesus, is also the Cause and Effect of Buddha, known as the Karmic Law. It is likewise the Compensation of Emerson, which he refers to as *the high chancellor of God*. All great souls have perceived this. Moses saw it when he said, *I set before you this day a blessing and a curse*. You will find it in all sacred literature and in every great system of spiritual thought.

We must cultivate a conscious and definite faith in the affirmative side of life. We must definitely train ourselves to believe. Now this is not as difficult as it seems to be. It calls for considerable mental flexibility and for quite a bit of self-discipline, but it does not call for any exercise of concentration, any storming of the Infinite, any outrageous demands upon the Universe. It is not a result of feasting or fasting, of having or going without.

Throughout the ages people in every walk of life have had this divine, sublime, and all-conquering faith. Some have been rich, some have been poor. Some have been fat and some have been lean. Some have been ascetics who have tortured their physical bodies to arrive at this faith, while others have traveled a pathway of peace and self-recognition to arrive at the same destination. Each in his own tongue has declared the glory of the God in whom he believed, and that God who is in all, over all, and through all, has answered each in his own tongue. How sublime, how divine was the interpretation of Jesus. How profound and yet how simple his announcement: *As thou hast believed, so be it done unto thee*.

As stated on page 157 of our text, we should have no confusion in our work. History has recorded innumerable instances of healing through faith. We know that the Principle governing faith is an inner conviction. The Universe is Its own pronouncement. It knows nothing outside Itself. As our text says in the fourth paragraph on page 158, faith is not confined to any age or station in life. For faith deals with an immutable, universal Principle, from which each draws according to his belief. We are learning how to make conscious use of this belief, how to set the Law in motion for specific purposes.

Summary

Asking in faith means to believe that you have what you ask for when you ask. There can be no qualification to this. It must be considered to be a definite proposition.

Inducing thought means the process by which we change our own inward mental patterns or habitual thought patterns and create new ones.

The Law of Mind is never coerced nor fooled. It always reflects with mathematical exactness what we think into It. The practitioner must know that he is dealing with a definite Principle, and that his work depends neither on an indefinite faith nor a law of chance. Everything comes through one Source through one Law. We are part of that Source and live in that Law. While we cannot neutralize the Law we can neutralize the effect of the way we have been using It.

Prayer, faith, and belief are closely related, but effective prayer must pass from belief through faith into the acceptance of understanding. One man's prayers are not answered above another's since God is the Eternal Giver, giving of Himself alike to each and all. If some people pray better and receive more, it is because they come closer to the nature of Reality.

Fear is misplaced faith. It is well to understand this; otherwise we shall be combating fear with faith rather than forgetting the fear and turning to the faith.

The Science of Mind reduces faith to a principle which can be understood and taught, and a technique which can be consciously used.

The prayer of faith acts in accord with Principle; therefore it acts like a law.

Questions

Brief answers to these questions should be written out by the student after studying the lesson, and the answers compared with those which will be included in next week's lesson.

1. Why do we say, *Prayer is its own answer*?
2. What do we mean by the statement, *The Absolute is in relationship to Itself alone*?
3. What is meant by, *Ask in faith*?
4. To what passage in the New Testament does our lesson refer when it states that Jesus told his followers to believe when they prayed?

5. When is belief automatically effective?
6. How can we change the subjective state of our thought?
7. What happens if we think affirmatively one day and negatively the next?
8. What is the basic principle underlying this entire philosophy?
9. If there is no limitation in the Law, why are we limited?
10. What develops the highest form of faith?
11. Why does our fear of lack deny the abundance of God?
12. Upon what belief are our principal fears based?
13. In what way are faith and fear similar?
14. In treating a person to heal him of fear, what would be your mental attitude?
15. How should we train ourselves to be affirmative?

Answers to Questions on Lesson 18

1. The Spirit creates by contemplation.
2. Contemplation in mental treatment means to know within the self.
3. The act of contemplation is likened to an object held before a mirror because as a mirror reflects the likeness of the object held before it, so the Law reflects into experience the likeness of the mental image contemplated.
4. Actual First Cause is independent of any existing circumstance. It is Its own reason for being. Relative first cause is dependent upon, and is in reality an effect of a previous cause. For example, holding a pencil before a mirror would be the relative first cause of the reflected image. However, the intelligent Life Principle within the one holding it would be the Absolute First Cause.
5. The Life Principle, as essence, is Spirit; the Life Principle, as Law, is a mechanical reaction.
6. In treatment will power is never used because it would be coercion or force. Willingness is used however, because it implies complete acceptance of the imagination.
7. Our consciousness means our entire mental life—both conscious and subjective.
8. Changing our consciousness through mental treatment means deliberately creating a new conscious and subjective reaction to life.
9. From the standpoint of mental healing, a spiritual consciousness is a mental awareness of Unity, Harmony, and Perfect Life.
10. A spiritual consciousness in mental healing is necessary because it produces the greatest faith, and therefore the greatest power.
11. Cosmic Consciousness means one's mental awareness of one's unity with Spirit or the Essence of life, and with all that lives.
12. The highest God and the innermost God is one because Life Itself is One, and everywhere present. Therefore man's life is the Life of God expressing through man.
13. The generally accepted idea of prayer is a petition, while mental treatment is a declaration.
14. God is an impartial giver because in the eyes of God, as Emerson said, *All people are dear to the heart of Being*.
15. Our prayers will be answered in such degree as we receive the desired gift.
16. We transmute limitation into freedom by using the One Law in a less limited way.

17. Each person has a unique destiny because no two persons being alike, each must have a unique and important place in the Cosmic Wholeness.
18. It is written, *But to as many as received him, to them gave he power . . .* (John 1:12), because while the power is already delivered, we must receive it.
19. We need salvation from thoughts of limitation, fear, bondage, and the sense of separation from good.

Practical Suggestion for Mental Treatment

Mind, the Only Creative Energy

No matter how seemingly impossible any situation may be or how difficult any problem may appear, the practitioner should never become discouraged. He must continue to do his work, knowing full well that he is dealing with the invisible Essence, the invisible Substance, the Great Reality back of everything.

It would be impossible for a person to do this unless he were firmly convinced that Mind is the only creative agency in the universe and that he has direct and conscious access to Its creativity. Moreover, he must be conscious that right thought and true statements are the enforcement of this Law of Mind.

Man's thought is the activity of Mind, for Mind without thought or directed consciousness would have no real existence. There can be no existence apart from consciousness, or if there be any existence apart from consciousness then there is no one, no thing, and no intelligence to be aware of such existence. It is evident that without self-awareness there is not only no realization of life, but no life to be realized. Hence we affirm that Mind in action is Law.

The practitioner who understands this will not become discouraged. He will know that if he persists in declaring the Truth, the pathway to Reality will be cleared, obstructions will be removed, wrong forms will be dissolved.

It follows that he will be both courageous and happy in his work. He will be happy because he is sure; doubts no longer assail him, fear does not possess him, negation no longer obsesses his thought. He continues to make his declarations with calm confidence and with Divine assurance.

The Servant May Become an Heir

Wherefore thou art no more a servant, but a son; and if a son, then an heir. How many of us claim our Divine inheritance? How many of us realize that the will or the nature of God was written before the foundations of this physical universe were laid, and that in this will each one of us was endowed with the faculty of true perception, bequeathed a life of perfection, and guaranteed immunity from all evil? For surely the will of God could be no less than this.

The will of God has been written by the invisible hand of Reality. It is still in probate as far as most of us are concerned; it has never been completely executed. We have not laid hold of our Divine inheritance. Perhaps we have been listening to the wrong counsel. We have accepted the false evidence of the senses. We have been cast into prison for debts which might have been paid had we recognized that

Substance already belonged to us. We have been a servant and not a son; hence we have not entered into the heirship.

In another place we are told that it is high time that we should awake from our sleep. Perhaps we have dreamed that we were servants and not heirs. Now we must awake from this mesmeric state. The heir must claim his inheritance; otherwise it is still kept for him and he has not the use of it. He must step forward before the bar of justice, which is the Law of Cause and Effect, and declare that he is no longer a servant, a slave, but a master, a son, an heir. He must announce that all that the Father has is his.

Thus he lays claim to his true estate, and laying claim in the name of God through Christ, the inheritance is at once delivered. That which had been kept in store for him is delivered into his hands.

Conscious Contact with the Infinite

It is written, *But the natural man receiveth not the things of the Spirit of God, for they are foolishness unto him: neither can he know them, because they are spiritually discerned*. This means that the objective senses, the intellect with all of its arguments might easily keep us from the Kingdom of Good unless we are careful to remember that spiritual things must be spiritually discerned.

There is an inner meaning to everything, an inside to every fact, a hidden cause within every visible effect. This Cause is Spirit.

If we spiritually discern this hidden Cause, if we inwardly know that It is operating for us, then we are thinking from the recognition of the allness of Good. We all have direct access to the Parent Mind but we do not all use this direct access because we are so used to judging from external facts. It is difficult for us to get away from the apparent long enough to judge the real.

When we know that there is but One Spirit in the entire universe we shall know that there is but One Source for all forms. We shall know that every form is some manifestation of this Source.

When we have found that this Source is also centered in us we shall know that we can come directly to It, and discerning that Its spiritual nature is love and truth and beauty, and particularly that It is responsive, we shall make known our requests with thanksgiving, with complete mental abandonment.

Your Word Operates Instantly at the Desired Place

Someone has said, *Rest in faith that your thought reaches the person, or condition to which it is sent*. Now we know that objective person, place, and condition are all effects following invisible causation, which is Mind. And we know that thought is the instrument of Mind. We know that Mind is ever present and is never divided; it is a complete and perfect unit. Therefore when we give a treatment we say, "This word is for this person," or, "It is for this condition."

From this viewpoint the word does not have to reach any objective place; it merely describes the place. Identifying itself in Mind with the place it is instantly at that place.

Some of the ancients have said that the Truth is that whose center is everywhere and whose circumference is nowhere. This is a good idea for us to keep in mind. It will help us to have a complete conviction that our word will always reach the desired condition; it will never fail to objectify where it should, when it should, and in the right way.

Nothing but absolute faith in the Law of Cause and Effect can give us this confidence. If we do not have this confidence we must start at the beginning again and ask ourselves the simple question: "Where did anything come from?"

It is self-evident that all things come from the Invisible, are projected by It, and remain within It. Our thought is an activity of this invisible Causation, and when we say, "This word shall manifest in this place," we may be and we must be certain that it will do so.

You Are a Spiritual Broadcasting Station

Did you ever stop to think that you are a spiritual and mental broadcasting station, and that messages are going out from you in all directions, perhaps even while you are asleep—messages which have an influence on your environment and the people around you? And since everything moves in circles, the messages you broadcast will come back to you.

We are told that the mental atmosphere of a home can influence a dog, a cat, or a canary to the extent that they become neurotic when surrounded by unhappiness or criticism. There is a place where our physical bodies begin and leave off, but the mind has no such limitations, and our thoughts penetrate everything around us.

We are all broadcasting stations, whether or not we know it. Our thoughts, feelings, and emotions, our faiths and fears, tend to make an imprint on our environment. We are also receiving sets, but it does not follow that we must tune in to every program being broadcast. When we want to listen to a certain program we tune our radios to its wave length. The program already is within the ether in the room, but it does not affect our instrument until we tune in to it.

It is fascinating to think that we are both mental broadcasting stations and receiving sets. And it will be even more wonderful when we learn to broadcast only the kind of messages that we wish to have return.

If a person's mind is filled with animosity and resentment people will feel it, whether or not he says a word. This animosity arouses within others, who have resentment and animosity, a feeling like his own. His thoughts tune in to theirs, and theirs immediately respond by flowing back into him. One accentuates the other.

On the other hand, if you are surrounded by people who have resentment and animosity but you have none, you will not tune in. Their vibration bypasses you, and their antagonism does not arouse an equal antagonism in you because you are not broadcasting on the same mental wave length.

It is the same with everything in life. A person whose thought is filled with the fear of failure tunes in to and picks up vibrations of failure wherever he contacts them, and to his own negative thought there is added a great mass of negative thoughts until finally it seems that the only thing he can think about is failure. In a way both his will and his imagination become hypnotized, because he is tuning in to so much negation. When a person's mind is upset, disturbed, and unhappy, all he mentally hears is discord because his inner ear is listening to a continual turmoil.

Conversely, a person whose thought is filled with the idea of success, who has faith and confidence in himself and what he is doing, will tune in to the successful thoughts around him, the thoughts of faith and optimism and happy expectancy.

A person who confidently expects good things to happen, who expects everyone to like him, and who expects to find happiness in life, wherever he goes will not only be broadcasting these thoughts which will make other people happy; he will be receiving them in return. Because he feels friendly, people will respond with friendliness.

We all wish to be like this. We not only want to be whole ourselves, because no one can be happy unless he is whole, but we want to help others. We not only wish to broadcast good news; good news is what we want to receive.

We should decide to think on the affirmative side of life, or accentuate the positive and eliminate the negative. In doing this we must make up our minds that we are not going to receive the criticism or the negative state or the animosity of anyone. And let us not forget the importance of keeping our minds in a state of good-natured flexibility. If a tree did not bend with the breeze it would break under a strong wind.

We have to be flexible and tolerant as well as positive and affirmative. And even if someone throws a brick at us we need not catch it. It is far better just to step aside. When we catch the bricks that are thrown at us, it is generally for one purpose only—to throw them right back. And the first thing we know the air is full of bricks, and what a mess that makes. It will help if we decide to play the game of life in a happy way.

Another thing we can learn is not to dwell on the obituary notices. Remember that for everyone who passes out of this world someone else comes in. Life is a river always flowing, and life itself never gets tired, worn out, or exhausted; it never depletes itself. Yes, there are a lot of things in the papers beside the obituary notices. We do not have to morbidly scan all the accidents any more than we have to listen to negative conversation. More and more we are coming to see what it means to accentuate the positive and eliminate the negative.

It is true enough that birds of a feather flock together, and birds do come home to roost. But if we use the mind that God has given us, we can build our own roosts. We can even change the color of our feathers, if we want to. For the Divine Mind has created a plumage for each one of us, and has built a nest in the Secret Place of the Most High for every living soul.

All of us are rooted in the Mind of God. We did not plan it this way; this is the way it is. God is still the Supreme Power, and the Divine Spirit is still present with us no matter where we are. We must learn to tune in to the Mind of God, for when we do we are tuning in to the most dynamic reality in the universe.

Do not be afraid to talk to God, always remembering that God speaks a certain kind of language and there is nothing negative in it. We believe in prayerful, affirmative meditation above everything else. We believe in actually talking to God and then letting God answer. But perhaps in our confusion we have talked *at* God rather than *to* Him. We have told Him how terrible everything is, how unhappy we are.

Try this: Sit or lie in complete repose, and then tell God how wonderful He is and how glad you are, how grateful. It is at times like these that we are really tuning in to the Divine, and the Divine will always respond to us. We shall always receive the comfort and consolation we need, the inward sense of security and well-being that everyone must have to be happy and whole.

Let us find a new wave length for our mental instruments, and as surely as we do this we shall begin to broadcast on this wave length. We shall discover that we are not only helping ourselves but are helping everyone around us. Let us tune our mental instruments to success and happiness, to the idea of physical wholeness, and above everything else to the comforting thought that there is a love in the universe which by its very presence dissolves all hate; there is a faith that neutralizes all fear; there is a confidence that brushes aside every doubt.

God never deserts us, and we shall never have to convince God to be good. All we have to do is reverse our whole mental and spiritual outlook on life and then the miracle will take place, because what goes out must return.

The skeptic may call this a Pollyannaish attitude and say that we are living in a world of unreality. Well, I have dealt with skeptics all my life and I have no awe of them—none at all. They are forlorn and unhappy people who have no guideposts to go by, no chart, no compass, and no pilot. Learn to say with Samuel Walter Foss:

Let the howlers howl,
And the growlers growl,
And the scowlers scowl,
And let the rough gang go it.

For behind the night,
There is plenty of light,
And the world's all right,
And I know it.

No, this is not an empty or an idle dream. This is an intense reality. Somewhere along the line we must find a faith greater than all our doubts and fears and uncertainties. Somewhere along the line we must find a love greater than all animosity. And we must find a peace beyond our confusion. This is the pathway that we are all seeking, whether or not we know it, and we are being guided by a loving Intelligence which evermore seeks to bring us peace and comfort, cheer and good-will, happiness and success, health and abundance.

First of all we must be sure that we are right inside, and then learn to trust ourselves because we have faith in God. We must learn to get our own broadcasting station in order. We must re-tune our own receiving set. It may take time and effort, but the goal we seek is worth the journey, and the prize that is offered is worthy of our effort. Heaven is lost only because we lack the idea of harmony; it was destined from the foundation of the world that right finally should win, and that love should conquer all.

We all are spiritual and mental broadcasting stations. There is a silent force flowing from us in every direction at all times. How necessary it is that we assume the role of the announcer and the broadcaster. How necessary that we write our own program and deliver it ourselves.

When a person speaks into a microphone in a broadcasting station his words are carried to the far corners of the earth, where they are reproduced. But the force that carries them is mechanical. It is a law, a vibration. And it is a law which actually reproduces the words he speaks, the intonations, the inflections.

And now along with this word which is broadcast goes a picture, an image of his personality. This is what we see in television, as though he were suddenly present everywhere, and the picture looks like him because it was his image, his likeness, that created it.

And so it is with the reaction of the Law of Good from a Power greater than we are. It always tends to bring back to us exactly what goes out. But we are always the broadcasters, and we can always change the pictures if we will.

Meditation

Out of the abundance of the heart the mouth speaketh. Today I am keeping careful watch that I think and speak only those things that I wish broadcast from my mind and returned to me.

I desire that everything I think shall be from the heart as well as from the head. I wish to broadcast kindness and love, sympathy and understanding, peace and joy. No condemnation, judgment, nor fear shall go from me to anyone or anything.

Tuning my mind in to the Divine, I draw into my own soul the essence of everything that is good, true, and beautiful. I draw into my own mind the realization of the Divine Presence and the Power of Good until my whole being responds.

And this is all I wish to broadcast to the world—something that will help and heal and bless, something that will cause everyone I meet to feel a new strength, a new hope. Desiring to receive the Divine blessing in my own life, I wish to broadcast it to the whole world. And so I say to the whole world:

> *The Lord bless thee, and keep thee: The Lord make his face to shine upon thee, and be gracious unto thee: The Lord lift up his countenance upon thee, and give thee peace, both now and forevermore. Amen.*

The Doctor, the Psychologist, and the Metaphysician

When the physician and the metaphysician come to understand each other better they will cooperate with each other. It is self-evident that each is seeking to alleviate human suffering. No intelligent person would deny the need of physicians, surgeons, and hospitals. On the other hand it is generally agreed that a large percentage of our physical troubles are mental in their origin, and that all have some relationship to mental processes. It is important, then, that we understand and appreciate the work of the sincere metaphysician.

It is not at all probable that the psychologist can take the place of the metaphysician. For just as the healing of the body without an adjustment of mental and emotional states is insufficient, so the adjusting of mental and emotional states without introducing spiritual values will be ineffectual. Hence there is an important place for the metaphysician, and his cooperation should be sought.

In the early days of spiritual therapeutics it was believed that a practitioner could not successfully treat patients if they were being attended by a physician, or if they were using material methods for relief. Now we know that this was based on superstition. We no longer give it any serious thought. The metaphysician feels it a privilege to be called into consultation with a physician or with a psychologist. He has learned to appreciate the field of medicine and surgery.

The day is certain to come when the field of medicine will recognize, deeply appreciate, and gladly cooperate with the metaphysical field. Such cooperation is far more common even today than the average person realizes. When the metaphysician stops denying that his patient is ill he will find a greater inclination toward cooperation from the medical world.

Today most physicians recognize the power of thought in relation to the body. All realize the dynamic energy of the emotions. Psychiatric hospitals are being built, and psychiatric wards are being added to hospitals already in existence. Just as psychology and psychiatry are being introduced into the medical world, so the metaphysical field will be gradually understood, accepted, and appreciated.

Already there is a tendency among many psychologists to affirm the necessity of a spiritual life. Spiritual values must be introduced into the healing art, and who is going to meet this need unless it be the metaphysician?

In our experience here at the Institute of Religious Science we have been most fortunate in this connection. Our practitioners have had the opportunity of cooperating with many of the leading physicians in our community, and this experience has been happy and beneficial to everyone concerned.

In such friendly cooperation the metaphysician has the opportunity of receiving a correct diagnosis from the physician, which enables him to do better mental work. There is also an added comfort in the mind of the patient when he knows that he is having proper physical care, proper diet, and right medical and surgical attention when necessary. His mind is in a more composed state, and this enables the mental practitioner to do more effective work. It is easier to work for one whose mental attitude is poised than for one whose thought is distraught. If a patient must undergo a serious physical operation, what is more important than that his mind be at peace? This alone would reduce the element of risk.

Progress is inevitable, and cooperation among all right-minded workers in the healing art is certain. Let us do all that we can to remove superstition, intolerance, and bigotry, which are the result of ignorance.

All should unite not only to alleviate physical suffering, but in so far as possible to remove its cause. If much of this cause lies hidden in the realm of mind, then surely those who are equipped to work in this realm are contributing their share to the meeting of a human need.

Not only should the physician recognize this, but the clergy should as well, and religious institutions should have a department for this purpose. The reason that this has not already taken place is that few such institutions have recognized the possibilities of this work.

When it is more thoroughly understood that trained workers in this field should be recognized as professional men and women entitled to compensation for their services, then something very interesting will happen. This has already been done in some religious institutions, but the majority of them have not yet recognized the necessity of making a definite profession of the healing work in order that men and women may give their entire time and attention to it, just as physicians and psychologists do.

We look forward to the day when there will be greater cooperation between physician, metaphysician, and religious leader. When the misunderstanding and superstition which separate these three fields shall have been removed, inestimable good will be accomplished. The dynamic energy of spiritual conviction can be definitely used for the purpose of healing, but this should be done by trained workers who must be compensated for their work if they are to give their entire time and thought to it.

So far the church has failed to recognize this field as the one most likely to revitalize it, to bring back into it the rich experiences, the fire of conviction that died with the waning fervor of prayer. The fundamental principle that the emotions often outwit the intellect has been overlooked. The dynamic power of spiritual conviction, consciously used for definite purposes, can again erect an altar of faith before which men will gladly worship.

The church has adequate physical equipment for carrying on metaphysical work. Why is it necessary that this equipment be reproduced in order to introduce a vital idea into the religious life of the world? It would be just as unreasonable to suppose that for every hospital now in existence there must be another one built if people are to receive proper mental and spiritual treatment. It is economically unsound to have to reproduce that which the church already has.

Sometime this more or less embryonic vision will become an actuality, with the physician, the metaphysician, the psychologist, and the clergyman all working together for the common good, each in his own field, each cooperating with the other. Today wherever the inclination toward such cooperation is manifest from any pulpit, that church is packed with eager and expectant people ready to support the institution which is bringing to them this new hope through a restoration of faith.

Meditation

I now recognize and fully understand that faith deals with a definite Principle; that this Principle is for me and with me, responding to me at all times. I know that the Universe honors this faith. All that I have hoped for and believed in I now accept.

There is no argument of unbelief within me. Nothing can arise within me to dissipate my faith, for I have this sublime conviction that the Spirit of the Almighty indwells my own soul, and that the Power of the Infinite goes forth through my word.

My word is the law of my life, bringing peace, joy, and happiness into my experience and into the experience of all who come to me for help.

I know that good is in my experience now, and that I am able to demonstrate this good today and tomorrow and always.

I know that in this good is everything that makes life happy and worthwhile, whether that is called money or friends or physical conditions—all are brought forth and harmonized and unified by the One Power which creates them and which holds them in place as long as they are useful, dissolving them when they are no longer necessary.

There is no longer any argument in my consciousness. I am not trying to acquire this faith. I recognize that I now have it. There is no sense of doubt or fear which can neutralize this faith.

My word cannot return unto me void. My word is not only with the Law, it *is* the Law, and that Law is perfect.

Faith and Treatment

Office of the Dean

My Dear Friend,

We think you are going to be especially interested in our article on *Energy and Mass*. It will help you to see from a scientific and mathematical viewpoint that mind and matter, or mind and form, or the invisible and the visible, are one and the same thing.

It will help you to see that your thought is not operating on something that is itself different from thought or a product of thought. The Universe is One System, and the visible and the invisible are the same.

You may be interested in the verse called *A Certain Man Had Two Sons*. I wrote it one evening after I had been thinking about the necessity of a spiritual body duplicating the physical, and that the physical must have a pattern in the spiritual. All of which shows that we draw ideas into our own consciousness by making some kind of a demand on the Principle from which all ideas come, or the Presence in which they originate.

We hope you are trying this, because this Principle and this Presence are no respecters of persons. It will be interesting for you to see what you can draw out of the Cosmic Bag.

Always bear in mind, as stated in the lesson, that treatment is a definite, concise, and moving thing; that when you give a treatment you are doing something definite in the Law of Mind, not just willing or wishing or hoping. You are to become a scientific as well as a spiritual practitioner. The one is a feeling and an art, the other is a consciousness and an act.

Sincerely,
Ernest Holmes

Lesson 20

Page 159 to bottom of page 164

As stated in our last lesson, faith is a mental attitude so inwardly embodied that the mind can no longer deny it. Real faith reaches a place not only of objective, but also of subjective acceptance. There is no longer any doubt in the subconscious thought which denies the affirmations made by the conscious thought.

We live by faith. But we wish to reduce this faith to understanding. In this instance we must practice acceptance, and wherever anything enters our thought that denies the reality of the good in which we are to have complete confidence, we must explain to ourselves why this thought of doubt has no power, for you will find that the explanation is the cure.

All of our explanations are to be built upon the belief, the conviction, the faith, that we are living in a Spiritual Universe which is perfect, and that all discord is the result of a misunderstanding of this Spiritual Universe. It is a denial of the Spiritual Universe, but this denial in no way changes Its reality.

When everyone believed that the world was flat their thought did not flatten out the world, but their belief in a flat world did limit their physical experience. They were afraid to travel for fear they would fall off the edges. But belief in a flat world did not change the round world, and when someone came along who knew the truth, the world as it is was revealed. Man's belief in a round world did not create a round world, but his faith and conviction that the world was round enabled him to circumnavigate the globe. Ignorance never changes the laws of nature, but it does restrict our use of such laws.

We must acquire a vitalizing faith. The one who hopes to practice successfully must have mental and spiritual enthusiasm. He must have a spirit of mental buoyancy. Even while his work is scientific he dramatizes his technique. He has the inner satisfaction of feeling that he is revealing the Truth to people. He is neutralizing fear and doubt by his affirmations of the presence of Perfection, of Peace, and of Wholeness. This comes from a complete faith in God, in the Universe, in the Universal Law, and in one's own ability to use It.

Spiritual thought force has as much power as we give to it, and reveals to us as much Reality as we are able to realize at any particular time. Spiritual thought force neutralizes doubt and fear just as light dissipates darkness. There is no effort in the process, and in such degree as we have implicit confidence in our ability to use spiritual thought force, just to that degree our word will be powerful.

It is impossible for us to have this belief as long as we think of ourselves as isolated from the Universe, but as we sense our unity with all life, our oneness with God, we better understand the use of the Universal Law of Cause and Effect. The whole process is a mental one, and thus it is evident that nothing can come out of a treatment unless we first put it in mentally. Unless we put conviction in, conviction cannot come out.

We must always know that the Truth which we speak is greater than any negative condition which needs to be changed. For as stated at the top of page 160, we should realize that when we speak from the standpoint of Spirit there is no opposition to our word. Turn to page 620 and read the definition of *Power*. You will notice that this paragraph says, *Man may transmute as much of the Infinite Energy into degrees of power as he chooses to use.*

The power which we use in giving a treatment is of itself merely an infinite possibility. We specialize it; that is, we determine what it shall do, how it shall operate, and for what purpose, and in such degree as we have absolute confidence that it will do so, it must do so. We are dealing here with the immutable Law of Cause and Effect, but we should never forget that the Spirit is always superior to the Law. The Spirit is Absolute Causation, the Law is Its servant.

If you will turn to page 633, under the definition of *Spirit*, you will see that First Cause must include all that is manifest on any plane. Your conscious thought is the same as First Cause, while the subjective reaction to it is the Law of Mind in action. Hence it is the *conscious* thought which gives the treatment.

We can never be too careful to remember this, nor too definite in stating it. It is the conscious idea which gives differentiation to the Law. If you will turn to page 580 and read our definition of *Conscious Idea* it will help you to see how this conscious idea creates form through the Law. The Law obeys the will of the conscious idea, but is not conscious that It is doing so.

The Law acts intelligently, and we must conceive of an intelligent operation of a Law which, even though It is intelligent, has no self-determination whatsoever. The Law is always the doer of the word. It is never a knower of what It is doing.

In your study you will never find anything more difficult to understand, nor more essential to our philosophy than this, both in the presentation of its Principle and in the performance of its practice. It was his knowledge of the power of his word over the Law which gave Jesus his authority. In the Meditation at the top of page 522 you will find a brief statement which may be used in helping you to realize your authority over the Law. If you will read the three Meditations on page 514, you will be helped to enter into a spiritual appreciation of your use of the Law.

The Spirit knows no opposition because It is a complete unity, and the Spirit within us is God. It is not something different; It is not a gradually evolving Spirit; It is *The* Spirit. Hence there is a place in us which is absolute, and a word which may be spoken that is all-powerful. The reason we seem to lack this power is because our psychological nature is not in complete harmony with the Unity of Good. As we let go of the human will, and of any and every idea of compulsion and strain, and through reason and intuition arrive at a place of complete acceptance, we come to exercise real spiritual power.

In order to do this we must rise above the belief in duality, for the Infinite knows no opposition and has none. (On page 587 read the discussion on *Duality*.) As we turn to Reality, It turns to us. That is, in such degree as our thought is affirmative the affirmation of the Universe immediately corresponds to it. This is the meaning of the saying, *Be firm and ye shall be made firm*. It is also what Jesus meant when, in describing the return of the Prodigal Son, he said that the Father saw him afar off and came out to meet him.

On page 466 you will find a further discussion of this, which we call the *reciprocal action* between the Universal and the individual. God looks at us as we look at God. Our looking at God is God looking through us at Himself. If this statement seems abstract and obscure, stop and reason it out for it contains the hidden secret of the ages, the key to the mystery of mysteries, the revelation of the self to the self.

It stands to reason that we cannot be effective practitioners while we entertain doubt and fear. We must come to realize that fear is not God-ordained. Doubt and confusion are a result of a belief in separation from Good. We must come to realize that we never have been separated from Good; Good has always been with us, but we have not recognized It. It is wonderful to contemplate the faith which Jesus had in the power of his word. We should arrive at the same conclusion about our own word.

In such degree as we cease contemplating evil we shall enter into a consciousness of Good. We must arrive at a basic conviction that Good is the only power there is; therefore our consciousness of Good can instantly annihilate any belief in evil. It is self-evident that this must be true, else the Universe would be divided against Itself; It would be a duality and not a unity.

Over and over we must reassure ourselves that there is One Power. This Power is operating through us. It is *our* power. There is One Mind, that Mind is *our* mind right now. There is One Law, that Law is effective in *our* lives right now. We must know and we must know that we know. For as our text says, in the third paragraph on page 161, *The Universe remains unlimited, though the whole world has suffered a sense of limitation*. We must be careful not to divide our thought against itself, but daily to reassure ourselves of our immunity from evil, our oneness with Good. All Power flows through us. The One Divine Presence is in us. The perfect Law responds to us.

The more clearly we can see this the more completely we shall demonstrate. But as you will find in the third paragraph on page 162, when we limit our faith to that which has already been done we are limiting the Infinite in Its action for us. But as our text states, *Principle is not bound by precedent*. Principle is forever the cause. It is, as our definition on page 621 states, *The Source or Cause from which a thing results*. Principle is never bound by anything that has gone before. We can speak the creative word today which will change all of our yesterdays and convert them into tomorrows of happiness, peace, poise, power, and prosperity. *Limitation is the result of an ignorant use of the Law* (last paragraph on page 402). Limitation is never a thing of itself; it is merely a circumscribed way of using one's freedom.

In treatment we must be careful that our thought is not influenced by any physical appearance whatsoever. That person is the best practitioner who is the least concerned over the objective manifestation which he wishes to dissolve. If the Spirit within him is God, then It can change anything that needs to be changed. While Jesus remained with his disciples his clear vision of this truth enabled them to perform mighty works. As the ages passed, this clear vision which he had was forgotten by his followers, the power which attended the vision waned, and the so-called miracles were relegated to history where they became mere symbols of the Divinity of Jesus.

We must realize that all men are Divine, all men have the hidden power. But to have the power is not enough—we must use it. We must sense this inner Divinity as a Divine Companionship, as explained on page 585, and then we must speak our word with definite intention, being conscious of what we wish it to do and knowing that it will bear fruit.

You will find many Meditations which will help you to this realization, from pages 507 to 550 inclusive. It is a good idea to read several of them and meditate earnestly upon their meaning. As this meaning becomes clear to you, turn directly to the problem you wish to solve, deny its existence, and in its place affirm the presence of that which is desirable. As the text states in the last paragraph, page 162, *No matter what the outside appearance, we must cling steadfastly to the knowledge that God is good.* Thus, *Effective mental treatment is propelled by a consciousness of love and a realization that the Creative Spirit is always at work* (page 163).

Read again the last two paragraphs on page 413, trying to sense that all the power of the Universe is flowing through you as you speak your word of liberation for yourself or for someone else. A mental treatment has only as much power as we believe it has, and only that can come out of a treatment which we put into it. Therefore when we give treatments there should be a sense of calm and poise and peace, a great freedom from any uncertainty or confusion or hurry. There should be no tension, anxiety, or strain. The mind should be relaxed but alert, poised but active, receptive to the good but conscious that it is giving direction.

A treatment is not mental mooning around. It is definite, concise, and always a moving thing. The thought which we use in a treatment is colored by our spiritual recognition, our consciousness of power, of light, of the Divine Influx, as suggested by the Meditation on page 530, *The Power Within Blesses All*. Read also the Meditation at the top of page 525. Such Meditations lighten the thought, open the intuitive perception, and actually permit an influx of power.

Once the power is delivered it must be consciously used. In giving the treatment, as our text suggests, we turn away from the condition and look to the opposite—to peace, poise, power, and perfection, claiming them as the only Reality, announcing that they are *now* manifest, and insisting that we recognize them.

This is not an act of the will in any sense of the term, any more than to look at a beautiful landscape would be an act of the will. We must have a willingness, but this is not to be confused with strenuous determination. It is to become what Emerson refers to as *a jubilant and a beholding soul*. In giving mental treatments, you become consciously aware of the Divine Presence in your patient, or the Divine Activity wherever your thought turns.

You must be definitely certain that wherever you are aware of Divine Action, there right action immediately follows. Theoretically, you convert things into thoughts and handle thoughts rather than things. In our work we must not only understand, we should also become accustomed to accepting the theory that thoughts are things, that wherever a true state of consciousness is generated, physical reaction will inevitably follow.

We invoke the Law, the Law evolves the form. Thus man is referred to as a husbandman of the Lord or as a dispenser of Divine Gifts. The Gift is already made, we specialize It. The consciousness of man is the enforcement of the Divine Law, and wherever this consciousness is harmonious, peace, joy, and prosperity follow.

All spiritual treatment is for the purpose of awakening this Divine realization at the center of our thought and for the purpose of directing the Law to do our specific bidding. Any type of treatment which will awaken this recognition will be effective, but no matter how great a realization of goodness we have, unless we give direction to it, it does no particular thing but remains merely an unused power.

Summary

Our belief does not change Reality; it merely changes our position in It.

Our thought has as much power as we believe it has at any particular time.

We could not believe our thought has power unless we knew it acted as a law.

The reason we can have faith and belief is that we know that belief and faith do act as Law.

We specialize the Law, that is, we use It for definite purposes; It is our servant. We must conceive of a Creative Law that works intelligently without Itself having any conscious volition or conscious intelligence. This is because the Law of Mind is a Principle and never a person. You are the person using It.

We must rise above all belief in duality to a consciousness that there is nothing to contradict our word in so far as it is true.

When we stop thinking about evil it will disappear. Limitation and ignorance go hand in hand.

All men are Divine. The most effective mental treatment is propelled by a consciousness of love.

A mental treatment is not hoping or wishing; it is definite, concise, and moving. It is not will, but willingness.

We invoke the Law, the Law evolves the form.

Thoughts are things in solution, things are thoughts in form, but the two are the same.

Questions

Brief answers to these questions should be written out by the student after studying the lesson, and the answers compared with those which will be included in next week's lesson.

1. What is meant by reducing faith to understanding?
2. In spiritual mind healing, why do we say that explanation is the cure?
3. Upon what premise are our explanations to be based?
4. Why should our mental work have a spirit of buoyancy?
5. Why must we put conviction into a mental treatment?
6. What do we mean by specializing the power of mind?
7. Explain the statement: *Spirit is Causation and the Law is Its servant.*
8. Does the Law which obeys the Spirit *know* that It is so doing?
9. Why did Jesus speak his word as one having authority?
10. Why does the Spirit know no opposition?
11. What is the spirit of man?
12. What is meant by the *reciprocal action* between the Universal and the individual?
13. What do we mean by the contemplation of good?
14. What should we add to such statements as, "There is One Power, One Mind, One Law, etc."?
15. Why is Principle never circumscribed by Its own effects?
16. Why should a practitioner not be influenced by appearances?
17. What is the difference between having power and using power?
18. In mental treatment, why do we handle thoughts rather than things?
19. Need we consciously assume the responsibility for creating conditions?

Answers to Questions on Lesson 19

1. Prayer is its own answer because prayer is an action which takes place within the realm of causation, while the answer is an automatic effect of such causative action.
2. By the statement, *The Absolute is in relationship to Itself alone*, we mean that the Absolute, being First Cause, is never limited by any effect, but governs all effects. The Absolute makes things out of Itself through the act of Itself becoming the thing It makes.
3. To ask in faith means to believe that we already have or that we inevitably must receive an answer to our faith.
4. The statement of Jesus to which our lesson refers is Mark 11:24, which is: *What things soever ye desire when ye pray, believe that ye receive them, and ye shall have them.*
5. Belief is automatically effective when it becomes a part of our subjective state of thought.
6. Since the subjective state of our thought is the result of our conscious or unconscious thought patterns, we can change it by deliberately and consciously creating new patterns of thought.
7. If we think affirmatively one day and negatively the next we are likely to neutralize our efforts.
8. The basic principle underlying this philosophy is that our thought deals directly with real Causation.
9. The Law, being Infinite, cannot be limited. Our limitation is the result of our limited use of It.
10. The highest form of faith is developed through a realization of one's unity with the Infinite.
11. Our fear of lack denies the abundance of God, because thought patterns of lack attract and create limited circumstances.
12. Our principal fears are based upon the belief that good is not always actively present in our lives and affairs.
13. Faith and fear are similar in that each is a positive mental attitude. For example, fear is a positive attitude toward evil, lack, etc., while faith is a positive attitude toward what we call good, abundance, etc.
14. Your mental attitude would be to deny fear and affirm faith.
15. We definitely train ourselves to be affirmative, not through any weird rites but by cultivating the mental habit of having faith in ourselves, in Life, and in the Universe.

Energy and Mass

One of the new propositions in physics is that energy and mass are equal, identical, and interchangeable. Now this is a harmless enough sounding phrase, but very few people understand the mathematics behind it. However, we can understand its meaning and apply to our own science.

Saying that energy and mass are equal, identical, and interchangeable is quite different from saying that energy energizes mass or that energy operates upon, in, or through mass to do something to it. When we say that energy and mass are equal, identical, and interchangeable, we are saying that energy, which is invisible, is the actual substance of the mass which is visible, and that the visible and the invisible are the same thing; they are equal, identical, and interchangeable. It is equal to saying that what you see comes out of what you do not see, what you do not see becomes what you do see, and what you do see and what you do not see are the same in essence.

Applying this to the invisible Principle of creation, it is no different from what we read in Romans 1:20: *For the invisible things of him from the creation of the world are clearly seen, being understood by the things that are made* . . . This is also equal to saying that what you see comes out of what you do not see.

Let us look at this proposition from a different light. Emerson said that there is one mind common to all individual men, and that we are all inlets to this mind. Spinoza said that mind is not one thing and matter another; they are the same thing. Quimby, upon whose teaching the New Thought Movement in America was pretty much founded, said, *Mind is matter in solution and matter is mind in form*. But he added that there is a Superior Wisdom, which he called the Science of Christ, to which mind as matter and mind as form is the substance that this Superior Wisdom uses.

It is of great importance that a student of this science understand the meaning of these rather abstract statements; that he reduce them to their utmost extremity and accept them as a part of his basic principle. He must be careful not to become so absorbed in some mystical or imaginative concept that he will be too confused or too far away from reality to think straight.

Einstein was a mathematician. Emerson was a logical thinker and a great philosopher. All of the greatest teachings of the Bible are inspirations and intuitions. Quimby gave us the key to spiritual mind treatment.

There could be no such thing as psychosomatic medicine or body-mind relationships if the ultimate substance on which mind works were different from the mind that works on it. A spiritual mind treatment is not a process whereby thought spiritualizes matter or materializes Spirit. Your thought can have no effect for, in, around, or through anything if it is unlike the thing that it affects.

Fifty years ago, to have said that mind and matter were the same thing would have caused people to think that one might be slightly out of balance mentally. But when a man like Dr. Einstein proclaimed that energy and mass are equal, identical, and interchangeable, we cannot laugh it off.

Remember again that Einstein was not saying energy energizes matter or influences it or hypnotizes it or does anything to it. Energy does not do anything to matter, nor does matter do anything to energy. They are the same thing. If either one does something to the other one it is because the two are one and not two, and the one is all there is.

Let us then apply this simple but abstract, profound but understandable proposition to our own science. Thought does not energize matter, nor does thought restore matter or a material form to a material harmony. There is no material universe.

This is true whether we are dealing with the Science of Mind or with Einstein's equation. Physical science no longer deals with a material universe. It deals only with a universe of undulating waves or streams of particles in some mysterious way hitched to a continuum or an endless stream of time. The sequence is not bound necessarily by any law of cause and effect such as science used to deal with, because at any moment it can be changed.

This is no attempt at a scientific or technical explanation of the new physics, but it is a new picture drawn for our imagination, and we might as well lay hold of it and apply it to our own science, for our philosophy is no more to be laughed off than is theirs. The time to laugh at one who deals with the Science of Mind passed on when physics discarded the theory of a material or a mechanical universe at least twenty-five years ago.

Translating the terms energy and mass into the terms mind and matter we have the same equation. But continuing with Quimby's theory that mind in solution and mind in form are the same thing, and that they constitute the matter of a Superior Wisdom which he called the Science of Christ, we see that we are using a force and energy that is both visible and invisible, and we are using it in such a way as to cause the invisible to become visible and the visible to become invisible.

Einstein's equation does the same thing in effect because it views energy and mass as equal, identical, and interchangeable. But we must also take into consideration that which views it, the physicist, the person. Here is one of the finest points in spiritual mind healing and in using the Science of Mind. Just as energy does not energize mass but is mass (or energy in form) so in our science there is considered to be no difference between the thought and the thing thought of or about. One becomes the other.

However, we must realize that back of all form or at the center of all creation there must be a Divine pattern which is the reality of that thing. What we change is not the Reality but our malformation of it, or quoting Ecclesiastes 7:29: *Lo, this only have I found, that God hath made man upright; but they have sought out many inventions*.

Cause and Effect

While it is true that science must deal with cause and effect in practical applications, it is also true that in physics the old idea of cause and effect has been eliminated, which means that things do not always work the way they are supposed to, basing the performance on precedent.

Here is a very interesting philosophic proposition, because we know that science cannot get along without dealing with cause and effect any more than a farmer can get along without planting crops if he expects to reap a harvest.

But at the same time we have to consider another proposition: the universe is not merely a gigantic machine. There is injected into its mechanism a will, a choice, a volition. From a scientific viewpoint it is no longer held that anything is predetermined or foreordained. (What a blow to theology!)

We still have the farmer, planting time, and harvest season, but we have also an alternative. He might plant his grain in May with the foreknowledge that, all things being equal, it will mature in September. But on the last day in July, being a free agent he might decide to plow it up and plant something else. There would be a sequence in the continuum, and there would be cause and effect operating unless it is intercepted, but there would also be choice and volition introducing a personal factor and spelling freedom.

This is the viewpoint the spiritual mind practitioner must take in working for himself or for others, whether for the healing of physical conditions, the betterment of circumstances, or whatever. He is to follow the injunction of Jesus and judge not according to appearances but to judge rightly. Whatever effect the appearance has on the mind, he is to say: "What if I do have a piece of ice in my hand? It will melt as it contacts the warmth of my flesh. What if there is an apparent obstruction in the physical body or in the body of my affairs? There is a truth which can dissolve it."

New causes bring new effects, and every sequence of cause and effect takes place in something which is neither caused nor effected. Freedom is where it is perceived and in such degree as it is perceived.

Such an attitude is scientific and mathematical. It is also intuitional and revelational, and from the standpoint of practicality gives us a vision that nothing is solid, everything is moving, shifting, changing. Emerson said that even though we view the universe as a mass of solid facts, God or the Supreme Cause views it as liquid laws, for matter is Spirit reduced to Its greatest thinness.

"A certain man had two sons . . ."

Time and eternity; man and his God;
Fate and its fortune; labor and load;
Birth, life and death—who has fathomed them?
The babe is born; the mother croons over the crib;
The father stands by, proud of his offspring.
Each would give his life that the child may live
And give birth to another.
To what end—for what purpose?

The toiler sweats at his bench,
The farmer turns his furrow,
The ship seeks its port,
The traveler his destination,
The man of affairs a fortune,
The leader a cause. Why?

The emperor or dictator—
It matters not which—
Sends his armies and ships to conquer another nation.
He wants oil and coal, and iron and gold—and sawdust.
The high caliph, or whoever, seeks converts to his faith.
They must drink his wine and eat his bread;
They must bow when he bows and in the same way,
Or he will have no part of them.

The man of science, he who knows all,
Must unlock the secrets of nature.
He must make new gadgets;
There is a big demand for them.
The patent office is crammed with ideas—
Millions of them—
From soup spoons to cyclotrons.
Some day, God willing, the man of science
May be able to blow up the whole world—
Himself included.
Here is what sticks—he hadn't realized
That he might be among them.
He tries desperately to rectify his mistake,
But he has overlooked the politicians and the generals,
And the kings and the dictators.
He will be lucky if he escapes with his life.

One half the world tears itself apart—
The other half tries to put it together again.
If the balance isn't too close, one side will win.
If not—what then?
It would seem as though whoever started the whole business
Must have had no sense at all—or else a lot.
Perhaps the "It," "Whoever," or "Whatever" that is responsible
Didn't know or didn't care, or else . . .
He or "It" cared more than has been guessed.
Wouldn't it be strange if someone or something really cared
But let the world alone just to see what would happen,
Thinking that some day it might become sane?
There is a tremendous loss of time and effort—ages of it,
And yet, if He or "It" cared, He or "It"
Still must be waiting to see what will happen.
What a fantasy! It couldn't be that way
And yet—perhaps it could.
There has always been that one half
Trying to sew up the mistakes of the other half. Why?

A very good and wise man once lived.
He was so good and wise that the otherwise
Thought he must be God.
But to get back to the man who was both good and wise—
He said that whoever or whatever made the whole thing

Really was all right;
That he was just trying an experiment to see
If he could somehow create beings whose company he could enjoy,
Who could give back to him the same love he had for them.

This good man told a story about a man who had two sons.
It seemed that one of them got the idea
That he would like to go his own way—
He wanted to do what he wanted to when he wanted to do it.
So he went to his father one day
And asked if it would be all right to leave home.
How here is the remarkable part of this story—
The father didn't argue with him;
He let him have his own way.
He said, "All right, son, I'll give you your freedom."
He even furnished him with funds and said goodbye and good luck.

He had a lot of fun for a while,
But in due time his money was gone
So he had to earn his living.
The only thing he could find to do was feeding pigs,
It wasn't much of a position in life
And, to add insult to injury,
He didn't make enough money to live on
And so he was always hungry.
But, the story says,
No one gave him bread, meat or wine.
He had had all these things in his father's house
But he had forgotten—almost, and yet not quite—
For, you will remember,
The father had buried in the son's mind
A memory of his original state.
This shows that the father never could forget—
And wouldn't wish to.

One day when the son was very hungry and terribly lonely
He began to meditate on his plight
And it wasn't a very pretty picture.
He was so tired and unhappy and forlorn,
But suddenly he remembered
What the father had planted deep in his mind—
Who he really was, and where he came from.

He remembered his old home, his friends, his father—
And even the servants.
He thought of the good things he had been missing—
Bread, meat, wine—
Yes, and song and laughter and dancing.
He hadn't laughed for ages, or danced—
What a pleasant memory it was!
The father really was a wonderful person after all.
So kind—so good—so true.
He would put aside his pride and go home.

He was overcome with joy by the thought;
However, he had such a sense of guilt that he was afraid—
What would his father say?
He almost gave up in despair, and he would have
If it hadn't been for the thoughtfulness of the father
Who knew what was bound to happen
When he made that imprint on the boy's mind
That could not be erased—
The impression that his father would receive him,
Somehow—somewhere—sometime.
He didn't think he would be received with love
But he might be accepted and perhaps cared for.
How good the beds were in his father's house!
He hadn't slept in a bed for so long.
Yes, he would go home, but he would be very meek and humble.
He thought: If I am meek, he will forgive and perhaps forget—
At least he will let me become as a servant in the house.

And so he returned, and a long way off—
No, it couldn't be possible!
His father was coming out to meet him!
Yes he was—he really was coming out to meet him.
Of course. How could it be otherwise?
The father was going to command him to leave the estate.
So he threw himself in the dust
And besought the father to have mercy—
He was so tired in body and mind, so hungry,
So weak from lack of food
That he never could remember
Whether he threw himself in the dust before his father

Or whether he fell down from sheer exhaustion.
At any rate, there he was at his father's feet.

Miracle of miracles! No, it couldn't be true—
And yet it was.
The father was speaking kindly to him.
He was telling him to stand up that he might embrace him.
Oh, that long embrace—
When all the years of fear and torture were swept aside.
The warmth of it—the love indescribable!
The father really was glad to see him;
He was asking him into the house.
He was telling the servants to prepare a bath of cool, clear water—
He hadn't had a bath for so long
He had forgotten the refreshing softness of it.
And food—not only food, a feast,
And friends and wine and song,
And dancing and playing on the harp,
And perfume for his feet,
And a soft couch for his head.

As he lay there, too happy to sleep
Lest he waken as from a dream,
He wondered why the father hadn't asked where he had been
Or what he had been doing or what had become
Of the money that had been given him.
Why—why—why?
And so, he fell asleep.

And while he was asleep he had a vision—
A vision of himself and the father
And all other sons, wherever they may be.
All belong to the Father's house
And all will return,
Somehow—sometime—somewhere.
Why, then, the suffering? Why
Fate and its fortune,
The toiler and the babe that was born?

Why did the ship seek its port
And the traveler his destination?
Why could the king send forth

His armies to conquer,
And the man of science unlock the secrets of nature
Before the world was ready?

All answers were one answer:
The father, even with his love and wisdom,
Couldn't have done it any other way.
Infinite though the father's love may be,
And complete his compassion,
Man was created to be free—
He must be let alone to discover himself.

This is what the wise man taught,
The man who was so good and wise
That the otherwise thought he must be God.
He said that the father had never left his house
Nor had the son strayed very far away.
The son need only turn to the father
And as he does so
The father will turn to him.
Thus does he return to the father's house
A free and independent soul.
Freedom—experience—evolution;
The freedom given—the experience gained—
The evolution certain.

. . . Ernest Holmes

Practical Suggestion for Mental Treatment

Disease Is Not First Cause

The basis for correct spiritual treatment starts with the idea that Being is already perfect. The idea of perfection is the spiritual power which heals.

From the standpoint of pure Spirit, an unknown or hidden false cause would be just as unreal as a known or revealed one. Therefore we must know that disease is neither cause, medium, nor effect. From the standpoint of pure Spirit, wrong action had no beginning, it has no duration, and it will have no climax.

The treatment we give is an activity of the Law enforcing this Truth. Your use of the Law, being on a higher plane of consciousness than the state of thought which produced the discord, must therefore erase it, and you must know that it will do so.

You know that Mind, or Spirit, is pure, perfect, and complete, manifesting Itself in physical form in and throughout all nature. The government of Good is enforced through the Law of man's own Divinity.

Power exists, and the action of this Power is upon your word, or your word acts upon the Power, no one knows which. For all practical intents and purposes, the Power acts upon your word.

The Silent One Within Us

We find this saying in the Upanishad: *The Silent One, the Knower, ever resting in us, may walk, stand, sit, lie down and not do anything at his sweet will.* And in our Bible it says: *I will work, and who shall let (hinder) it*? What are these but statements of the absoluteness of the Supreme as the all-conquerable power of the Spirit? And this all-conquerable power of the Spirit finds self-expression through man.

This Supreme Being is at the center of each one of us. To It we may come for guidance, and from It we may draw both the inspiration and the power to live, stand, walk, or sit. Every act is an outcome of consciousness, every movement is within the Divine Being, and since the Divine Being is everywhere It must also be at the center of our own life.

It is not only at the center of our own life; It *is* that center. Hence to think of It as the very essence of our own being is clear thinking. To know that Its being is our being is right knowing. And to declare that Its life is our life is to permit Its power to flow through us.

Healing Is a Revelation

The practitioner should know that at the center of every man's being there is an absolutely perfect Life, a complete Wholeness, and a deathless Principle. The work of the practitioner is to mentally uncover this ever-present Reality, this changeless and eternal Perfection.

In the uncovering process the practitioner may use many forms of thought. His thought may take the form of reasoning, logic, argument, affirmation, denial, or realization. The form of mental procedure is not important. The all-important factor is whether or not the form which he uses causes his own mind to believe, to understand, and to accept the perfect and spiritual nature of his patient.

Suppose we were told that a beautiful diamond ring lay at the bottom of a trunk filled with rubbish and that it was to be ours when we should succeed in uncovering it. Should we care very much what method we used to remove the rubbish? The main thing would be to find the diamond. We should feel justified in using any method which would enable us to do this. This is equally true in spiritual mind healing. We must uncover the perfect man; we must remove every obstruction of thought which denies his presence.

Spiritual mind healing is a revelation even though we go through a process to arrive at it. Each one must work out his own method and pursue his own logic. If his method and logic lead him to the right conclusion he will be rewarded by an affirmative answer.

Meditation

I know that I am the image and likeness of God. I know that I am spiritually perfect, mentally perfect, and physically perfect. I know that my thought reflects the images of good which are in the Mind of God, and I know that my body reflects His thought.

There can be no congestion or inaction in my thought, in my affairs, or in my physical body, and if there appears to be any congestion, this word completely obliterates it, for this word is the law establishing absolute harmony in my experience, removing every obstruction and casting out all fear.

I am fully convinced that I am a spiritual being. I am inwardly aware of this perfection now.

I sense the presence of the Living Spirit within me. I know that there is nothing in me that can deny this Divine Presence. I am not disturbed by any appearance which contradicts my thought about myself, for I know that any appearance which does contradict it will be changed.

I am conscious that I am free this very moment from every appearance which contradicts the Truth about myself. Everything that does not belong to me is being eliminated.

This word reveals the whole man, the heavenly man. That man was perfect, is perfect, and shall remain perfect.

Mental and Spiritual Treatment

Office of the Dean

My Dear Friend,
The first paragraph of this lesson is of great importance. After you have read it, think it over again and then again and still again, because there is a vast difference between science and faith, although of course we do have faith in science.

You are learning a system which is independent even of your faith—the way to use a creative Law that responds to your spoken word, to combine an inward feeling of the Divine Presence which is within you and which you feel, and the Law which you use. This is the key to the situation.

You will also notice the article on psychosomatics explaining our position relative to body-mind relationship. We think you will agree that to psychosomatic medicine must be added the spiritual relationship which we all have, not only to the Universe around us and to each other, but to some deep fountain of life flowing up within everyone. The discovery of this fountain is the discovery of Life Itself.

Note carefully the articles on the need we all have for forgivingness, and how to overcome the inferiority complex. In treating others you will find these two articles most valuable.

When you start treating a person for the first time be sure to include the consciousness that he knows the Universe holds nothing against him; that is, in a certain sense forgive him for his sins or mistakes, thus relieving him of the condemnation of the whole race which operates in almost everyone. Know that he belongs to the Universe and is safe and happy in it. Know that he has a sense of security and peace within himself.

As always, we wish you the greatest success and happiness.

Sincerely,
Ernest Holmes

Lesson 21

Page 165 to bottom of page 168

In order to treat scientifically we must have complete confidence in the working of the mental law or medium through which mental treatment operates. Turn to page 609, and read the definition of *Medium*. Turn also to the definition of *Creative Medium* on page 582. When we speak of using the Creative Medium of the Universal Law we are referring to the idea, basic in our philosophy, that we are surrounded by a Creative Mind which receives the impress of our thought and acts upon it. That is, this Creative Medium receives the impress of our thought exactly as we think it, and its tendency is always to return this thought clothed in form.

The conscious mind of man uses this Universal Creative Medium for definite purposes and causes it to bring that which he desires into manifestation for him. The Medium, of Itself, as suggested in the second paragraph of page 392, *is Mind in an abstract and formless state*. It is unexpressed until we bring it into expression. We do not bargain with the Universe. We use the laws of nature. We need not fear the Universe in which we live; what we need to do is to learn how to cooperate with it.

As stated in the lower section of page 383, we need not be afraid of God, for the Universe cannot demand anything of us other than that we live in accord with the laws of Truth, Justice, and Harmony. If daily we are doing this we may be certain that we are unified with both God and man. If so there is no reason why we should not use the Law for our own pleasure and for the benefit of others.

As suggested in the second paragraph on page 358, if we could stand aside and let the Law work we should always be successful. By standing aside we mean that if we could get our personal fears, doubts, and misunderstandings out of the way, and like Jesus practice a conscious realization of the Divine Presence, we too should know that within us is that which can say, *I am the way, the truth and the life; no man cometh unto the Father but by me.*

Jesus did not mean that men come to God through the personality of Jesus the man, but rather through the Principle of the Christ. Turn again to the definition of *Jesus* and of *Christ* in the Glossary. Certainly we could not come to the Father through the man Jesus, but because the man Jesus revealed the Divine Principle and the Universal Presence of the Perfect Law, we can come to the same revelation within ourselves.

Jesus the man was talking about Christ the Principle. For a more complete discussion of this turn to page 357. Christ is the son begotten of the only Father; that is, our true sonship is Christ, and Christ is the manifestation of God through the spirit of man, projecting authority upon the Law, which is the medium through which it exercises this authority. Within each one of us this Christ dwells and always has dwelt in all of His fullness. At first this Christ seems dormant, but when the human thought awakens to its own Divinity, then the new birth takes place.

We should daily turn to this living inner Presence, and believing implicitly in It consciously receive It as our real nature. This is not as difficult as it sounds since already we all instinctively believe in a Power higher than the human will. Beginning with the paragraph at the bottom of page 361 and running through to the third paragraph on page 362, you will find a more complete description of the meaning of the Christ, and if you study the life of Jesus with this in mind you will discover that he had implicit confidence in his own Divinity. This is why he said, *He that hath seen me hath seen the Father*. The reality of each one of us is the Father, and the Father is all Power.

The Universal Creative Spirit is absolute and unconditioned, and the Universal Creative Law is limitless. This Presence and this Law, operating as an active and a passive principle in each one of us, constitutes our Divine sonship and gives us authority in our own lives. Hence as the human gives way to the Divine in each one of us, that which is human becomes exalted. God indwells every man's soul. God is not more in one man than in another but the same Divinity is latent in all people, which explains the verses on pages 360 and 361.

The universal Christ has complete control over time and experience, and becomes the savior of any individual or group of individuals who learn to loose the spiritual energies which already exist within them. This Christ Principle, which has been taught under the name of many mysteries, must now be fully understood as that Principle which exists at the center of every man's thought. The Holy of Holies is in our own soul. We must learn that God is, not was. The Law is an ever-available experience in everyday living. Our work is more than the operation of a blind faith; it is the conscious use of a definite Law.

Now why is it, as described in the second paragraph on page 165, that the practitioner speaks to himself about his patient rather than speaking directly to the patient? In using the word *speaking*, we mean mental treatment. The reason why the practitioner does this is because there is but one mental Law and all people live in this Law. They not only live in It, but by It. When you speak the name of someone in this Law and give direction to your thought, the Law operates for that person, not for someone else, just as though you were sending a message by an intelligent messenger who would be certain to deliver it. The Mental Law or Mental Medium, as defined on page 611, is the Universal Mind.

The practitioner declares the Truth about his patient. *Truth* is defined on page 639 as *the Reason, Cause, and Power in and through everything*. We have shown (Lesson 10) that Truth, being Reason, Cause, and Power, must be absolute. Our concept of Absolute, as defined on page 575, is *unconditioned perfection*. Hence the practitioner in declaring the Truth about his patient affirms his patient' s spiritual perfection. He declares that his patient is a perfect being *now*, complete this moment. He seeks to build up this consciousness within himself, knowing that as he does so it will find a corresponding affirmation in the one whom he is seeking to help. His thought is based entirely upon the concept of Divine Love, which means Universal Harmony.

You will find *Love* defined on page 608 as the givingness of the Spirit, and *Harmony* is defined on page 597 as being in tune with this Divine Spirit. Therefore the practitioner tunes to the Divine Harmony of the Spirit, which is God, and recognizes that this Harmony is in his patient, and because the Spirit is a Unity It responds to the demand made upon Itself.

Turn to page 459 and you will find a discussion of the two great commandments which are, love God and love man; and as analyzed in this section we are to realize that God and man are not two, but One. The God Principle in each one of us must be called, not into being, but into manifestation, for the God Principle already exists at the very center of our life—It *is* our life and It makes Itself manifest as we recognize It.

There is no miracle in this form of treatment. A spiritual but natural Law is used. The Universal Principle of Harmony is called upon which responds according to the Law of Correspondence. It operates as the Law of Reflection which we have so frequently discussed. When we say in a treatment that John Smith represents the Principle of harmony and peace and perfection there will be a corresponding reaction within him which will equal our own knowledge of harmony, peace, and perfection. In other words, it is self-evident that the Law must and can respond only by following an exact pattern. Otherwise it would not be a law; it would be a caprice. Treatment is always definite; if it were not we would have no conscious or scientific method, for treatment would be subject to chance.

Mental treatment is not explained in the Bible. The Bible, of course, does teach the Law of Cause and Effect, that *whatsoever a man soweth, that shall he also reap*. The Bible teaches that the Universe is a spiritual system in which man is included, and it suggests that a person can control his world by the power of thought, but it does not tell us how to give definite mental treatments, nor does any other of the sacred literature of the ages with which we are familiar.

If there is such a thing as the Science of Mind and Spirit, then we must not only believe that the Universe is a spiritual system, but we must understand something of how this system works if we expect to use its laws with any degree of success. In other words, we must have a definite Science of Mind. We must know what we are doing and how to do it. Hence we must not only have a Principle, we must have a technique. We must not only understand that there is a Law, but we must know how to use this Law. The Law is the Principle, our knowledge of how to use It is our technique. This technique is suggested on page 458 under the heading, *A Formula for Effective Prayer*, which we have already analyzed in Lesson 6.

If we study the method of Jesus we shall discover that he always spoke an affirmative language. He acted as though there were a Law which obeyed his will or his word. He had implicit faith and confidence in this Law. This we must learn to do. This in no way contradicts any religious conviction which one already may have. It merely teaches one how to use the power which any true religious conviction should generate. For if God is, and if God is all there is, then surely that which is contrary to the Divine nature can be neutralized.

If you will turn to page 446 under the heading *The Cause of Human Troubles* and carefully consider the meaning of this section relative to regaining our lost Paradise, I think you will find that negation is not born of Truth, but of ignorance. If the Universe in which we live is infinite, then it stands to reason that that which is limited or which limits us is not Principle, but lies in our use of It. Moreover, the same power that binds us will free us, since there cannot be two infinities, but the Infinite is to each one of us a reflection of our finite comprehension of It. It will not be less, It cannot be more, It must therefore remain true to Its own nature.

The very bondage which we experience is in reality the Principle of Freedom used as bondage. The one who uses this Principle to help himself and others we refer to as a spiritual practitioner. We discussed this in Lesson 14 but you may turn again to the definition of *Practitioner* on page 620 for the sake of refreshing your memory.

A practitioner is one who uses Mental Law. The question might then be asked, "Why should a practitioner think of the spiritual side of this Law?" The answer to this is obvious. While the Law of Mind is a Law of Cause and Effect, and of Itself is entirely neutral, our ignorance causes us to use It destructively until spiritual enlightenment dawns. There is no negative liability in using the Law provided we use It only for constructive purposes. When we use It for any other than constructive purposes the reaction will be one of self-suffering until the lesson is learned. Hence the Spirit of Christ, which means the harmonious use of the Law, always takes precedence over all other uses of the Law. This is because the Infinite is a perfect Unity.

A practitioner is one who uses the Law for constructive purposes. He greets the Divinity in his patient; he senses God in him. He tries to understand that God must be in him. Every declaration he makes about his patient is for the purpose of revealing the indwelling Christ.

Turn to page 601 for the definition of *The Indwelling Christ*, and also for the definition of *Incarnation*. You will see that the practitioner forms his statement in such a way as to bring about a mental recognition of this Indwelling Christ and this incarnation.

Heaven is defined on page 598 as being not a location but a state of consciousness. The practitioner must arrive at a state of consciousness in his own mind where he senses a heavenly state for his patient. He declares that this Divine Harmony is now manifest in all of Its fullness in the life of his patient. In doing this the practitioner frequently must deny that which seems to contradict his affirmation about the patient. Turn again to the definition of *Affirmation* on page 575, and the definition of *Denial* on page 584. This will help you to see exactly how you should proceed in treating.

A professional practitioner (see page 168) takes on a moral and an ethical responsibility never to disclose the intimate confidences which must exist between a patient and practitioner. The patient bares his soul and the practitioner must honor his confidence and never violate the trust which is imposed upon him.

It is the practitioner's business to uncover God in every man, and to make those statements about man which he feels must be true about God. Hence the more conscious the practitioner is of the Divine Harmony the more power his mental statements will have.

Summary

We must have complete confidence that our word is operated upon by a Power greater than we are. There is nothing in the Universe to be afraid of because we are unified with both God and man.

Getting all of our littlenesses out of the way makes it possible for that thing which is greater than we are to flow through our consciousness. This is the Principle of Christ or the Christ Principle, or as Troward states, the son begotten of the only Father.

Jesus, the man, understood the nature of the Christ within him.

We must court the Divine Presence and use the Universal Law. Both are unconditioned. The Christ Principle within us transcends time, place, and experience, since it creates new times, new places, and new experiences out of Itself.

The practitioner speaks to himself *about* his patient rather than mentally addressing his patient. Tuning in to the Divine Harmony, he recognizes this same Presence in his patient.

We must always know what we are doing and why we do it. We must have both a Principle and a technique, and we must speak an affirmative language.

The Power that binds us can as easily free us, for it is not the Power but the way we use It that decides what is going to happen to us. Therefore freedom is not opposed to bondage, nor bondage to freedom. In a certain sense they are the same thing, although our experiences of them are different.

It may seem strange to say that freedom and bondage are the same thing, but they are identical in the same sense that water and ice are the same thing. The ice could just as well be in a different shape and the water is not limited because the ice is large or small, nor is ice evil because we freeze something with it, nor is water evil because we can boil something in it. Actually there is but One Power, One Presence, and One Law, but many ways of expressing the One.

Questions

Brief answers to these questions should be written out by the student after studying the lesson, and the answers compared with those which will be included in next week's lesson.

1. In treatment why must we have confidence in the mental law?
2. What does *Mind in an abstract and formless state* mean?
3. When is it right to use the mental Law for our own benefit and for the benefit of others?
4. What is the difference between Jesus the man and Christ the Principle?
5. When does the new birth take place?
6. What is the active and passive principle within each one of us?
7. What gives us authority in our lives?
8. Why, in mental treatment, does the practitioner speak to himself about his patient rather than directly to his patient?
9. What is our definition of Truth?
10. Do we call the God Principle into being or into manifestation?
11. Does the Bible teach a technique for mental and spiritual treatment?
12. In mental treatment, what do we mean by having a Principle and a technique?
13. What is a spiritual practitioner?
14. If the Law we use is a mental law, why do we speak of using It spiritually?
15. How does the practitioner greet the Divinity within his patient?

Answers to Questions on Lesson 20

1. Reducing faith to understanding means to no longer believe blindly, but to understand the Law in which we believe.
2. In spiritual mind healing we say explanation is the cure because explanation removes fear and doubt and paves the way for faith and conviction.
3. Our explanations are to be based upon the premise that we are now living in a spiritual and a perfect universe.
4. Our mental work should have a spirit of buoyancy because spiritual enthusiasm vitalizes faith.
5. We must put conviction into a mental treatment because we can take out of a mental treatment only what we have first put into it. For example, if we are working mentally for some particular thing, we must first have the conviction that that thing can come into our experience.

6. By specializing the power of Mind we mean using the Law of Mind, which of Itself is impersonal, for both definite and personal purposes.
7. *Spirit is Causation and the Law is Its servant*, means that conscious intelligence directs while the Law obeys.
8. The Law which obeys the Spirit does not know that It is doing so because the Law has no conscious intelligence; It is merely a mechanical but intelligent reaction.
9. Jesus spoke his word with authority, because he knew that the Law had no choice other than to obey.
10. Spirit knows no opposition because being the only Cause there is, It could have nothing to oppose It.
11. The Spirit of man is God.
12. *Reciprocal action* between the Universal and the individual means that the Law of Mind responds to us by corresponding. Hence it is done unto us as we believe.
13. The contemplation of good means thinking about and mentally dwelling upon such ideas as peace, poise, harmony, a sense of security, etc.
14. To the statements, "There is One Power, One Mind, One Law, etc.," we should add (to make these statements meaningful in our experience), "This Power, Mind and Law is our Power, Mind, and Law right now."
15. Principle is never circumscribed by Its own effects because It is the Creator of such effects and can change what It has created. Hence the power which impoverishes us can just as easily enrich us.
16. A practitioner should not be influenced by appearances because appearances are in the realm of effects, while his word is in the realm of causation.
17. *Having power* implies only a potential possibility; *using power* is the practical application of such possibility. For example, having gasoline in our car does not mean taking a trip. Spiritual consciousness undirected does not necessarily demonstrate anything.
18. We handle thoughts rather than things in mental treatment, because thoughts are the causes of things.
19. We need not consciously assume the responsibility for creating conditions. Our responsibility rests only in giving direction to or invoking the Law.

A New Look At Psychosomatics

I once knew a man who developed arthritis in his feet to the extent that he was unable to put on his shoes. After a little questioning I found that one of his duties was collecting rents from people who were unable to pay. He was a very sensitive person, and unconsciously he developed a physical condition which made it impossible for him to walk to the places where he must meet a situation that was so distasteful.

I have in mind a woman who became so anemic that she was at the point of exhaustion. Her real emotional trouble was loneliness. Her family had grown up, married, and established their own homes. She was left alone, in beautiful surroundings but with no inward, enthusiastic interest in life. We might say that Life had gone out of her—as though it had flowed away.

Well, these are body-mind relationships that we are hearing so much about under the general heading of Psychosomatics. Psychosomatic is rather an ominous sounding term until we understand what it means. *Psyche* means the mind, and *soma* means the body. But the Greeks, from whom these terms come, also spoke of the *pneuma*, by which they meant the spirit. This we do not hear very much about in psychosomatics, but the Greeks evidently considered it of importance. They felt that man was, as our New Testament says, spirit, soul, and body, and that these three together constitute the whole man—the man who is a spirit with a mind and a body.

One of the ancient philosophies of China taught that man has a spiritual body, a mental body, and a physical body. And to show how intuition often precedes scientific discovery—and by thousands of years as in this case—this Chinese philosopher said that the physical body cannot be in health unless there is physical circulation. Today we know that there must be proper circulation, assimilation, and elimination if the body is to be normal.

Our ancient philosopher said that man also has a mental body, and unless the mental body circulates through the physical there will be improper circulation, physically. This, too, precedes our modern knowledge of body-mind relationships, particularly as they pertain to our emotional reactions to life. For we now know that most mental and emotional congestions, with their inner repressions and unconscious conflicts, are due to a lack of proper assimilation of emotional ideas.

But to get back to the ancient Chinese idea. It concludes that there cannot be proper circulation in the mental body unless the spiritual body, to which the mental is attached, circulates through the mental; that we cannot even be physically whole until there is a circulation of the Spirit through the mind, and the mind through the body. This is why the Greeks spoke of the whole man as made up of *pneuma*, which is spirit; *psyche*, which is mind, and *soma*, which is body; and why the Chinese said that the three are one and must have proper interaction.

Let us now take a look at the ideas of one of the chief exponents of the teaching of Platonism, a man by the name of Plotinus who lived somewhere around the Third Century A.D. and who is considered to have been one of the most illumined souls of all the ages. Plotinus said that our physical organism is attached to a spiritual idea, which he called a Prototype or a Divine Pattern, and that when any physical organ becomes detached from its Pattern it begins to have pain, and longs to return to that which will make it whole.

And we have this idea expressed in still another way in our own Scriptures, where it says that we should be perfect, outwardly, even as the Divine Spirit already is perfect, inwardly. *Be ye therefore perfect, even as your Father which is in heaven is perfect.*

This is what we call taking a new look at the modern idea of psychosomatics, upon which so many books are now being written—books well worth reading that deal with body-mind relationships. And let us see if we do not find something missing even in this new outlook on life. Not that it is not wonderful as far as it goes, and altogether true, but it so happens that man is a spirit, having a mind and a body. So it is not enough to say that there must be proper relationship between the mind and body. There must be proper relationship between the spirit and the mind also. And I think we may coin a new expression (one that is entirely intelligent and without which the idea of psychosomatics can never be quite complete), which is *spiritual psychosomatics*.

We believe that man is rooted in pure Spirit; that he is a spiritual entity, right now, here in this world, and that it is impossible for a person to be completely well physically unless he is happy mentally. Equally we believe that it is difficult for him to be happy mentally unless his mind has the assurance that it is rooted in something stable and permanent, something transcendent and altogether whole within itself.

Man is spirit, soul, and body. To try to live in the physical organism without the mind is impossible. To try to live on intellectual thoughts without feeling is equally impossible. But not to realize that even the mind, wonderful as it is, is dependent upon something greater than itself, is disastrous. For if many of our physical troubles are the result of an inward emotional conflict based on a sense of inadequacy, defeat, and an unconscious feeling of guilt and rejection, then nothing is more certain than that the mind and the feeling must have the assurance of a Power greater than themselves, governing, guiding, and enveloping.

We get right back to the old thought, so simple but yet so direct, and one of the most exalted concepts the human mind has ever conceived—*In him (in God) we live, and move, and have our being.*

We do not deny the body, nor do we deny the mind. What we do is affirm the Spirit. We believe the body should be properly cared for—that is the office of the physician. We believe the mind should be oriented—that is the office of the wise counselor. But in addition to this we believe in the Spirit which should govern the mind. Consequently we have developed what we call a new order of spiritual meditation, where an individual takes time definitely each day to remind himself that he is a spirit, that he is one with God, and to try to bring about a deep realization that there is a Power greater than himself sustaining him; a Wise Counselor guiding him; a generous Provider who is ready and willing to meet the needs of everyday life.

No, we do not deny either the body or the mind, but we do affirm the Spirit as the Supreme Presence and the Superior Principle of all life. We do come from this thing that we call Life, or God, and we are fundamentally spiritual beings even while in the flesh. How, then, can we hope to be whole unless we establish a right relationship between this trinity of our being, which is thought, feeling, and action?

Spiritual psychosomatics is a reality, and all our modern systems, wonderful as they are, must fall short of the ultimate goal unless and until the whole man is recognized, and we try to live from the viewpoint of Divine government in human affairs—Divine Life flowing through the physical body; Divine Intelligence governing the thoughts of the mind. For it is in God, and in God alone, that there is absolute security. Every great and gracious soul who has ever lived has recognized this and taught it.

Let us, then, think of *spiritual* psychosomatics, and consciously and deliberately unite the mind with the Spirit. For if so many of our troubles, physically, are due to inward conflicts that arise as a result of feeling isolated, unwanted, unneeded, and unloved, with the attendant sense of guilt, how can we find wholeness without first discovering some wellspring of Life within us, some Divine inward assurance that we are all on the pathway of an eternal unfoldment? It is my belief that it would be impossible.

Perhaps Jesus had this in mind when he said we do not live by bread alone. And yet he realized the need of bread, for he fed the multitude. He never denied any of the objective things, nor any of the things which today we call subjective and unconscious, which he understood better than we do. He included the lesser within the greater, and said that if we seek the Kingdom first, all these things will be added.

It is evident that since he went about healing the sick and doing good, Jesus never rejected the idea of our objective lives as though they were illusions. He knew that the body must be fed and clothed and the mind comforted. But he knew where the real Substance came from. And so he taught a most simple method of practice—to go into the inner chamber of our thoughts and feelings, meditate upon the Divine Presence until it becomes a reality, and then conform our whole thinking to this invisible Pattern of ourselves, which the Bible tells us is *hid with Christ in God*.

Our Need for Forgiveness

We are all human beings and we all have made mistakes. We all carry an unconscious burden of guilt and we all need a sense of being forgiven. One of the most revealing things in the new Science of Mind is our need to feel that we are right with God, with life, and with each other.

We know that a continual state of resentment can produce many types of physical disease. This does not mean just diseases of the imagination. It means diseases that the imagination creates in the body through psychosomatic relations, between the mind and the body. A continual state of resentment against others can badly affect the digestive system. It can produce many forms of physical irritation. It can cramp our whole style of living and block the spontaneous flow of enthusiasm, without which there is very little joy in life.

Much of our inability to forgive others comes from a deep-seated inferiority complex. Often our antagonistic attitude toward others rises from a need within our own minds to be relieved of our unconscious sense of self-condemnation, as though we have such a burden of guilt within our minds that we can hardly bear it. And so we project it to others just for the relief it gives ourselves.

This brings us back to one of the fundamental thoughts of Jesus: *Forgive, and ye shall be forgiven*. Of course Jesus knew that we do not make bargains with God, but the more carefully we study his method the more clearly we see that he often removed emotional blocks before he healed people. On one occasion he forgave a paralyzed man, much to the dismay of some of those around him who told him that he had no right to forgive others. Jesus' only answer was to ask them whether they thought it was easier to forgive the man or to tell him to get up and walk, but, he said, to show that the son of man does have power to forgive, I will tell the man to get up and walk.

There is a definite tension which accompanies the emotional state of condemnation, and so Jesus forgave the man and removed this tension. In view of what we know today, he was practicing a perfect spiritual science. He must have been able to look inside people, mentally, and he probably knew exactly how people thought, and why, and of course he knew that anything that stops the flow of life, anything that blocks our God-given right to live happily and with faith in the universe, must affect the physical body.

Probably Jesus knew more about spiritual psychosomatics than anyone else who ever lived. He also knew something that most of us have yet to discover: we cannot give what we do not possess. And certainly he knew that we all have a need for a feeling of being one with God.

No one can feel one with God who hates anyone or anything. You will remember that in the Lord's Prayer Jesus said, *Forgive us our debts as we forgive our debtors*. For he knew that it is only as we forgive that we can be forgiven.

At first thought this looks as though we were bargaining with God, but such is not the case. God is life and love, and how can life and love flow through us if we stop them at any point? It is not because we bargain with the Almighty that Jesus said, *Forgive us our debts as we forgive our debtors*. The real reason is that it is impossible for us to have a sense of being forgiven while we condemn others.

And now we are putting the proposition in the only place where it can be handled—within ourselves. For when there is nothing in us that would condemn others, then there will be no condemnation left, either toward the self or others. It is then and only then that we unblock the stream of life which so freely flows to all and through all, when we permit it.

Jesus also said, *Give, and it shall be given unto you*. Life intends and wants to give us every good thing, but when the circuit is stopped at any point it is retarded at every point. A good enough illustration is the circulation of blood in our physical bodies. Stop the circulation anywhere and it retards it everywhere, and wherever the circulation is stopped, stagnation sets in, and infection is likely to follow. We never drink from stagnant pools because we know they are poisonous. We seek the free-flowing water which purifies itself as it flows.

Our minds are mental pools through which flow the thoughts of good, which are thoughts of love and generosity, good will and peace, poise and power. Wherever there is stagnation in our mental lives we shall discover that the reason is because we have not permitted this flow.

Everything moves in circles. This is the way of life, and what we refuse to give we refuse to accept. Nothing is more important than that we learn how to forgive both ourselves and others. Jesus carried this proposition to a complete finality when he forgave the man who died on another cross beside him. It seems to me that this forgiveness was one of the greatest lessons of the cross.

There is another instance in history which shows the same sublime attitude as that of Jesus. When Mahatma Gandhi was assassinated, his last act after receiving the mortal wound was to make the sign of forgiveness with his hands. Jesus and Gandhi—two of the greatest spiritual geniuses of history. Each knew the necessity of the human mind to relieve itself of the burden of condemnation, and each made the supreme sacrifice as an object lesson to all humanity that even God cannot give us what we refuse to accept.

The great lesson we learn from this is that it is impossible for us to feel the relief and the release from self-condemnation while we bear condemnation toward others.

We long to be free from burdens. How we yearn for a sense of release from fear and doubt and uncertainty. How greatly we long for a security which takes fear from our lives. We pray for a certainty and a faith that will make us whole.

The physician and the surgeon can patch up this physical body of ours, and the psychologist or psychiatrist can help us to straighten out our emotional tensions, for all of which we should be grateful. But only Life can give life. Beyond this body and deeper than this mind there is a perennial wellspring of Life which can flow through us to eternal givingness and to everlasting forgivingness.

Who would not be in Paradise? If we felt that someone beside us had the power to say to us, *Today shalt thou be with me in paradise*, in the Garden of Eden of the soul, in the fields that bloom forever, beside the still waters—if we knew that there was someone who could do this for us, would we not exchange everything we have for this gift? Of course we would.

Emerson said that the universe remains to the heart that is unhurt, and Jesus said, *It is your Father's good pleasure to give you the kingdom*. This Kingdom is something we do not earn; it is the gift of heaven. This heart that is unhurt is the heart that God gave us. We alone have refused to receive the gift; it has never been withheld. From the day we are first ushered into this world, until that last moment when the soul takes its silent flight into the unseen, our life is drawn from an invisible source.

It is intended that we should be happy. It is meant that we should live to the full; that we should sing and dance and be glad; that we should love and be loved in return. But in our ignorance we have inhibited the action of God in our lives, and so we have cut ourselves off from the only Power that can help us.

The only sensible thing to do is retrace our steps and start all over again. We should not do this with any sense of morbidity or fear, but rather with the feeling of an explorer who knows that there is an undiscovered country, and who is willing to take time to find it. There is an undiscovered country in our own minds. It is the world the way God made it. There is a humanity that we have not yet met. It is the Divinity hidden within each one of us. There is a God who exists everywhere. We shall never see this God until we look through the eyes of our own Divinity.

Let us start with this simple proposition in mind:

> *God is all there is. God is love. Love is the motivating power of the whole universe. God is in everything; God is in everyone.*
>
> *Realizing that love is the great motivating power of life, and knowing that God must be at the center of everything, today I am meeting this God in everyone, and seeing the manifestation of His life in everything.*

If there is any condemnation or animosity in me, I gladly loose it. I loose it and let it go as I turn to that silent Presence within me which gives all and withholds nothing.

I enter into the harmony of eternal peace, into the joy of knowing that I am now in the Kingdom of God, from which no person is excluded. My yesterdays are gone forever, my tomorrows stretch forth into an endless future of pure delight. And from out the invisible there comes to me these words: TODAY THOU ART WITH ME IN PARADISE.

Overcoming Fear and the Inferiority Complex

Fear not, little flock; for it is your Father's good pleasure to give you the kingdom. Here is the implication that some kingdom over which we should have complete dominion has already been given, and if there is such a kingdom, and if we should have dominion over it, then we should act as kings, not as vassals, not as slaves, and not as those who cringe before an inexorable fate.

If all people are made in the image and likeness of the Divine Being, then surely one person should not be afraid of another. And if Life Itself is a unity of good, which our study has led us to conclude, then why should we be afraid of life?

Experience has proved to us that some people are afraid of life; they are afraid of each other, and seldom do we find anything which even resembles a kingly attitude. Moreover, in those rather rare instances where we do find a kingly attitude it is too often attended with arrogance. It is of the utmost importance to solve this perplexing problem which every priest, physician, metaphysician and psychologist meets in his daily contact with people.

Under analysis it has been found that an inferiority complex is based on the fear of life. The basic fear is an inability to properly adjust to everyday living.

An oversensitive person is always handicapped, and too often assumes an attitude of arrogance or blustering bravado to cover up his inward hurt. Generally speaking he will not admit that such a hurt is there. And even though he train his will and study every psychological method known with which to combat life, unless he has overcome the fundamental fears of life he has only covered them that much deeper by his mental maneuvering.

Anyone who is familiar with mental reactions knows that a man who goes blustering around saying he has no fear, asserting loudly that he is just as good as anyone, and who always demands the attention of others, is sick inwardly. He is attempting to cover up some part of himself, although this is impossible to do. The Chinese sage said, *How can a man conceal himself?*

Though we crowd all of our emotions back into the unconscious, they always come up in another form. It is impossible to bury a living spring. We can merely change its course. It is just as impossible to destroy that dynamic urge which some call the libido, some the will to power, and others—more rightly perhaps—designate as the Life Force seeking self-expression.

If we would heal the inferiority complex we must arrive at conclusions more basic than merely teaching our student or patient to shout that he is self-sufficient. For the louder he screams the more frightened he becomes, until finally his scream is a shriek and his attitude toward life becomes hysterical.

We are told that inferiority complexes often arise from youthful frustrations, from early childhood repressions, from emotional reactions which have shocked the finer sensibilities when they come for the first time in contact with the hard realities of life.

This may be true, and proceeding upon this theory it becomes necessary to uncover the psychic stream of previous experiences and unconscious memories. In this process of uncovering, this analysis of the soul or psyche, if the incident which started the stream of consciousness in the wrong direction (which turned it back upon itself) is brought to the surface and self-seen, it is generally dissipated.

To analyze every person psychologically is out of the question, and it seems just as impossible to convince everyone of the truth of certain religious dogmas. All people do not wish to become orthodox religionists, nor do they wish to believe in some particular form of spiritual philosophy. What, then, are we going to do? The answer is so simple that it seems surprising when we arrive at its correct conclusion.

We should not overlook the fact that there are innumerable persons who have been what we call twice born. Through religious convictions their whole lives have been instantly transformed and the entire psychic stream of previous experiences reversed. Fear has been overcome through faith and through spiritual conviction, and morbid neuroses have given way before some spiritual force which we cannot completely analyze but which no person who has investigated the facts would think of denying.

All religions which have helped people have helped them because of one common denominator running through each, and that is faith in something greater than the isolated self. Equally, all psychological processes which have been beneficial in removing fear and the inferiority complex have been able to do so because of one common denominator running through that process, namely, the giving back of the self to the self followed by the re-education of the self and the readjustment of the self to life, in confidence, in faith, and in self-assurance.

This should teach us that there is one basic negation, which is a denial of the Life Principle, and one basic affirmation, which is an acceptance of the Life Principle. And that the affirmation reduces the negation to its native nothingness.

It would be impossible for a man to remain filled with fear if his confidence in the indwelling Spirit were greater than his fear. For such confidence would automatically neutralize fear. This is what has taken place in that particular type of religious conversion which has caused an individual to become "twice born." What his religious convictions were is of no consequence if by them he arrived at the truth and the salutary effect took place.

In recognizing this we do not dishonor his religious conviction. Rather we affirm it. But in such degree as we understand the working of any principle we need no longer approach it along the spasmodic and more or less uncertain avenue of some peculiar form of conversion. The same may be said of the different schools of applied psychology. They all arrive at practical results, and these results generally depend upon the practitioner more than upon the methods involved, since the principle underlying all of these methods must be one of faith.

However, the religious faith has a certain superiority over the psychological, for it naturally follows that if a man can be brought to have faith in God, his faith in God will be greater than any faith he could have in an individual or a group of individuals.

It is not only important, but necessary to discover what kind of belief we must have. In what way shall we use faith to overcome fear and to heal the inferiority complex? The answer is obvious—faith in God, faith in each other, faith in life, faith in destiny, and above all, faith in the eternality of our own souls.

The uninformed may indulge in a smile when we speak of having faith in the eternality of the soul. Nevertheless, if he cares to investigate the matter with great thoroughness he will discover that without this faith in the eternality of the soul the other types of faith of which we speak are weakened. The reason, I think, is apparent. We could have no real faith in God or in the integrity of the Universe unless such faith included a definite relationship on the part of the individual soul to the Universe.

Now if that relationship is only a temporary one, the relationship of a candle to its flame, then it bears no weight whatsoever. Such a conviction would lead most people to despair, for they would exclaim, *For what shall it profit a man, if he shall gain the whole world, and lose his own soul?* (Mark 8:36) Faith in immortality is necessary to a real healing of the inferiority complex and fear. Our faith in life must be so great that in our imagination it bridges the gulf which we call death.

A careful analysis of the great characters of history who have had this faith would soon prove to us that with its advent the sense of inferiority and fear has lessened. The chapters of religious history are filled with the accounts of those who have passed from weakness into strength, from timidity into courage as a result of the transforming power of faith. Whether or not we choose to call this a psychological reaction makes no difference, since all mental reactions are psychological.

If, on the other hand, we wish to call such experiences spiritual we are equally right. The spiritual experience has come to the mind, has convinced the intellect, and has penetrated the emotions. When such experiences have sunk deeply enough, they have become subjective, which means that they have become permanent.

The thing we wish to do, then, is to find a faith greater than our fears, whether they are fears of people, of conditions, of life, or of death. Such faith is born out of a complete conviction of the eternal destiny of one's own soul and of all other souls.

We cannot fail to realize that fear and the inferiority complex are always a turning of thought back upon the self. This is why it has so often been called a form of selfishness, but it is more than this. It is self-centeredness rather than selfishness in the ordinary sense of the term. We have all known many unselfish persons who have made a complete sacrifice of themselves to good causes but who have felt martyred in so doing, persons who have devoted their entire lives to others but who have been very conscious of doing so.

This self-centeredness often accompanies the inferiority complex and it too must be healed. It is healed by realizing that there is but one final Self in which all selves converge. The Infinite desires neither martyrs nor those who sacrifice anything of their true nature. The Law of the Infinite is toward self-expression, and self-expression in the individual means the expansion of the individual, the evolution of the individual, an eternal on-goingness. Hence the self-centered person must be given a goal or an ideal greater than his individualized self. He must surrender the smaller self to the greater self.

This is the sacrifice which he is called on to make. He must die to his concept of the limited self and become resurrected to the consciousness of that self which is one with all persons, places, and things, one with all ages, one with God. He must give up his fears and his hurts. After he has learned to look upon all other persons as he looks upon himself, then he will know that the true self cannot be hurt, nor does it wish to hurt. His soul will have entered that mental atmosphere where hurt is no longer possible.

In such degree as all vindictiveness, hate, and animosity disappear, he will find himself merging with the spiritual atmosphere of others. He learns to respect and admire others, and expects that others will respect and admire him. He overcomes his fear of life by understanding life, not by fighting it. He overcomes his fear of people by coming to understand rather than shun them.

This type of understanding is beyond the ordinary concept of tolerance. He does not learn to tolerate people; he learns to understand them. There is a vast difference. He sees through the weakness and frailty and inconsistency of human life, even its fears and morbidities. He no longer cringes. With calm placidity he faces his inevitable exit from this world, knowing that as glorious as this life has been, he is certain to go to a better.

If we would eliminate fear and morbidity this is what we must realize. Human experience has never found a better way. Indeed, it is the only way which is certain to produce the desired results.

In actual experience this work is done somewhat after this manner, with the understanding that if you are treating yourself you say, "I am thus and so," or if you are treating someone else you say, "He is (or she is) thus and so." This is the method of procedure for all treatment:

> *I know that I am one with Life. I now understand that Life Itself is perfect, complete; that there is a spiritual Presence and a Divine Unity running through everything. I understand how it is that this Divine Unity personifies Itself through all people. I see clearly how it is that this Divine Unity operates every form and animates every event. I am conscious of this Divine Presence at the very center of my own soul. It is the Reality of myself. This Reality is strong, positive, certain, confident, and whole.*
>
> *I see that the Reality within me is the same as the Reality in all people whom I shall ever meet, and that the Reality within them responds to the Reality within me; therefore in our human greeting there is a Divine Unity. All my human relationships are established in this Divine Unity.*

All of my relationships flow from It. There is no fear, no sense of inferiority. I am conscious of my ability to meet every situation. I am conscious of my ability to meet every person with perfect frankness, perfect openness, and in complete understanding.

Moreover, I know that every person wishes me well. Every situation which I experience tends to promote my well-being, to increase my happiness and self-expression, and all the good that there is, is my good today.

My faith in good is complete, my union with Life is perfect, and I shall always meet appreciation, helpfulness, encouragement, and certainty. This is the Law manifesting Itself in my experience today, tomorrow, and always.

Practical Suggestion for Mental Treatment

Arguments Logically Presented to Mind

Arguments logically presented to Mind will produce definite results. What does this statement mean? It means that we are surrounded by a Universal Mind which is creative, which receives the impress of our thought and acts upon it. It receives the conclusion of our thought and acts as though it were true. Hence a mental argument logically presented to Mind in such a way that its conclusion is definite, must produce a definite result.

The argument should be made with a consciousness of harmony, of wholeness, of peace, of power, and of perfection. When we make the statement that God is all there is, our argument must support this statement by strong mental proof that since God is all there is, there is nothing else. We must know that both cause and effect are spiritual and our every argument should tend to demonstrate this position in our own thought. For whatever we demonstrate in our own thought is logically presented to Mind to be acted upon and projected into form.

Creative Mind of Itself has no specific intention as far as we as individuals are concerned. We give It the only intention It has for us, and the fact that we find ourselves in confused and limited circumstances, instead of disproving this theory is a positive proof of it.

These uncertain circumstances in which we find ourselves are themselves a direct result of confused thinking. When we reverse the process and start with the proposition of the allness of Good and logically present to Mind the idea that Good is the only power, we shall see definite changes take place in outward manifestation.

Do Not Deny the Physical

In spiritual mind healing we do not deny that the patient has a stomach, lungs, arms, etc. We affirm that they are ideas of mind; that they are spiritual substance. The only thing we deny is a material sense of the physical body. The spiritual body is in mind and is pure Spirit.

The practitioner does not deny the body. He affirms that body is a combination of right ideas; that right action takes place in every organ. He supplies the material sense with an opposite spiritual realization.

The body is the sum total of right ideas, and all right ideas are eternal, universal and perfect. Therefore God, or Spirit, is the life of the real body and the essence of it.

We must be careful to tell our patients not to condemn the human body; certainly never to deny its reality nor the reality of any of its organs or functions. There is nothing wrong with the sum total of right ideas which make up the real body, which is spiritual. Every organ and every function of the human body has a universal prototype behind it. It is an idea in the Mind of God, and a perfect idea.

To dwell morbidly on any organ or function of the body is to condemn it, to retard its action, to congest its movement, to impede the circulation through it, and, of course, wherever the circulation is impeded the elimination is also impaired. We must know that there is Divine circulation, perfect assimilation, and right elimination.

The function of the body is not something apart from God but is something *within* God. We must learn to love all of these functions as being attributes of Spirit, and to sense the Divine Universal Harmony underlying all.

Methods of Treatment

Office of the Dean

My Dear Friend,

If fear is contagious, we wonder how many of us catch the germ. No doubt we all do at times. To overcome fear is one of the main essentials of our study. If fear is contagious we may be certain that we are either sending it out or drawing it into our own consciousness. By the same token we may be certain that if we are not tuned into fear we shall not be affected by it, even though it appears in our environment. Love, confidence, and faith are the great antidotes for fear.

People who are practicing the Science of Mind must generate faith in something bigger than they are. The best way to do this is through a great love based on complete confidence in the Universe in which we live, and on an underlying feeling or sense of this, which comes through intuition. There is nothing to be afraid of in the Universe, and Love is the greatest impulsion in life.

We are not at all concerned with the viewpoints of the materialist who might deny this, for he is like the fish who jumped out of the frying pan into the fire and will have to be left to stew in his own juice.

Life to us is either good or evil, depending upon our philosophy of life, and no matter how intellectual this philosophy may be, it is not sufficient unless it contains an inner warmth and color. We should never forget that there are many things which may be considered unscientific according to our present knowledge, that are not necessarily nonscientific according to laws which we are discovering, and no doubt will go on discovering.

We know you are thinking these things over with me.

Sincerely,
Ernest Holmes

Lesson 22

Page 169 to bottom of page 172

The tools of thought which the mental practitioner uses are ideas. These ideas are formulated at the center of his own consciousness, in his own individualized mind. It is self-evident that he cannot think outside himself nor away from himself. As a practitioner be sure that you make no attempt to send out thoughts to anyone for any purpose. You think within yourself, no matter for whom or for what purpose you are working. The movement of thought within your own mind produces a vibration in the Universal Mind, which is the Medium for all thought action.

Turning to the Absolute means turning within. It means turning away from objective conditions or situations, from pain, suffering, fear, want, and unhappiness. We turn within to the unconditioned, for the Absolute is unconditioned; that is, It is neither bound nor limited by anything which now exists.

We turn within to a quiet contemplation, a recognition that the things which we desire are already accomplished facts in our experience or in the experience of those for whom we are working. A scientific treatment cannot be conditioned. In our mental work we turn entirely away from the thing as it appears to be, and taking the thought that with God all ideas are perfect, and with the Law all things are possible, we create a form which is more desirable than the one we are now experiencing.

We must have absolute confidence and faith in our own word. We must never doubt its effectiveness through the Law, for if with God all things are possible, and if there is but One Mind, and if that Mind is our mind now, then in such degree as our thought functions in the consciousness of that Mind, it *is* that Mind. Thus we also may say, *The words which I speak unto you, they are spirit and they are life*.

Turn to the paragraph called *The Seeing Eye* on page 451 and you will again realize that Spirit created all things by the power of Its own Word, and that we are spiritual beings. It is because we are spiritual beings, and because we are universal on the invisible plane that our word has power. One of the most important things we have to realize is that our word has as much power as we recognize that it has. Yet we do not put the power into it. This seems almost like a contradiction, but as a matter of fact it is really an intelligent idea of potential energy and action.

Power already exists, just as God already exists, just as all laws already exist. They exist forever. Power already is and we use it, and since the Ultimate Power is Absolute Intelligence or Creative Mind acting as Law (moving mathematically), then it logically follows that our concept of this Intelligence is this Intelligence functioning through us at the level of such a concept. In other words the Infinite responds to us by corresponding with our states of consciousness. (Read again the lesson on *The Law of Correspondents*, page 483.)

The Spirit always responds by correspondence; therefore it is done unto us *as* we believe. Belief is not the power; it is the avenue through which the power flows. This power is eternal and nothing has ever happened to it. On page 468 under the heading *The Father's House Always Open*, we have a description of the return of the Prodigal Son to his father's house. As he turned to joy, joy turned to him. It mattered not how long he had been sad, nothing had happened to joy. *And lo, I am with you always, even unto the end of the world*. Reality cannot change. And so the returning Prodigal found that nothing had happened except that he had made a journey into a far country.

How wonderful to realize that the Kingdom of Heaven is at hand! That what we need to do is not to coerce, but to perceive. This, which is the most simple thought imaginable, is still perhaps the most difficult to realize—we need not struggle, we need not strive but we must know. To realize that that which is known is demonstrated is to enter more completely into the Absolute.

In treatment we withdraw from the contemplation of appearances. The source of power is tapped at the center of our own inner contemplation. God goes forth anew into creation through our creative act. Hence we are practicing scientifically when like the Prodigal we return to the Father's house. The Secret Place of the Most High and the Holy of Holies is in our own souls.

In our work we treat neither physical bodies nor diseased conditions, nor do we treat disease as though it were an entity. In fact the practitioner must be careful to separate the belief from the believer, the experience from the one who is having it; otherwise he will more firmly establish such experience in the consciousness of the one for whom he is working. He endeavors to realize his patient as a living embodiment of perfection. He must recognize the fact that the Divine has never been touched by any discord.

On page 415, fourth paragraph, the statement is made that *there must be a universal standard of Reality*; that is, there must be a Divine Intelligence which coordinates everything in one complete unity, and whether or not we realize this we must be part of such a unity. The creative power of our thought cannot change our unity with Good, but temporarily it can cause us to appear separated from Good. Since Good is always at hand, our recognition of It, causes It to spring immediately into our experience.

In spiritual mind healing the practitioner turns definitely from the physical condition from which his patient suffers, and endeavors to think of him as being a perfect spiritual entity. He declares that this spiritual entity is now perfect and that every organ and function represents Divine activity.

In such degree as the practitioner is successful in convincing himself of this, his patient should respond with a higher recognition of his unity with God. God will become to him the Infinite Person back of his own personality. He will become a true worshiper, as suggested on page 362 under the heading *God—Infinite Personality*. Unless this spiritual awakening does take place in the mind of both patient and practitioner there will be no permanent healing. Faith must be restored, for it is of very little value to change one limited concept for another. We must awake to larger possibilities. A consciousness of the spiritual Presence awakens a creative feeling within us which nothing else can.

In the fourth paragraph on page 398 you will find these words: *The creative power responds to feeling more quickly than to any other mental attitude*. We know this to be true both psychologically and metaphysically. Turn to page 588 for a definition of *Emotion*, and read again the definition of *Healing* on page 597. Turn also to page 511 and try to capture the spirit expressed in the Meditation, *Majestic Calm*. We are part of the unity of all life.

Now turn again and read the whole of page 493—*One Lord, one faith . . . One God and Father of all.* There is a Divinely conceived man, there is a spiritual organism and a harmonious relationship in this body of divine ideas which we call the human body. The physical body which we objectively contact is a condensation of these ideas in a form or at a rate of vibration which is essential to this plane, but the life-giving Energy which sustains this physical form springs from an invisible Force. This is the water of which Jesus spoke to the woman at the well when he said that whoever drank from the well which springs up from within himself, would never thirst again. This is what Emerson means when he tells us to learn to listen greatly to ourselves.

There is a place in man which is ever perfect. It states on page 467 that God knows no sin. When the Prodigal Son returned filled with self-condemnation, God did not condemn him. Our consciousness must rise above both the mistake and the one who is suffering from it. The consciousness of the practitioner must see through the apparent to the reality.

The practitioner is one who uses his conscious thought for the purpose of giving direction to a definite Law which he recognizes as functioning at the center of his own being, and which operates upon his own conviction. He neutralizes or erases the discordant thoughts in his own mind about his patient; he speaks not to him but *about* him. He talks to himself about his patient; he demonstrates the patient's perfection in his own imagination. Here at the center of his own being he neutralizes the fear, the doubt, the unhappiness, the sense of pain, and in its place supplies a sense of harmony, of peace, and of wholeness.

It states at the top of page 170 that the one who has the most complete faith will be the best healer. This is a logical deduction if we start with the premise that all is Mind or Intelligence. For if all is Mind or Intelligence, any thought, being an activity of Mind or Intelligence, must produce a reaction which is exactly equal to the conviction which is in the thought.

We come now to the discussion of different types of mental treatment, chiefly the *argumentative* method and the method of *realization*. As our text implies, the argumentative method is a logical presentation of conscious thought to the Principle of Mind. The logic of this argument is based upon the premise of Perfect Being. Of course this presentation of thought takes place within one's own mind. The practitioner argues to himself about his patient, claiming that the eternal Reality is harmony; therefore his patient cannot be discordant. The eternal Reality is wholeness; therefore his patient cannot be sick.

He is talking about the spiritual man; he is never thinking of the physical man. All the claims he makes are about the spiritual man, and if he never tries to treat the physical man he will never be confused over his thought about the spiritual. We become confused in our thought about the physical only when we feel that our thought in some peculiar way must do the healing. But when we realize that it is a recognition of Truth that does the healing, we may make our declarations about the spiritual man without any mental disturbance caused by the appearance of things as they seem to be.

In the argumentative method the practitioner is an attorney stating a case, pleading a cause, presenting all the arguments in favor of perfection, and denouncing all the arguments opposed to it. Because the God of the practitioner's spiritual understanding is perfect, the person of his patient also is perfect. Silently the practitioner pleads his case in support of this all-good, this eternal Presence at the center of his patient's being. He must be convinced in his own mind of the truth of his argument.

The method of realization is a more definite establishment of the thought that the work is now done, complete, and perfect. There is very little argument used, and at times none. There is a sense, an atmosphere, a feeling, but always there is definite intention, for where there is no definite intention we are merely tuning to the indefinite and nothing practical will happen. This has been the great weakness among most idealists and in most mystical presentations. The practical man joins Heaven with earth. It is not enough to say there is one Life and that Life is God; we must know that this Life is our life now. It is not enough to say the energy exists; we must use it.

Whatever method a person uses, this is the end toward which he works—that he shall realize the perfection of his patient, state it definitely, declare it positively, and believe in it completely.

As suggested on page 171, there is but one Medium between all people. Therefore there is no absent as opposed to present treatment. When you treat a person at a physical distance you follow exactly the same method that you would use if he were in the same room with you. You always say, "He is thus and so," never "You are thus and so." The moment you begin to say "You are," you will wonder if your patient is receiving your thought.

In this method we never try to send out thoughts, hold thoughts, concentrate power, or influence anyone. It is the exact opposite of all such ideas. It is a method of self-realization for the patient. This method is not only simple, but it is direct and effective. It also has this advantage—the practitioner need not be bothered by any appearances. His power over the appearance is equal to his ability to judge, not according to the appearance but according to his concept of Reality. There is nothing opposed to Good. An absent treatment is the same as a present treatment, since there is no absence in the One Presence. New York City and Los Angeles are in one Medium. All people are in one Medium.

The practitioner does not wonder what is going to happen or hope something good will happen. He is making a series of definite statements. These statements are conscious, consciously directed, and they are definitely believed in. He is convincing himself, never anyone else. Therefore, whether he is using the method of argument or realization, he is really doing the same thing. Probably in most cases at the present state of our spiritual unfoldment, we shall have to combine these two methods. That is, we generally start with an argument, affirming all the things we feel must be true and denying those things we believe should not be true, finally arriving at a sense of spiritual realization.

As a practitioner works daily, he gradually comes to a realization of the perfection of each patient. This is what constitutes the element of time in spiritual mind healing; not that it takes time to perform the healing, for the miracle of life could be instantaneous and the Absolute knows no processes. The process is in the accumulation of thought, in the time it takes to recognize, to arrive at a conclusion, to reach the spiritual goal, which is a sense of perfection.

This experience of time usually does take place in our work and we should not be much concerned over it one way or another. Each individual treatment, however, is complete within itself. No treatment is good until it arrives at some definite conclusion, and the statement should always be made that the work is complete and perfect.

Summary

As far as the individual is concerned, all personal causation starts at the center of his own being. Therefore the practitioner must have complete confidence in himself, in the kind of God he believes in, in his own word, and in the way he uses it. This confidence is not merely self-confidence. It is a confidence in the real self based on the theory that the real self merges with God, the One and Only Presence.

The Divine Presence is, and we entertain It; Power is, and we use It. The realization that this Power and this Presence are not only at hand but already within us furnishes a key to our understanding of the Presence and to our use of the Power.

There is an Intelligence and an Integrity beyond ours, and yet it is a part of the Reality of our own being.

The practitioner envisions the patient as a perfect spiritual entity, and he tries to bring out a higher recognition and a greater appreciation of the Divine Presence in everyone and in everything.

Since feeling is the basis of everything, there is a certain emotion or feeling that should accompany every treatment.

One kind of thought can erase another kind. Yet at the same time we must never forget that the thought of the practitioner does not go anywhere. It is centered in his own consciousness about some person, place, thing, or condition.

What we call an argumentative treatment is a series of arguments presented to the Mind Principle. This argument is devised to unite Heaven with earth, or the Invisible with the visible.

Whether the treatment is what we call absent or present, it always takes place in the mind of the one giving it.

Questions

Brief answers to these questions should be written out by the student after studying the lesson, and the answers compared with those which will be included in next week's lesson.

1. What are the tools of thought a mental practitioner uses?
2. How can ideas, realized at the center of a mental practitioner' s consciousness, affect his patient?
3. What do we mean by turning within in mental treatment?
4. What do we mean by thought functioning in a consciousness of the One Mind?
5. What is meant by our being universal on the invisible plane?
6. What is the Ultimate Power?
7. Is belief the power or the avenue through which it flows?
8. What do we mean by separating the belief from the believer?
9. Can any thought separate us from our unity with Good?
10. How should a spiritual practitioner mentally view his patient?
11. In treating to heal physical ailments what principal declaration does a mental practitioner make?
12. What is meant by the statement, *Our consciousness must rise above mistakes and suffering*?
13. Name the two types of mental treatment used in spiritual mind healing.
14. Describe the argumentative method of treatment.
15. What is meant by presenting an argument to the Principle of Mind?
16. In the argumentative method of treatment why do we say that the practitioner is like an attorney?
17. Describe the realization method of treatment.
18. Toward what end does a practitioner work, regardless of what method he uses?

19. In treatment where does the argument or realization take place?
20. Should we use both methods in treatment?
21. What constitutes the element of time, not merely in giving a mental treatment but in its actual demonstration?
22. What is the difference between an absent and a present treatment?
23. Why must a treatment arrive at a definite mental conclusion in order to be effective?

Answers to Questions on Lesson 21

1. In treatment we must have confidence in the mental Law because It can respond to us only as we believe; hence mental states must reflect their correspondents, i.e., confidence reflects certainty, fear reflects confusion, etc.
2. Mind in an abstract and formless state means that Mind of Itself is without form until thought gives form to It.
3. It is always right to use the mental Law for ourselves and others when we are using It in accord with truth, justice, and harmony.
4. Jesus the man was a human being. Christ the Principle is a realization of the Divine nature of all men, or the Universal Sonship. Jesus the man became Jesus the Christ through this realization.
5. The new birth takes place when man recognizes the presence of the Christ Principle within himself.
6. The active principle within us means the self-assertive word, while the passive principle within us means the Law obeying the activity of this word.
7. The knowledge that we use a Creative Principle gives us authority in our lives.
8. In mental treatment the practitioner speaks to himself about his patient rather than directly to his patient, because the Mind and Law with which he deals is omnipresent. Hence it is both at the center of his being and his patient's being.
9. Our definition of the Truth is that it is the Reason, Cause, and Power in and through everything.
10. The God Principle already exists within us; hence we do not call It into being but into manifestation.
11. The Bible gives us no technique for mental and spiritual treatment. However, the Bible does tell us that the Universe is a spiritual system and that thought is a creative agency.
12. The principle of mental treatment is the Law of Mind. The technique of mental treatment is a definite procedure in using this Law.
13. A spiritual practitioner is one who uses his mental technique for helping himself and others.
14. We speak of a spiritual use of the mental Law because spiritual, in this sense, means thinking in accord with the Divine nature.
15. The practitioner greets the Divinity within his patient by recognizing the God within him.

The Contagion of Fear

John Jones was humming a gay tune and seemed to exude great confidence in himself and the world as he boarded the streetcar. He sat down next to a man who was filled with fear and apprehension. By the time John Jones got off the car he was in the grip of a terrible anxiety which he could not explain.

It is possible for us to catch fear from others much as we would catch a cold, for we are all unconscious mental, emotional, and spiritual broadcasting stations. This takes us back to a thought in the Bible which says that a man's enemies shall be those of his own household, for our real enemies are our fears and phobias, our doubts and uncertainties, our anxieties and our inner conflicts.

Many years ago I discovered—and, of course, others had discovered before me—that nervous, fretful, and agitated children, who have nightmares and who cannot retain their food, are affected by the inner agitation of their parents' thoughts and feelings.

But let us broaden this field and say that the whole world is filled with the thoughts of the people who live in it, and that perhaps we are all more or less subject to the passing emotions of the race mind. A leading psychiatrist has told us that fear can render a person completely unconscious as far as his brain is concerned. He tells us that it paralyzes the memory, and if a person is afraid he will forget something, he is likely to do so. We know that in cases of amnesia people are so frightened by some unconscious thought that they even forget their own names and who they are and where they came from.

Fear produces a mysterious chemical which is released into the blood, but this chemical disappears when the anxiety is over. We all have our little fears and anxieties. And we all wish to get over them. The healing of fear and anxiety is not to be found in any drug or physical manipulation. The cure is to be found only within our own minds. Where fear is the disease, we have to be our own doctors.

The Bible tells us that perfect love casts out fear, and that where love is, fear cannot remain. We can apply this principle of faith and confidence to ourselves as individuals, to our families as the first unit we deal with, and to all the people we contact in the everyday walks of life. Did you ever notice the effect of just being with a person who is calm and poised and unafraid? How differently you feel, how buoyed up and confident you become! Why should not each one of us become a broadcasting station for faith?

The world is too largely governed by fear. We are afraid of this and that and something else; we are afraid of what has happened and what is happening and what we think is going to happen. If fear is contagious and does in some mysterious way secrete a germ which acts negatively in the physical body, I think it is not too much to say that it also secretes some kind of a mental germ in the whole race mind which affects everyone with a sense of confusion and uncertainty and anxiety.

There is no doubt that this is true, and we should do something about it. Not that we have to become heroic figures who consider themselves the liberators of humanity, for we are probably not in a position to do this. What I mean is that each one of us should analyze our own thinking to determine what is wrong, and replace every fear with faith and confidence.

But where are we going to get this faith and confidence? Certainly not out of the weakness of our previous experience, and perhaps not out of the thoughts that we had yesterday—those thoughts that were so filled with anxiety. It seems to me that we will have to begin all over again. And we must find some reason for having a faith that is stronger than all our fears. So far the world has never found this reason outside what we call a religious or a spiritual idea. And by this I mean a direct faith in God.

There is nothing for God to be afraid of. And if we can, and do, tune in to the thoughts of others, and if they can affect us, as they most certainly do, why should we not learn to tune in to the Mind of God, which is free from fear and doubt?

This is what is meant by prayer and meditation. For in the act of prayer and meditation we commune with the invisible Spirit; we draw Its strength, Its peace, and Its serenity into our own souls. And as a result of this we become strong and self-reliant, because we have built up a confidence in life, a faith and conviction which wards off all fear. Just as a germ of physical disease is less liable to infect a strong body, so the germ of mental fear is resisted by a whole and happy mind.

It would be interesting if some day we should read a headline in the daily newspaper which said, *A germ of fear is now operating in a certain locality,* or, *infecting a whole community*. And it would be interesting if the same article were to tell us that a group of people were working to counteract this fear germ by broadcasting faith. And then after a while we would pick up another newspaper which had a headline reading, *We are now inoculated with faith and the fear germ has disappeared*.

Well, perhaps this sounds a little far-fetched today, but I have complete confidence that the time will come when we shall see such headlines in the papers.

The quickest and most effective method to get rid of fear is to get quiet and lift up the whole thought in confidence and faith to something bigger than we are. It is like going from a cold, dark room into the sunshine and just sitting there, letting the rays of the sun penetrate the whole being with warmth and color until the darkness and the dampness are gone. So it is with the life of prayer and faith, of affirmative Meditation and of communion with that Divine Spirit which is closer to us than our very breath.

Let us not forget that if fear is contagious, faith is doubly so. How wonderful it is to realize that we can so influence our environment that everyone who steps into it will be benefited. If this is what we are doing, the very stars in their courses will conspire to aid us.

And we may be certain of something else—there is at the center of our being a strong fortress of faith, placed there by a Power greater than we are, by an Intelligence that knows everything, and forevermore held in place by a Divine Presence which is God in us. It is to this indwelling God that we must turn. So how would it be if we worked out a method for doing this?

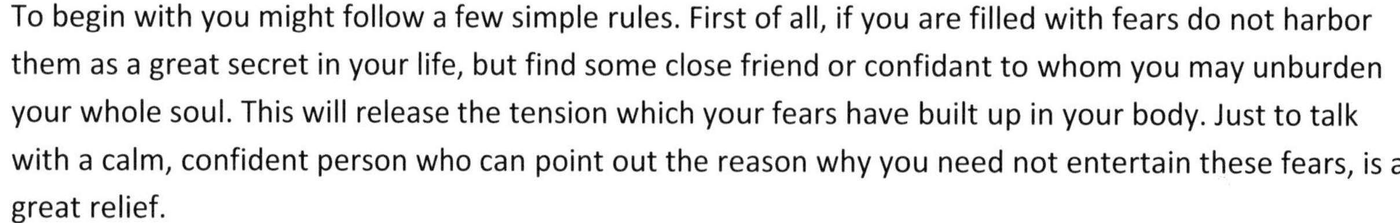

To begin with you might follow a few simple rules. First of all, if you are filled with fears do not harbor them as a great secret in your life, but find some close friend or confidant to whom you may unburden your whole soul. This will release the tension which your fears have built up in your body. Just to talk with a calm, confident person who can point out the reason why you need not entertain these fears, is a great relief.

This is, however, but a temporary thing, for next you must learn to face the fears. It will do you no good to run away from your fears. You should not be afraid to analyze them and you should explain to yourself just why you know there is nothing to be afraid of. Whenever you find yourself brooding over some fear or entertaining some anxiety, begin at once to do something about it.

And the next thing to do is convince yourself that you would not be here were there not a Power greater than you are that put you here. And learn to have confidence in this Power. Never be afraid to say to this Power and this Divine Presence: "I now lay down all my fears and doubts and anxieties. I pass them back into the great and perfect Life of which I know I am a part." Confess your fears to yourself before this Power, and then reach just a little higher in faith than you were in fear and you will discover a miracle is taking place—fears will begin to recede, until finally they appear as a speck on the horizon of your mind, and then they seem to walk over that horizon and disappear entirely, like darkness running away from light.

This is not as difficult as it sounds, if you just become as a little child. We all need to resurrect this little child within us, who unfortunately has been so buried in our unhappy experiences that we have almost forgotten that he was ever there. But we have not quite forgotten, have we? We all need to resurrect the confidence in life which we had in our youth.

To recapture this dream of youth is the wisest and the most intelligent thing any person can do. Fear has brought confusion. Faith will give birth to confidence. Anxiety has brought days filled with conflict and nights full of dread. Faith alone can heal this confusion and drive from our minds all thoughts of fear, and dissipate all anxiety. Love alone can bring harmony into our lives. So say to yourself:

> *I lay all fear aside, and in confidence and complete faith I turn to the one perfect Divine Presence, knowing that the light of Truth shines upon my path even as Divine Love guides me into the Secret Place of the Most High, where I dwell under the shadow of the Almighty.*
>
> *I know that there is nothing to be afraid of in God's world. Fear cannot operate in me, nor can it go forth from me. At the very center of my being there is complete confidence, complete faith. At the very center of my being there is a consciousness of the protection of Divine Love, the guidance of Divine Wisdom, and the strength of Divine Power.*
>
> *And so I turn in thought to the whole world and know that my word is bringing light and life and a feeling of strength and confidence to everyone. I turn in thought to the leaders of the world everywhere, and know that love and intelligent guidance is directing their thoughts and actions.*
>
> *I turn in thought to all the nations of the earth and awaken in them the realization that there is good enough to go around; that there is a Divine government under which they all may be protected from the fear of each other.*
>
> *I turn in thought to the great creative imagination of the human race and assure it that there is a feeling and a presence at the center of everything waiting to make itself known.*
>
> *And I turn to the great God, who knows all things and who can do all things, and say: "Lead, kindly light, amid the encircling gloom; lead Thou me on."*

How Old Are You?

How old do you think you are? How old is old? And when does a person get too old to enjoy life? Could it be possible that even age is something that happens to our minds rather than to our bodies? And could a person be as young at eighty as he is at eighteen?

We are told that each cell of the physical body is completely replaced every fourteen months. It seems funny, does it not, to think that no one is even a year and a half old, physically.

We are also told that there is no reason to suppose that our minds grow old; that the mind is as young at ninety as it is at nine; that the only thing that is added to it is experience. Most psychologists agree that we learn less rapidly as years advance, but just as certainly and just as accurately. Some of the scientific minds today are telling us that while time exists, age does not; that in reality time is not a way of measuring years and months and days, but rather a measurement of experience in a limitless life.

If it is true in a broad sense that neither the mind nor the body actually grows old, it is time for us to ask what produces this aging process.

Suppose we think of mind in the same way we think about space. Space is everywhere. Many things exist in space. But space itself is never crowded and it never gets old. No matter how much stuff you put into it there is still just as much space. You cannot wear it out. It never grows tired and it never becomes burdened with care.

And now let us introduce another thought that we have often talked about. God's Mind is the only mind there is and God is eternal. The whole proposition is this: We live because God lives in us, and we are able to think because the Mind of God is in us.

Our trouble is that we have thought of ourselves as separate from God, and in doing this we have stored up a burden of care and worry in our minds. We also take on a feeling of responsibility which we are not equipped to handle when we come to the place where we think, "I am separate from God. If I am facing life and all its problems with my little mind I feel inadequate to handle the situations that come along, because I am working all on my own, alone and without help from the Power that is greater than I am."

What a load we shall get off our minds when we learn that there is but one Mind that carries every load. Is not this what Jesus meant when he said, *My yoke is easy and my burden is light*?

And now let us consider what wonderful miracles Life is always working in our bodies. When even one minute cell is injured there is an Intelligence that immediately puts all the chemistry of our body to work to replace it with a new cell, one that is whole, complete, and perfect. This is how wounds heal.

It is almost startling how Divine Intelligence works for us to give us health and comfort. Even in such a simple instance as stepping from a warm room into cold winter air, if we had eyes to see it, we would witness a miracle of the One Life at work for our comfort. This Life immediately causes the circulatory system, the respiratory system, and the digestive system to go to work in such a way as to bring about an inner balance of temperature to counteract the cold wind and keep the body free from pain and discomfort.

But nature does not seem to interfere with our thought processes in the same way, and this is because we are individuals and have the right of self-choice. And so we are permitted to store up liabilities in the mind which tend to perpetuate our discomfort.

Life maintains a wonderful factory in the human body. It has a furnace room to generate heat. It has a chemical plant to purify and dispose of poisons. It has a maintenance crew that keeps the machinery in order. It even has a lubricating system which keeps the joints oiled. And there is a transportation system that carries supplies from one part of the factory to another. And an interoffice communication system that would stagger the imagination of the greatest engineer.

This One Mind, which is God, is capable of running the factory of this human body in perfect order. When Jesus said, *Consider the lilies*, he could have been saying to us: See how beautifully the factory is run when there is no interference with the laws of God. It is self-evident that God's Mind would be capable of running this factory of ours which we call our bodies if we would not throw wrenches of fear and doubt into the machinery, and if we would not overload the communication system and the transportation system with the burdens of grief and worry.

This is so simple that we should ask ourselves: "How is it, and why is it, that we have arrived at a place where we have stopped trusting the Divine Architect who created the factory and who is capable of operating it so perfectly?" I think if we could answer this question we would know what is wrong with us.

In Job 33:23 we read: *If there be . . . one among a thousand, to shew unto man his uprightness: . . . His flesh shall be fresher than a child's: he shall return to the days of his youth*. Of course we should not interpret this as meaning that we want to go back to childish ways or former years, but that we do wish to keep the child always with us and not be burdened with the years that have passed. This is what repentance means. It means to think in another way. It means a new birth in the mind of that Life that comes fresh and new every moment of our existence. Every day is a fresh beginning, every day is the world made new.

Nor does this mean that we have to recapture the physical body we possessed years ago, but rather that we recognize the youth of the physical body which we now have because there is not one cell in it that is over a year and a half old. Youth is in every muscle and in every fiber of our being. It is no wonder Jesus likened the Kingdom of Heaven to a child. So let us consider the mental attitudes of a child if we would recapture the dream we seem to have lost.

When we were young we had so much to look forward to. The days were crowded with happiness and fulfillment. We could hardly wait to get up in the morning to begin over again, because we had such enthusiastic expectation. The first third of a person's life is spent in the enjoyment of the day in which he lives, always with something more ahead. He is learning, studying, finding out how to do things, getting ready to live in a larger way. He has the security of home and parents. He is not afraid.

He reaches maturity, and the world is still ahead of him. He falls in love, gets married, has children, and the cycle repeats itself—he lives in his family and all the things that he had done for himself he now does for then, only in a bigger way. This is about what happens to the average person for the first half of his life. People do not grow old when they are busy with the pleasures of living, the enjoyment, the expectation, the enthusiasm, and the thought of the more that is to come.

But too often, when these first two periods have passed, there is not enough left to look forward to. The kick has gone out of life. For no man is happy who chases mad ambition. We are happy only in creative things, and in those things where we share the joys of living with others. We must keep our interest in life so active that there will be an element of wonder and surprise in simple everyday things.

Life is activity, and when we stop being active we turn away from the newness of life. And the person who grows old in years without an inward expectation and assurance that he is going to live forever, somewhere, will find the last part of his life burdened with the thoughts of yesterday. Let us make up our minds that yesterday is gone. Tomorrow has not yet arrived. But today can be filled with wonder if we know that we stand on the threshold of that which is wonderful and new.

I have never yet met a single individual who maintained this attitude in the last part of his life unless he had faith. And I am talking about the kind of faith we all understand the meaning of—faith in something bigger than we are, in a Power greater than we are, and a complete assurance that we are going to live forever, somewhere.

It is an interesting fact that whether or not we know it, and whether or not we like it, our lives are so tied in with God, the living Spirit, that we cannot even remain young and enthusiastic unless we know that we are one with that which knows no age and has no burdens.

Youth is not a time of life—it is a state of mind. Nobody grows old by merely living a number of years. People grow old only by deserting their ideals. Years wrinkle the skin, but to give up enthusiasm wrinkles the soul. Worry, doubt, self-distrust, fear and despair—these are the long, long years that bow the head and turn the spirit back to dust.

Whether seventy or sixteen, there should be in every man the love of wonder, the sweet amazement at the stars and the star-like things and thoughts, the undaunted challenge of events, the unfailing childlike appetite for what next, and joy in the game of life.

You are as young as your faith, as old as your doubt; as young as your confidence, as old as your fear; as young as your hope, as old as your despair.

What Is Your Dream?

Did you ever have a nightmare? I once ran across a cartoon which showed the picture of a man sound asleep, and apparently having a terrible dream in which he saw a gigantic figure at the foot of the bed leaning over him, as though it were about to seize him. The man was nearly prostrated with fear and said to the phantom, "What are you going to do with me?" The phantom replied, "I don't know. What are you going to do with me? I am your dream, you know."

How many phantoms we all carry around with us in our imagination. How often we have such morbid and unhappy thoughts that they actually appear as gigantic and menacing figures about to seize us in a deathlike grip. And how seldom do we face these fears and try to find out exactly what they are and where they came from. What a shock and what a surprise it is to us when we realize that we are the ones having the dream; we are the ones who are creating the phantom, and in a certain sense running away from the shadow of our own fears.

What, then, are our dreams? Are we dreaming of success or failure? Of happiness or misery? Of sickness or health? For our dreams are mental patterns that can lead us into a fuller and richer life, or they can create phantom monsters that make our lives a nightmare, whether we are asleep or awake. Every man is the dreamer of his own dreams, and within each is the spiritual power to choose the patterns that he wishes to experience in life.

Psychosomatic medicine has been developed to help people get rid of the monster-phantoms that come up out of their own minds. For what is a neurosis other than a group of mental images that arise to disturb the mind? Take the case of a person who feels that no one likes him. Just think of the monsters that he creates in his own mind through his feeling of being rejected. He looks at his fellow men and imagines that they do not like the way he wears his clothes, the way he talks; he feels that they are criticizing him in their own minds.

The fact is that his own morbid dreams are putting negative ideas into the minds of everyone he meets, for there is a mental contact we have with others which registers in them. He begins to shrink from life, and instead of throwing back his shoulders and facing life openly and squarely, he begins to round his shoulders and close in on himself. The passing world looks at him and says, "Here is a person who is defeated and miserable."

The dreamer who feels that he is unliked is so blinded by the monsters of his own mind that he does not realize that everyone around him is simply responding to the way he feels. He does not know that the phantom of hostility which he encounters is in his own mind and is actually following the dictates of his own thought. One of the interesting things that we have learned in the Science of Mind is that the very thought patterns we create, in a certain sense gradually obsess us. They can reach a point where we become hypnotized by them, and we go around in a dream state, imagining that everything and everyone is against us.

The unfortunate thing about this is that the dream is real enough to the one who has it. The man who was asleep and having the nightmare which nearly paralyzed him with fright, awoke in the morning and was greatly relieved to know that there was no ominous form threatening his safety. He was relieved to find that it was only a dream. And so it is with most of our troubles. They are real enough to us while we are having them.

But there is another part of us that was never caught in this dream. And just as the man who saw the gigantic figure at the foot of his bed finally awoke to a realization of its unreality, so there is some part of us that can awake to the unreality of most of the things that bother us. The very fact that one can rouse a man who is experiencing a nightmare shows that there is something about him that is superior to the experience he is having.

One of our most common dreams is that we are unhappy, that nothing ever works out right for us, that people do not like us, that life is against us, and nothing good is ever going to happen. And because there is a law of mind which operates on our thought we begin to create the situations which look like our dreams. And in reality they are our dreams. Then we bow down before them in fear, and feel that we are the victims of a fate beyond our control.

A parable is told of an angel who came to visit the earth. He found himself in the usual stream of human activities, and he listened to the conversations of people. For the first time he heard negative comments. Someone who was supposed to be an authority said that there might be a war and human life would be destroyed. And he read in the newspaper of a great epidemic of illness. And someone who certainly should have known explained in great detail that financial hardships were certain to limit all of us. He heard that there was not enough good to go around, the world was not going to be able to produce enough food for everyone, and people were going to starve to death.

He began to wonder if these things might not be true, and even as he entertained the thoughts of negation to which he was listening, the brightness of his angelic presence faded into dark shadows. His form seemed to shrivel, and looking at himself he saw that he was dressed as a human being, walking the earth in fear, doubt, and uncertainty.

And so the weary years went by, years of unhappiness and impoverishment and dread, years so filled with anxiety that he wished he were dead, that some oblivion might forever swallow him up. And yet, even in the midst of all this, something within him remembered that he was once an angel of God, living in a heaven of beauty and a place of peace and joy, living in a Garden of Eden which God had provided for him. And remembering, a determination arose within him to somehow or other find his way back to this lost paradise.

This determination grew into a great hope, and as hope was renewed a light seemed to shine in the distance; and he seemed to have the courage to travel toward the light. And gradually a miracle took place. As he traveled toward the light he found that shadows were being cast behind him, until finally he so completely entered into the light that no shadows were cast at all, and he realized that he had been asleep, that he had had a bad dream from which he was awakening.

To what extent are we all dreaming, and in our dreams seeing the monsters with terrible forms that we have unconsciously built up in our own minds? And we too are asking these forms, "What are you going to do with me? What terrible future do you have in store? What awful experiences are to come now?"

Perhaps we are still asleep and have not had quite the courage to ask these phantom forms what they are going to do with us, or to listen to the only reply they can make: "There is nothing we can do to you. What are you going to do to us? We are your own creations, you know."

St. Paul said, *It is high time to awake out of sleep*. So let us wake up, and let us be certain that we no longer drug ourselves with the sleeping potion of fear and uncertainty and doubt, but awake into faith and confidence, into peace and joy, into love and happiness. For there is something in us too, like the angel in the fable, that has never forgotten. There is a silent witness at the center of every man's being which evermore proclaims with the great and the beautiful Jesus: *Come unto me, all ye that labor and are heavy laden, and I will give you rest.*

Practical Suggestion for Mental Treatment

Simple Acceptance

Until a person has demonstrated the Truth so completely that he can never again be shaken in his conviction about It, he should not talk much to others about his belief. For the conscious and subjective reaction of their doubt might confuse him unless his own mind is already so firmly planted in understanding and faith that it remains calm in the midst of confusion and doubt.

Particularly is this true when one is making a demonstration for one's self. It seems to scatter his force. Some power seems to go out of him. It seems as though there were cracks in his mind through which conviction oozes. Others will see the evidence of his demonstration when it takes actual form.

Remember, the intellect argues, but the Spirit *knows*. The intellect examines; the Spirit has no opinions. This is why Jesus likened the Kingdom of Heaven to a child, for the child expects his parents to meet his needs. When he asks his mother for a drink of water he expects a drink of water, and he would be the most surprised person in the world if he did not receive it immediately. Equally, the mother expects to give it.

It is the nature of the Creative Mind to respond to us, to give us what we ask when we ask it, and in the way in which we ask it. Thus the childlike mind of absolute acceptance is likened unto the Kingdom of Heaven. In actual practice we must let go of the mental images which we dislike, and cling to only those which are more nearly after our heart's desire.

When you give a mental treatment you should feel that all the power there is in the universe is flowing into your word. It is impossible to feel this way if you think that you are dealing with will power, mental coercion, or even mental suggestion. It is equally difficult to do so if you feel that you are dealing with some masterful mental concentration, but it is very easy if you simplify it in your thought and realize that you are dealing with an Eternal Presence which when called upon responds to you.

What Is a Demonstration?

Office of the Dean

My Dear Friend,
We hope you will pay particular attention to the article, *The Will to Live*, since it is now known that those without the will to live unconsciously begin to destroy themselves. Of course they cannot destroy the Spirit or the Soul or the Mind, but the mind can destroy the body when the will to live is absent. We ought, then, to find plenty of reasons why we love life and why we can live it enthusiastically.

Everyone should find some creative work to do, because it is not enough just to know that everything is all right; we must do something about it. Life is meant to be lived, and it ought to be lived in joy and happiness and with a deep sense of peace which arises from a conviction of security.

We not only should have the will to live but to live the more abundant life. We should have a fuller, richer experience, coupled with a deeper and more meaningful consciousness that we all are enveloped in the Divine Presence. Those who have this feeling will know this Presence and will never have to ask anyone else whether it is true. They will know by having experienced it.

Nothing can be more important than that we feel the family life to be a part of a larger livingness. Right here on earth the Kingdom of Heaven should be established in the family life, and great joy should be experienced in doing this; the creating of a perfect whole in the family, love and consideration, compassionate understanding, joy and happiness, and the placing of the whole family under Divine protection.

Surely this would create a Heaven on earth.

Sincerely,
Ernest Holmes

Lesson 23

Page 173 through page 176

The argument that one uses in a mental treatment tends to produce an affirmative conclusion in one's own thought. It is the conclusion and not the argument that makes the treatment effective. If one could instantly arrive at the correct conclusion, which is Perfect God, Perfect Man, and Perfect Existence, then mental argument would be unnecessary. If one could always use a method of pure realization it would undoubtedly eliminate much repetitious work. However, from a practical viewpoint, one is not always sure of reaching a pure spiritual realization. Therefore in ordinary practice it is better to rely on technique, adding to it as much spiritual realization as possible.

A series of statements made in Mind and believed in will produce a definite result. Nearly a hundred years of experience in this field has proved this to be true. Moreover, unless it were possible for one to produce desired results without first having reached an exalted state of spiritual consciousness, it would be impossible for the average person to use this Science. But science is a knowledge of principles reduced to usable technique. We do not instantly recognize our perfection or the perfection of others; hence we should not hesitate to go through the mental processes necessary to arrive at such correct spiritual conclusions.

All of our arguments are built upon the theory that the Universe in which we are living is a spiritual system governed by laws of intelligence. All methods of procedure in this Science are definite and conscious. A practitioner does not put his mind into a negative state, as if to see what influence he may pick up. He does just the opposite—he creates a positive and aggressive state of thought. He makes a series of declarations about his patient, all of which tend to produce mental evidence in favor of the patient's perfection.

He starts with the assumption that his patient is spiritually perfect right now and that every apparent imperfection is the result of a covering up of that which is perfect. The work of the practitioner is to uncover this hidden perfection, to declare the truth about it, to argue in Mind that his patient is perfect, disregarding all appearances to the contrary, and inwardly to know that his argument is correct.

Turn again to the definition of *Treatment* on page 638. Treatment is an art, an act, and a science; an art because it is a thing of feeling; an act because it is a movement of consciousness; and a science because it is based upon a definite technique of a proved principle. Treatment is always a self-conscious act of the mind. The only office that will has in this treatment is one of direction. The Spirit does not will things to happen, as is shown under the definition of *Will* on page 645. It proclaims rather than wills, and we must have a willingness to proclaim the supremacy of Spirit, to argue for the potency of the All-Good.

Turn to page 553 for an example of treatment for alcoholism. You will find there a series of statements which tend to free one from the belief that one is subject to this habit. This treatment tends to unify man with the Universal Life Principle which is God. It declares for the intimate unity between the Universal and the individual, and ends by specifically saying: *I do know the Truth and I am free*. This is a good example of treatment. For an illustration of a more inspirational method of treatment turn to any of the Meditations for Self-Help, pages 507-550 inclusive.

We must recognize that the Reality back of all appearance is complete and perfect. In treatment we must present our case in a way which will convince the mind that the person for whom we are working is one with this perfect Reality and that he is now expressing the harmony of his real being. As our text states, *This argumentative method of treatment is a series of affirmations and denials, for the purpose of building up in the mind of the practitioner a state of realization and acceptance* (page 173, third paragraph).

Let us repeat, the treatment takes place entirely in the mind of the practitioner, but because his mind is in the same medium as is the mind of his patient, his work takes place in a unified field. Therefore whatever he realizes at the center of his own thought rises spontaneously and instantaneously at the center of his patient's thought and has an effect equal to the practitioner's own realization of the truth of his statement, and to the patient's conscious or subjective acceptance of the truth of those statements.

The practitioner must believe in his own statements. He need never try to crowd them into the consciousness of his patient. He knows within his own mind. He must remain true to his conviction. As far as he is concerned nothing else matters. If we turn to page 453 under the heading *That Which Defiles* we find that we must keep our mental house free from that which contradicts the truth of our being. Everything that contradicts this truth must be ruthlessly uprooted. We must come to see the patient in thought as a living embodiment of the Divine Ideal, a personification of Christ, the incarnation of God—perfect in every part, complete in every attribute, whole in every organ. We must, as stated on page 447, approach the Spirit in Its own nature.

Turn again to Lesson 6 and read the discussion of the paragraphs on this page (447). We must learn to embody, that is, mentally realize the truth of our own statements. As stated in the last paragraph on page 414, *the letter without the Spirit does not quicken the flesh*. Feeling is at the very center of the Universe, and this feeling must be reflected in the thought of the practitioner; not feeling as we ordinarily think of the average emotion, but rather feeling as a deep, positive, calm, and exalted consciousness.

From this standpoint feeling is more than emotion; it is the very cause of emotion. It is a conviction so great that thought no longer denies it. It is an acceptance so complete that the mind no longer conceives its opposite. As stated at the top of page 400 this conviction is first established in the conscious thought as the starting point of any activity.

Since the subjective Law knows only to obey, having no will of Its own, in such degree as this spiritual conviction is arrived at in the conscious mind, it is automatically imparted to the Law, which is the only actor. Again and again we realize the essential necessity of knowing the Truth. There is a Truth which known, is demonstrated.

Turn to the last paragraph on page 331 and the second and third paragraphs on page 332 and study carefully the method which Jesus used. First there was a realization, a recognition of Divine Power; then there was a consciousness of his unity with this Power; then he spoke the word as one having authority. We must have an abiding sense of the unity of good, the Fatherhood of God, and the brotherhood of man. It should seem perfectly plain to any student of this Science that if we are dealing with a Mind Principle it must follow that the more exalted the thought the more power it will have.

It stands to reason that if we are dealing with such a mental Principle, thought should not be divided against itself. It should always be peaceful, but it should never be passive to negations. (Turn to page 616 for a definition of *Passive Activity* and to page 617 for a definition of *Peace* as used in this text).

There is a passive activity which to some might seem to be a negation. This passive activity is referred to by the ancient sage who said that all things are possible to him who can perfectly practice inaction. He did not mean inaction as we think of action and inaction, but his concept of inaction was that calm, frictionless activity of pure acceptance poised in perfect Spirit. Jesus used this nonresistant but intensely active method. He consciously warded off the ideas of race suggestion and calmly proceeded with the supposition that all power was delivered unto him.

To meditate upon God is to inbreathe the power of God; to meditate upon Good is to embody Good. (*Meditation* is defined on page 609.) We meditate on our oneness with the Whole. This is the method Jesus used: recognition, unification, and command. *Father, I thank thee that thou hast heard me. And I knew that thou hearest me always*. These statements were followed by the command that Lazarus come forth from his tomb. Jesus' conviction was so great that he said, *Heaven and earth shall pass away, but my words shall not pass away.*

We must have faith in the power of Spirit, faith in the willingness of Spirit to respond to us, and absolute conviction that the Law cannot help corresponding with our states of consciousness. Turn again to our definition of *Correspondence* on page 581. Our work should be simple but direct. In giving treatments we turn from the condition to the contemplation of its opposite. We do not try to concentrate; we try to believe. We do not will; we have a willingness.

The practitioner does not try to fathom the exact way in which the Law works. He takes it for granted that It will work, and then he states that It is working and believes in his own statement. His work is entirely removed from the field of will, concentration, and coercion, into the field of willingness, consecration, and acceptance. As stated on page 174, a demonstration is made when the prayer is answered, when the treatment finds fulfillment in actual objective affairs, when the word of the practitioner takes form.

We cannot demonstrate beyond our ability to mentally embody an idea (page 174). What does this mean? It means that we cannot demonstrate beyond our capacity to inwardly give birth to the idea we wish to see demonstrated. Love will overcome hate when love is greater than hate, when the idea of hate is swallowed up in love, when the embodiment of the idea of love is more complete than was the thought which produced the hate. This is what is meant by embodiment.

From this viewpoint embodiment is not so much an image of thought as it is an atmosphere of Reality. It is a feeling, a sense of the Divine Presence in the patient, an intellectual acceptance backed by spiritual realization. It is more than a belief, it is a solid conviction.

As stated in the second paragraph on page 344, *The highest mental practice is to listen to this Inner Voice and to declare Its Presence*. This cannot lead to illusion, but to Reality. It is not a psychic experience but a self-conscious one. This experience of the unity of Good and the all-conquering power of Love is sometimes accompanied by a consciousness of light. This light is the natural atmosphere of the spiritual universe. It is, as our text says, something which pre-exists. No ordinary use of the power of concentration or will can produce this light, but the ascension of consciousness through the expansion of the mind does frequently produce a manifestation of this light which already exists.

Turn to page 334, third paragraph, for a further discussion of the power of Jesus which lay in his recognition of the Infinite that was personal to him and of the Law that responded to him. It is a combination of a sense of this Divine Presence and of authority over the Law which makes a good practitioner. Therefore our ability to embody an idea means more than the mere words would signify. It means an inner sense of Reality which, as it were, lights the darkness around it; a light whose beams shine through the prison door and reveal to the captives that there are no chains to bind them. This is the Power of God operating through the Divine Presence in man.

We must have such a conviction of our authority over the Law that it becomes natural for us to use It instantly and on all occasions for any purpose. We must know, as our text states (pages 174 and 175), that *the possibility of demonstrating does not depend upon environment, condition, location, personality, or opportunity. It depends solely upon our belief and our acceptance*. Further we are to realize that the art of creation is an act of giving form to the formless.

Turn again to page 582 and reread our definition of *Creation* which has already been referred to in Lessons 2 and 5. If we think that our ability to demonstrate depends upon any given condition, then naturally we are limiting that ability to the condition already existing. It is certain that our thought must transcend the condition it wishes to neutralize; otherwise it will be caught in it.

A treatment is good only when it is given in complete independence of any objective situation. Does the artist feel that his ability to paint the picture of a desert scene depends upon anything other than his capacity to visualize this desert and to outline it on the canvas? He knows that he can give form to his idea. Nor is his idea limited by any other man's picture of the desert. The creative art is always independent of any created thing. It is always new. This is the meaning of the saying, *Behold, I make all things new.*

The Universe cannot deny us anything when our demand upon It is made in the right way. Turn to page 583 for our definition of *Demand*, by which we mean recognition and acceptance, not coercion. Read also on the same page the definition of *Deductive Reasoning*, which will help to explain why it is that the Universe cannot deny us anything which we conceive provided that what we conceive is consistent with the nature of Reality. Therefore we all receive as we ask and it is done unto every man as he believes. The conscious belief must become a subjective embodiment before our desired good can be a permanent experience, for it is the subjective state of our thought which is the automatic medium between the Absolute and our relative.

As our text says, we must not fool ourselves, for demonstration means an actual objective manifestation of some definite form or condition or situation. We can check up on this kind of a demonstration, and unless we can check up on it we have not made a demonstration but have only fooled ourselves. We do not believe in saying *Peace* when there is no peace. If, then, we are treating for the removal of a false growth, the only way we can possibly know our treatment is effective is to have the growth disappear.

You need have no superstition about this. Your patients may go to a physician for a physical checkup, and unless the undesirable condition is being removed you are not meeting the case. On the other hand, if the condition is being removed you most certainly are meeting the case and you may continue in joy until the demonstration is complete. The day will come when physicians and metaphysicians will work together in the healing art, and that day will come when each realizes the importance of such cooperation.

As stated on page 176, the next to the last paragraph, there need be no self-deception in our work. Nothing can be more specific than a mental treatment, and if a demonstration is made nothing can be more definite. The treatment should be continued until there is a definite demonstration. We should insist that we have this proof in our experience; otherwise we shall soon be spending our time merely in spiritual daydreaming. This type of thought produces no good results, and from a psychological viewpoint is detrimental to our psychic well-being.

When, as a result of meditation, prayer, or treatment we find conditions actually changing in our objective world, or in the experience of those for whom we are working, we shall know that we are working correctly. As our conviction grows, so will its evidence accumulate. This evidence will then be so objective that anyone can see it.

Summary

We are made up of our thoughts; therefore our main endeavor should be to learn to think constructively, until finally our subconscious reactions become entirely constructive, filled with faith and confidence and peace and joy. We are living in a spiritual universe right now, and our lives should be a living proof of this truth.

In spiritual mind treatment the particular words we use are not of as much consequence as is their meaning to us. That is, every statement must find a corresponding feeling and meaning in the mind of the one who makes it. Consequently we do not think so much of the statement as of what it means to us, for all words of a spiritual treatment must come from the heart instead of the intellect. The head or intellect makes the words coherent and builds up an argument to present to the Mind, which draws a logical conclusion, but we must never overlook the need of a feeling back of this argument which causes us to give it. The argument is merely the way in which the feeling is put into form.

A demonstration takes place when our whole consciousness, both objective and subjective, agrees, and particularly when the subjective state of our thought no longer denies what we affirm. We have complete authority over the Law but should listen to the Spirit; that is, we should develop the intuition so that we are consciously aware at all times of harmony, peace, happiness, and poise.

Our work is like that of an artist; the picture he is about to paint is independent of anything already created. We need have no superstition about this, but a definite feeling of being one with the invisible forces of nature.

No matter how much good we may experience today, tomorrow we should expect more good.

Questions

Brief answers to these questions should be written out by the student after studying the lesson, and the answers compared with those which will be included in next week's lesson.

1. What do we mean when we say it is the correct conclusion rather than the argument which makes a treatment effective?

2. Is it possible to produce results without first arriving at an exalted state of spiritual realization?
3. What do we mean by mental procedure in treatment being definite and conscious?
4. What is the office of the will in mental treatment?
5. What unifying mental action takes place between a practitioner and his patient for effective treatment?
6. How does the realization of the practitioner's thought rise into expression in his patient's experience?
7. How shall we keep our thought free from that which contradicts the truth of our being?
8. What steps did Jesus use in demonstrating the truth?
9. Does passive mental activity imply mental inaction?
10. What was the fundamental supposition in the philosophy of Jesus?
11. Upon what premise should our mental work be based?
12. What does the mental practitioner take for granted?
13. When is a demonstration made?
14. What is the limit of our ability to demonstrate at any particular time?
15. Why must thought transcend any condition it wishes to change?
16. Why do we say treatment is independent of any situation or circumstance?
17. What do we mean by *the* Absolute and *our* relative?
18. What do we mean by conscious belief becoming a subjective embodiment?
19. Why is it that the subjective state of our thought is the automatic medium between the Absolute and our relative?

Answers to Questions on Lesson 22

1. The tools of thought a mental practitioner uses are the ideas formulated at the center of his own consciousness for himself or someone else.
2. Ideas realized at the center of the practitioner's consciousness affect his patient through the medium of the Universal Mind.
3. Turning within in mental treatment means turning from all external things and confusion, to the thought that with God all things are possible.
4. By thought functioning in a consciousness of the One Mind we mean thought that is so unified with good that no opposites can possibly suggest themselves to the mind.
5. By being universal on the invisible plane we mean that while objectively each is a separate entity, subjectively each is unified with the whole.
6. The Ultimate Power is Absolute Intelligence, or Creative Mind acting as Law.
7. Belief is not the power, but the avenue through which it flows.
8. When we use the expression, *separating the belief from the believer*, we mean mentally repudiating negative thought or belief and affirming spiritual perfection of being.
9. Thought cannot separate us from our unity with Good; it can only appear to separate us.
10. Definitely turning in thought from any negative appearance, a practitioner mentally views his patient as a spiritual and perfect entity.

11. The principal declaration which a mental practitioner makes in treating physical ailments is that his patient, being a spiritual entity, is perfect in every organ, function, and activity.
12. By consciousness rising above both mistake and suffering we mean that the mental attitude which heals must rise above the condition which it seeks to change.
13. The two types of mental treatment used in spiritual mind healing are the argumentative method and the method of realization.
14. The argumentative method of treatment is a logical presentation of conscious thought to the Principle of Mind.
15. By presenting an argument to the Principle of Mind we mean a series of affirmations and denials based upon the premise of perfection.
16. In the argumentative method of treatment we say that the practitioner is like an attorney because he argues in favor of perfection and denounces all arguments opposed to it.
17. The realization method of treatment establishes an atmosphere or feeling that the definite desired result is complete and perfect now.
18. Regardless of what method a practitioner uses he always works to the end of building up within his own mind a positive acceptance of his patient's perfection.
19. In treatment the argument or realization takes place within the mind of the practitioner.
20. Generally speaking, we combine both methods, i.e., we begin treatment by using any argument or line of thought which leads to a spiritual realization.
21. The time element in spiritual mind healing is not objective but subjective; hence the manifestation depends upon the time it takes to acquire a mental subjective acceptance of the desired result.
22. Since there is no absence in the One Mind, and because both practitioner and patient live in this One Mind, there is no difference between an absent and a present treatment.
23. A treatment must arrive at a definite mental conclusion in order to be effective, because without the definite mental conclusion the result would be vague.

Psychosomatic Medicine and the Infant

To begin with, all people are born with a predetermined desire to express life, to come to self-fulfillment through love and accomplishment, and to live creatively. We call this the cosmic urge to express something that seems to be inherent and fundamental in man, in animals, and in all nature.

Two of the basic principles back of the emotional drive which everyone has are that the ego must not be rejected, and the libido must find an object.

Libido means the emotional craving for self-expression. This is based on the idea of love seeking an object upon which it may lavish its affections, and thus finding fulfillment in the object of its desire. This impulsion seems to be born with life itself, and we are told that from birth, and even prenatally the infant should be surrounded by an atmosphere of love and attention.

Of course the infant does not reason these things out; it merely feels them. This feeling is born with the infant; it is put there by nature. The infant born into a home where it is unwanted feels an unconscious repulsion, and everything in its life becomes conditioned by this feeling. Often such infants shrink from the very touch of the hand. This is why one of the new innovations is to place the babe in a basket beside the mother where she may reach out and touch and fondle it.

The whole atmosphere of the home should be one of wanting and needing and loving the infant. Otherwise the emotional reaction of the infant is that it is not wanted, needed, or loved. Its libido, which means its emotional craving for finding a love object, is pushed back into the infant mind, and unconsciously it feels itself to be an alien in its environment. This early conditioning is a great influence throughout its life, because these are the first impressions the infant receives.

This law of our emotional being, that the ego must not be rejected, is fundamental. If this is true the infant should be welcomed at the time of birth as though it were a gift from heaven, a gift of God, an offering of love to humanity, the greatest treasure on earth and the hope of the future.

The infant should be fondled and held not only to its mother's breast but in its father's arms. There is no danger of spoiling the child through love. Quite the reverse. The future life of the infant may be wounded without it. What more wonderful concept can we entertain than that of Jesus who said, *Suffer little children, and forbid them not, to come unto me: for of such is the kingdom of heaven.*

It is better to have no children than to have those who are unwanted and unloved. Parents assume a tremendous obligation when they permit themselves to have children. From the earliest point of conception there should be preparation in the parents' minds, an atmosphere of thinking, feeling, and longing for the new birth. There should be definite, daily meditations centered around the idea that the child is conceived in love and welcomed with joy. Such daily meditation will relieve tensions and assist nature in making the birth normal, natural and easy. There must be no confusion or anxiety. Everything should flow along with a calm and delightful expectation of wonderful things that are going to happen.

The mother should feel that she is carrying a Divine treasure, the highest gift of life. She should daily sense the formation of this embryo into a perfect being, and always with great tenderness in her heart and mind.

The father too should have the same mental attitude, for he is a part of the mental and emotional family life and without him the child could not be born. Some part of him enters into this birth since he is an instrument of nature in its accomplishment.

The ego must not be rejected, which means this: in the early formative years particularly, the child must feel itself to be a part of the family life. This does not mean that the child is to have its way willy-nilly, but it does mean that it is not to be harshly rejected as though it were of no importance. The counsel of children should be sought by parents, that they may feel a community of interest and spirit, for they are working out the family life together. They all are now some part of it.

Particularly when another child is born the older one or ones should feel that they too are playing an important part in the birth. The new babe has not come to take their place in the affections of the parents, but rather that they all may enjoy it together. This is of vital importance. Too often this process is reversed and the older ones feel something is taking their place. With this inward feeling comes an unconscious sense of antagonism toward the newcomer.

All of this, too, must be taken up in quiet meditation, in spiritual unification of the family life. If these two fundamental needs are fulfilled the child will be conditioned early in life to meet anything that may come up in its experience. This is why people who speak with authority on the subject maintain that these early formative years are of vital importance.

To show how true this is, there are cases on record in which an unconscious resentment of the wife to the husband centers in the child, and babes have been known to suffer with continual diarrhea when this unconscious resentment exists. It is known too that in early life children often have attacks of asthma in order to gain the notice, affection, and care of the parents.

Psychosomatic medicine is wonderful. What it teaches is of vital importance to all of us. We agree thoroughly with the findings of those who are giving their whole endeavor to the subject. We not only agree with them; we will go a step further and introduce the idea of spiritual values, the deep inward feeling that the family is a household of God, a Kingdom of Heaven on earth in which the parents are seeking to play the role of Heavenly Father. How can this take place unless the parents themselves believe there is such a Divine Presence, unless they believe that all conception is immaculate and that all birth is holy.

And we would add this other thought: everyone is in partnership with Life, with Love, with God, with Truth, with Beauty. To rear a family without some spiritual concept that is adequate, whatever religious form it may take, is going contrary to the first law of our being, which is that we are all rooted in the Divine Spirit, in Perfect Life. We are all children of God.

The Will to Live

We are told that we are born with a will to live and an almost equal will to die; that when we look forward to more pain and unhappiness than to peace and joy in living, the mind begins to destroy the body so we shall not have to suffer the pain we unconsciously anticipate.

The will to live and to be happy is necessary to our physical well-being. The more we study the way the mind works the more we realize that most of our physical ills, and perhaps all of our unhappiness, come from certain deep-rooted reactions to life that generally are built around the idea that we are not wanted or needed or loved. We feel some deep sense of guilt, and this gives rise to a feeling of insecurity and anxiety. Thus we reject ourself, and suffer because of this self-imposed condemnation.

So the morbid race goes on in the inner conflicts of the mind, until finally the frustration is so great that the mind begins to destroy the body because the impressions it has received are destructive. When this reaches a point where there is no longer a will to resist it we say the person does not have the will to live and so even nature cannot restore him, and generally in such cases he passes on.

What we need is a deep, underlying faith or conviction about life that will remove this inner conflict and frustration and let the original Divine pattern come to the surface, for we all are rooted in God, the living

Spirit. There would have to be perfection at the center of our being or we should not be here. This is what Jesus meant when he said, *Be ye therefore perfect, even as your Father which is in heaven is perfect.*

Our roots run deep into the creative soil of the Infinite Mind, and if we had not stopped drawing straight from the roots of our being we should be all right.

The Science of Mind, under different names and schools and methods, recognizes this, and its endeavor is to find out where and when and how we started on the wrong path—the pathway that leads to destruction rather than life, the pathway that leads to unhappiness and frustration rather than joy through self-expression. Man is born to be happy, to live creatively, to love, to sing, to dance, and to express himself to the full. When he does not do this he feels unhappy, sad, and alone, and wishes he were dead—he no longer has the will to live.

We must find a method that can easily and quickly reach the seat of our trouble. Instead of probing the mind to see just where, what, when, and how this whole negative chain of destructive thoughts started, we can go back to that which is more fundamental. We can go back to God, the creative Spirit and say:

> *I was born of God. There is one Life, that Life is God, that Life is perfect, that Life is my life now. Nothing has interfered with that Life, nothing can interfere with it.*
>
> And then: *I know that there is nothing in the universe that holds anything against me.*
>
> And following the thought of the Great Teacher, *Forgive, and ye shall be forgiven*, we can say:
>
> *I forgive myself. I forgive everyone else. The past is gone. It need no longer affect me. I know that God holds nothing against me, and if I have done anything to hurt others, or they have done anything to hurt me, I now forgive myself and them. Therefore I am conscious that I have complete clearance. There is no judgment, no condemnation.*
>
> We must also know there is no fear. Perfect love casts out all fear. Therefore we can say:
>
> *I have confidence in life. I have a deep faith and a complete conviction that God is all there is and that I am wanted and needed and loved, not only by the Divine Spirit but by everyone I meet. I belong to Life, it belongs to me, and I am going to enter into it with joy. Life is ready to give me everything that is good, and I am ready to pass it on to others. I am a channel through which good flows in every direction. Giving and receiving, and receiving and giving, the channel is never stopped.*
>
> We can say to ourselves: *I have no sense of insecurity or anxiety. I feel secure in God. I know that I will be guided and guarded and loved into fulfillment. I have no anxious thought for tomorrow, for I shall know what to do when tomorrow comes. I shall be guided to know what to do. Having no morbid regrets over the past and no anxiety over the future I live today as though God were all there is, because God is all there is. There is no other power, no other presence, and no other life.*

Jesus knew what was in people's minds. He knew about what today we call the blocks and conflicts, the repressions, the inhibitions, which go under the names of inferiority complex, or superiority complex, or a sense of rejection or guilt. And he took people's minds straight back to Life and told them that it did not matter so much what had happened in the past because they could get a complete clearance from it. What mattered was that they should forgive themselves and others, know that they are forgiven, and that no longer indulging in what is wrong, they would feel a new will to live surging up within them.

You remember how frequently Jesus spoke of the joy that was his and how he said that he had come that they might have life and have it more abundantly. He placed great emphasis on the will to live creatively and to enjoy life.

Jesus did not say that life held anything against us, or condemned us, or judged us. He said that at any hour of the day we can get a complete clearance. This is what he meant in the parable of the laborers, where the man who came in at the eleventh hour received the same compensation as the ones who had labored all day, as though he were saying: "What if you have been lurking in the dark or damp shadows of previous experience until you are so depressed that you don't know what to do because you are surrounded by darkness, the very moment you step out into the sunshine you are in the light. Just place yourself in the position so that all shadows will be cast behind you, so there will be nothing between you and the sun and let its warmth and energy fill you with a new will to live."

No person has the will to live unless he feels that life is worth living. And he cannot have a deep sense of the will to live unless he feels that he is going to live forever somewhere. It is impossible to divorce this will to live eternally, this belief that we are immortal beings, from the best possible mental hygiene. This is why Jesus laid so much emphasis on eternal life—that there is always something worthwhile to look forward to. The play has just begun and it will never end.

It has been my opportunity to consult with thousands of people over a period of years, and my experience has taught me that Carl Jung was right when he said he had never yet seen one single permanent healing from neurosis without a restoration of spiritual faith, and that it is impossible to get the most out of life while we are here unless we believe in immortality.

There is nothing complicated about this. We should stop thinking it is so difficult to get our thought straightened out, and begin to realize how easy it must be, for there is no mystery about it. We know that thoughts are things, and we know that our inward emotional reactions to our ways of thinking do produce inward psychic or mental diseases, which in turn give rise to most of our physical afflictions. And we know that the reason this happens is because our thoughts are based on the negative rather than the positive, on fear rather than faith, on disappointment rather than fulfillment, and on all the other negative attitudes we could name.

We know that the battle for the right to live happily through the will to live rightly is half won when we have correctly diagnosed the trouble. And if we have been walking down a road that leads nowhere, where the trail runs out and stops, all we have to do is reverse our steps and remember the Power that took us down the wrong road can just as easily lead us back on the right one.

It takes less energy to live constructively than it does destructively. It takes no energy to have faith, while fear devastates such energy as we have. It takes no energy to love; it is hate that is destructive. It does not take mental or physical energy to be happy, but unhappiness and morbidity consume so much energy that it devitalizes us mentally and physically. It does not take mental or physical energy to build up hope; it is despair that blocks us. All it takes is faith.

It sometimes seems strange that Life should have delivered such power into our keeping, such a will and imagination, and then let us alone to make the great discovery for ourselves. Sometimes we wonder why it did this, as though we were questioning the providence of God. But a little thought will show us that God never made any mistakes, and never can. This is the only way we could have been created as free people, for the very idea of freedom carries with it the obligation of ignorance and the reward of understanding.

And now it is high time that we awake from our sleep and come back to a direct and intimate relationship to the Power greater than we are and to a Law of Good acting creatively on our prayers of affirmation, our meditations of faith, and our hymns of praise. The Science of Mind conspires with us because it has led us back through the dim and dark caverns of our own thinking to the original source of our being which it has hesitated to call God but which it knows is a Power greater than we are.

No one can travel the new road for us but ourselves. Science may put up a sign: *This is the way; walk in it*. But even as the Prodigal of old remembered who he was and resolutely turned his steps homeward, so must we decide that Life is for us and not against us, and turning from everything that denies this, take our journey into the Promised Land.

Insecurity

It is believed that there are four different subjective or unconscious components underlying the insecurity and anxiety complex. In order to understand this let us go back to the idea that the ego must not be rejected.

When the infant or the adult suffers from an unconscious sense of being rejected, not wanted, needed, or loved, he unconsciously receives the impression that there must be something wrong with him. Without the objective faculties being aware of it, he argues with himself somewhat after this manner: "Nobody likes me, no one wants me around; I am in everyone's way. There must be something wrong with me or this wouldn't happen." Thereafter he develops an unconscious sense of guilt, of self-condemnation.

But nature has provided that certain processes of the mind, which seek to protect the ego, keep this inward feeling covered so that it never gets to the surface. For most of our inner conflicts are never brought to the light of day. If they were they would cease to exist. From this sense of not being wanted, needed, or loved and this unconscious sense of guilt and self-condemnation which is not permitted to come to the surface because the ego must not reject itself, there comes a sense of insecurity, a feeling that "I am not safe anywhere; I don't fit anywhere; everything about me is wrong." And out of this sense of rejection, guilt, and insecurity, a feeling of anxiety is generated.

You can easily prove this for yourself by talking with people who have a continual anxiety complex. There never seems to be any specific reason for this feeling. They cannot put their finger on some point of experience and say, "This is it." Rather the inward conflict, seeking release from its tensions, projects the anxiety first into one situation and then another, as though it were a searchlight seeking out an object for itself.

It does this to get rid of tensions, for inward conflicts are a result of the out push of the desire for self-expression which has been crowded back upon itself through repression. Since the ego must not be rejected because it would lose its self-esteem if it were, a certain mechanism of the mind pushes the stream of desire back into the mind. The conflict is between the desire for self-expression and the repression which shoves it back into the unconscious where the conflict silently goes on.

This is a simple and altogether too brief an explanation of the nature of our inner conflicts. Yet as simple as it is, it is fundamental, and you will notice in any book you may read on the subject, some reference is made to these few simple facts. In psychiatry and analysis, and in most psychological counseling, the purpose is to uncover these inner conflicts and cause them to come to the light of day where they will be self-seen and understood, on the theory that when they are self-seen they will disappear. That is, we shall understand why we feel as we do and why we need not feel that way.

This process is cumbersome, time-consuming and therefore expensive. However, it is scientific and the techniques for exposing the inner conflicts when successfully used should and often do completely relieve the pressure and thus rehabilitate the individual, causing him to be a normal, happy, and spontaneous person.

But we believe there is more to it than this. Man is rooted in pure Spirit; he is some part of Life; he is an incarnation of God, and no matter what his inward conflicts may be or what may have occasioned them, there is a way for him to get a complete clearance from them without the elaborate process of analysis. If he could forgive himself for all the mistakes he may have made, if he could get a clearance in his mind from the fear that there is some God condemning him, that some terrific evil awaits him hereafter, he would get complete relief.

This is one of the salutary purposes of the confessional, and perhaps this is why Jesus so frequently told people that their sins were forgiven them.

If it is true that at the core of every neurosis there is a sense of being rejected, attended by a consciousness of guilt from which arises a feeling of insecurity and an attitude of anxiety, why could not we with our method get a complete clearance by attacking these four fundamental native attitudes and silently assuring ourselves that there is nothing in the universe that holds anything against us. We have not done anything so terribly bad after all. Why should we feel insecure in the universe in which we live, or have any anxiety if our whole confidence is placed in God or good?

This brings us right back to the fundamental proposition upon which our whole thought is based: God is One, God is good, God wills only good, God is right where we are, God is within us and around us.

If self-condemnation is an unconscious thing, and as a result of it we protect ourselves from inward conflicts by projecting condemnation to others, then it would follow that if we could relieve the tension of the burden of guilt and condemnation from our own unconscious thinking we should no longer project it toward others.

Perhaps this seems too simple to be true, but great truths are simple, and the most effective methods are the most direct ones. The starting point for a clearance of the inward burdens that are too heavy to bear and the conflicts that tear so many people apart, is to get a clearance in our own mind about ourselves and our relationship with God.

Some might think that this is a way whereby one excuses oneself for wrongdoing. Nothing could be further from the truth, for while the sense of condemnation for others remains, one has not reached a clearance in one's own mind. A consciousness of love would be the basis for the assurance we need, a feeling that Divine Love gives of Itself, that we give of ourselves, and that there is nothing in us that can project anything but love and peace and joy to others.

It has been my experience that whenever any individual arrives at complete self-forgiveness while also understanding that any cause he sets in motion toward others will react upon himself, he has reached a place where his judgments are no longer harsh. He becomes a kind and lovable person and he has peace within his own mind. There can be no peace until this clearance is made. In one of the great books of wisdom of the East it says that the self must raise the self by the self. There is no other way, for the blind cannot lead the blind. There must be a seeing eye.

Not only can you do this for yourself, but you can do it for others by using the same method. For the only difference between treating yourself and others is that when treating yourself you say that "this is the truth about me," while in treating others you say, "This is the truth about him (or her)." Forgiving and being forgiven, loving and being loved, living and letting live, is the simple basis for it all. Just to be yourself in God. Just to be simple and spontaneous. Just to live as though today is God's day and you may rejoice in it.

I would like to make this further suggestion for your careful consideration: Is it not possible that the belief in a devil or devils and in a future state of judgment from which one must shrink in horror, are themselves a result of projecting our own unredeemed lives into the universe, judging God by our own misfortunes, our own lacks, our own fears, doubts, and uncertainties? It is my belief that the unconscious imagination of man has made this projection, for there can be nothing to fear from God. Man's problems are within himself alone, and to himself alone, and from himself alone. Suffering is not designed by the All Creative Wisdom.

There is still another reflection that must be made. Jesus said, *Judge not, that ye be not judged. For with what judgment ye judge, ye shall be judged; and with what measure ye mete, it shall be measured to you again* (Matthew 7:1,2). Is this not a veiled statement of an immutable law of cause and effect from which we cannot hope to escape?

This is not an easy philosophy. It is the toughest that ever confronted the mind and imagination of man. Many people may be under the mistaken concept that the metaphysical philosophy is attractive to people because it says God is good and everything is all right; therefore there is nothing to fear. This is far from the truth. What it says is this: Do you wish to be loved? Then stop hating. Do you want to be happy? Then be sure that you are never the occasion for unhappiness in others. Do you wish to stop shedding tears? Then be sure that you are never the instrument which causes others to shed them.

Am I certain there is nothing in me which can hurt anyone? Then as surely as God is God and justice is justice nothing can harm me, but the harm I would do to another, I myself must suffer. Only from a cleansing of the self comes redemption.

Treatment

There is one Divine Presence filling this whole household, personified in everyone.

This household is a Divine family living, moving, and having its being in that which is the very essence of love, confidence, and peace.

Every member of this family is united, happy, and whole.

There is no fear, no anxiety, no criticism, and no condemnation.

There is great joy and happiness in this family.

Each member belongs to the One Divine Family, each is secure and whole in the One Perfect Presence, and all together are united in an atmosphere of love and beauty.

The children in this family are children of God. The parents are God's instruments on earth for the rearing of these children in close and intimate consciousness of their oneness with all life, with each other, and with the world in which they live.

The food that this family eats is blessed. Every act of each and all members of this family is blessed.

There is a joy and a song, a feeling of lightness and happiness permeating this household by day and by night.

All members of this household sleep in peace and wake in joy and live in the consciousness of good. Therefore the benediction of Heaven rests upon everyone here.

Practical Suggestion for Mental Treatment

We Cannot Take Out More Than We Put In

We must know that the doorway of opportunity is never closed. Man is always receptive to the Divine Ideas. It is never too late for him to manifest opportunity; it is never withheld from him for a single moment; there is no sense of limited or restricted opportunity.

Treat to know that your patient is at the doorway of limitless opportunity, forever expanding in his experience. Everywhere he goes a new and better opportunity for self-expression opens before him; he is compelled to recognize this opportunity and to act intelligently upon it. His imagination is continuously increasing, new ideas come to him every day, and he knows how to execute these ideas.

And right here be sure to remember that nothing can come out of a treatment that is not first put into it; hence it is not enough to state that God is limitless, for though this abstract statement is undoubtedly true no concrete manifestation of it can take place in the experience of your patient until you specifically designate that it is taking place.

Know that your patient is receptive to the influx of ideas. Feel that he is now the object of every infinite solicitation, that friends are impelled toward him, that he is compelled to recognize them, and that his talents are appreciated and he is adequately compensated.

Free every belief about him which he has brought to you. Ask him why he thinks he is not getting along better and then deny every negation which he affirms, immediately affirming its direct opposite. Handle the case specifically and definitely; formulate your statements in such a way that if the words were actual things and immediately formed before you, the form which they would take would be desirable.

Spiritual Mind Healing

Office of the Dean

My Dear Friend,

Alcoholism is one of the great problems of our day. The article on Alcoholism in this lesson views the problem as an emotional one and shows how we would handle it in the Science of Mind.

So far, Alcoholics Anonymous has handled the problem better than most anyone else. They all have been alcoholics; therefore they know how an alcoholic feels. They start with the simple proposition that there are but three things that can happen to an alcoholic: he will become mentally unbalanced, die of the disease, or be healed.

Their first step is to recognize this, and then come to realize that there is a Power greater than they are. They have added a significant thought to their concept of God which is that everyone must find God in his own way. This certainly would be true according to our philosophy of life, which is that everyone is an individualized center in the consciousness of God, and of course no one can approach the Ultimate Reality other than through his own consciousness.

In dealing with alcoholics, then, if you follow these simple rules in helping people to meet God in their own way, being sure that they do believe in something greater than themselves, and then treat them, I am certain you will be successful in helping them.

Alcoholism is the result of two things: an emotional sense of insecurity and the desire to escape from it, and the fact that certain people are allergic to the habit because of the chemistry of their bodies. Therefore Alcoholics Anonymous claims, and we believe rightly, that the addict who wishes to be free from the habit must completely abstain from now on.

Sincerely,
Ernest Holmes

Lesson 24

Page 177 through page 180 *

Spiritual mind healing is a process of thought by which an individual consciously directs the Law of Mind.] *
As a result of such direction a definite physical reaction takes place either in his own body, in his objective environment (circumstances), or in the body or the objective environment of someone else. In spiritual mind healing the practitioner entertains thoughts and ideas within his own mind for the definite purpose of helping others, whether it be changing their environment or working for betterment in their physical condition.

It follows that since this whole process is one of thought, the theory upon which this science is based is an understanding that we are surrounded by a universal medium of Mind which reacts to our thought in accordance with exact and mathematical law. Not only is this the theory back of spiritual mind healing and demonstration, but it is also the most plausible theory back of any and all belief in faith or prayer as effective means to definite ends.

We must become accustomed to the thought that as practitioners we are using a Power which we do not create nor coerce; we only use It. Power is before we use It, and until we learn how to use It consciously It may present Itself to us in a chaotic form, as disease, discord, or unhappiness. But this same Power brought under the control of conscious thought, when such thought is poised, harmonious, and peaceful, will produce harmony and peace instead of discord. We never deal with two powers. We always deal with One Power which may be employed in two different ways.

There is a difference between believing that we are dealing with two powers, and knowing we are dealing with but one. Read again the definitions of *Duality* on page 587 and of *Unity* on page 640. The spiritual practitioner is conscious that the ultimate of all form is one Universal Stuff existing in one unified Medium which is intelligent. This Intelligence is responsive to thought.

The practitioner starts with the assumption that man is a spiritual entity in a perfect Universe. He is unaware of the Truth about himself, but since his thought is creative, through ignorance of the nature of the Law he creates bondage and experiences it until he becomes aware of the creative power of thought. There can be no God who cares for one more than for another or prefers one cause to another. The Universe, as Law, reacts to each through a law of reflection or correspondence, which means that the subjective world around us reacts to the images of our thoughts exactly as we think them. Read again the definition of *Equivalent* on page 589 and the central section of page 500, *The Law Is No Respecter of Persons.*

The Law responds by corresponding, not capriciously but as cause and effect—immutable, invariable, and inevitable. Yet changeless as is the Law of Cause and Effect, when we change our position in It, Its reaction to us is instantly reversed to meet our new position. If you will turn to page 466, *God Does Not Condemn*, you will see that this is the lesson Jesus was teaching when he told the story of the return of the Prodigal Son. The Father, whom Jesus is depicting, turns to the son as the son turns to Him; that is, the attitude of the Law corresponds with our attitude to It.

When we change our attitude the response is different, but the Law of Cause and Effect cannot change. The only thing that changes is the form. Read again the definition of *Form* on page 594, the definition of *Space* on page 633, and study the definition of *Time* on page 638. You will at once see that time, space, and form are conditioned by our consciousness of them, and that our consciousness of life is the starting point for our use of Universal Power.

Study the definition of *Universal Power* on page 641. Everyone has access to all of this Power, which is the ultimate of all causation. Examine the definition of *Ultimate* as used in our studies on page 639 and you will discover that both Cause and Effect are Spirit, and that in the Ultimate there is no evil for God is all there is.

What we now need to do is reverse our position in Spirit. In so doing we do not introduce any supernatural power (read the definition of *Supernatural* on page 635) for there are no supernatural powers, but when we reverse our position in Mind, then Mind reacting as Law at once reverses Its position in relation to us. This reversion is not conscious as far as the Law is concerned, but automatic.

Our knowledge of this truth becomes our savior. (See the definition of *Savior* on page 631). Each has a savior within himself because each may decide whether he will meditate upon lack, want, fear, unhappiness, disease, and death, or whether his thoughts will be independent of existing conditions. This is to judge not according to appearances but righteously, for while any created thing is real it is never a thing in itself, nor a law unto itself. (Read again the definition of *Law* on page 605 and refer to Lesson 7).

Spiritual mind practice is based on the theory that the Universe in which we live is already perfect, that man is necessarily some part of this perfection, that he is on the pathway of self-discovery, and that because he is an individual he must awake to his true relationship with Reality, for a constructive program is never imposed upon him. The process is one of awakening to what man already is, the ignorance of which has caused the Principle of Freedom to appear in his experience as bondage. One of the greatest truths we can ever realize is that the power which binds us is the only power that can free us, for there are not two powers, but only one.

We do not say that people are not sick, poor, or unhappy. What we do say is that sickness, poverty, and unhappiness are negative uses of the Truth; that they may be converted into wholeness, harmony, and joy by a reversal of our use of the Law. From this viewpoint sickness is not a spiritual reality nor is it an entity of itself. It is, however, a real enough condition to those who experience it, and it is not at all necessary for us to deny this experience. What is necessary is that we affirm that it need not be. On page 454 under the heading, *Who Would Save His Life Shall Lose It*, we find that we need not give up anything that is real in order to understand the Truth. We need to lose the sense of living apart from life, and realize that we are immersed in the Infinite Godhead which is perfect.

We are powerful only as we unify with this power in our own consciousness. It was never meant that we should give up pleasures or any human benefits or privileges, provided such pleasures and privileges are constructive. What we need to give up is the negative use of the Law. We must surrender the idea of isolation and accept our unity with Good, our oneness with the Whole. This is done by making definite statements, arriving at definite mental conclusions, coming to a realization of the indwelling God as the Reality of our own lives.

Turn to page 366, the bottom paragraph, and read through the Meditation in blank verse on page 367. There you will find a discussion of the attitude which Jesus seems to have taken toward the Universe, followed by a Meditation for the purpose of arriving at the same conclusion. Turn also to page 343, the second and third paragraphs, for an explanation of Illumination, which is the result of conscious communion with the Universal Spirit. God is not external but indwelling. The Kingdom of Heaven is in our own consciousness.

More and more we should seek to realize the Divine Reality which already is inwardly present. Say: "There is One Life, that Life is God, that Life is my life *now*." It is not enough to state that there is One Life, or even to add that this Life is God. This statement is complete as a treatment only when we add:

"This Life is my life now." We must consciously recognize our unity with the Universal Life while at the same time realizing our authority in directing the Law. The Law of Itself, having no purpose to execute, must operate upon the images of our thought as we think them. To an enlightened soul there is neither condemnation nor salvation external to his own thought. (Read the first paragraph on page 420 under the heading of General Summary.)

When we come into this world, as our textbook states, we bring with us an accumulation of race suggestion. We are largely the sum total of what all people have believed. Read the definitions of *Race Suggestion* and *Race Thought* on page 624. An understanding of this will help us to realize that we need not consciously think negation in order to experience it. The sum total of race belief dominates most men's subconscious selves at all times and controls their destiny. To rise above race suggestion is to find salvation. We are mesmerized by the race consciousness until we consciously extricate ourselves from it.

Turn to the Meditation on page 526, *The Seal of Approval*, and to the last Meditation on page 516. They provide excellent examples of how one works definitely to free oneself from the mesmeric spell of race belief, which includes inherited tendencies, prenatal conditions, and the belief in previous births and deaths. One works, when necessary, to know that neither stars, dates, numbers, horoscopes, nor any other related practices have power over the Spirit, and that man can be freed from the hypnotic spell of all these negations. We must therefore immediately free ourselves, and using the dynamic power of our spiritual affirmations dissolve the condemnation of human thought, for *if God be for us, who can be against us?*

Turn to the Meditations on page 537, *Command My Soul,* and *Despair Gives Way to Joy*. Read these words thoughtfully and meditate on their meaning until you feel something loosen within you, something very definitely let go, and you know that the sense of evil and condemnation is actually leaving you. Thus we find that prayer is its own answer according to the immutable Principle of Cause and Effect.

One should have faith in oneself and in what one is doing. The spiritual practitioner is a person who uses his spiritual faith for definite purposes, working in the silence of his own thought for the redemption or freedom from bondage of the one whom he seeks to help. His work is done through the medium of the One Mind. He sets the subjective Law in motion, basing his thought upon his belief in the Unity of Good and the Perfection of Being. The more spiritual the thought of the practitioner, in the true sense of spirituality—which means harmonious and whole—the more power his treatment will have.

As stated at the bottom of page 178, absent and present treatments are identical, as far as the practitioner is concerned. There can be no absent in the One Divine Presence. Hence the practitioner knows the Truth in his own mind, which means knowing It within and upon the One Principle. Because this Principle works both creatively and mathematically It must respond in accordance with the directions which the practitioner gives It. In giving these directions he does not assume an attitude of commanding some reluctant power; he merely seeks to realize the Truth within himself. That is his command; that which follows is automatic, or reacts in accord with Law.

If you were treating someone at a physical distance you would act exactly as if your patient were in the room with you. Since you never try to speak *to* him personally but always to yourself *about* him, it is evident that an absent treatment and a present treatment are given in the same manner. If you will turn to page 408, the last two paragraphs, including the paragraph at the top of page 409, you will see that the practitioner deals with the spiritual man and not with a sick body. The first man to be healed is the practitioner. This is one of the most difficult things to understand and yet it is of the utmost simplicity. It becomes clear to us the moment we perceive the principle of unity involved.

As explained in the second paragraph on page 179 of our text, *There is no personal responsibility in healing*. Our responsibility lies in approaching the Spirit within us through an affirmative attitude of self-recognition. (Read the whole of page 447). The practitioner directs the power but he does not hold any thought over it; he believes something into it which is quite different from holding thoughts. He looses thought, and never tries to influence anyone.

Since there is no coercion, compulsion, nor strain in a mental treatment, right spiritual mind healing should not tire anyone, but rather it should refresh him. If you find yourself becoming strained over mental work you should recognize that you have been using will power rather than the Principle of Mind, you have been using coercion rather than consciousness, you have been trying to compel rather than to acquiesce. Well did Jesus say, *Agree with thine adversary quickly*. This we must learn to do. We must learn to believe. We should have the childlike faith to which Jesus referred when he said that *wisdom is justified of her children* (page 442).

Personal magnetism has nothing to do with spiritual mind healing, which is neither hypnotic nor magnetic. It deals with personality only in so far as one person realizes the Divine Presence in another and states that this Divine Presence is functioning harmoniously and that the Law of Wholeness is made manifest.

In making this statement he may deny certain conditions which exist, while he affirms that the desired condition is ever-present in the experience of the one for whom he is working. This has nothing to do with either physical magnetism or mental mesmerism; neither does it come under the head of hypnotic suggestion. It is entirely a process of self-realization in the mind of the practitioner, with the definite intention that this self-realization, or the statements which he makes to himself, shall be immediately and permanently effective for his patient.

Healing, according to our text, is more of a revelation than it is a process. By revelation, as defined on page 630, we mean becoming consciously aware of the hidden Reality. The Gift of God is made but we must accept it. As far as we are concerned it is not made until we do accept it. The process of healing is the time and thought it takes to become mentally aware of this and to let go of the false and accept the true.

When you give treatments you are making definite statements in your own thought, and clearing up points in your own mind for someone else or for yourself. Therefore anyone who believes he can use this Principle can do so. It is not merely snapping one's mental fingers; it is a definite mental process producing a definite mental recognition. In doing this the treatment theoretically resolves disease into thought and changes the thought about the disease, the lack, or the limitation. This is what a spiritual mind practitioner does. He seeks to find the spiritual equivalent of good which is greater than the belief in lack, which has produced the wrong condition.

Suppose one lacks proper physical circulation. The practitioner seeks to realize mentally that since Spirit circulates everywhere It circulates through the body of his patient. Thus he provides a spiritual equivalent of circulation which produces a faith or belief in circulation greater than the mental acceptance which denies it. In healing hate he must provide an equivalent of love, a mental and spiritual concept of love greater than the thought of hate.

You will find in your practice that this will work out quite naturally and normally as you go along. You will learn by doing, which in the last analysis is the only way any of us can learn. Your work should always tend to produce mental evidence of the spiritual perfection of your patient, the ever-availability of Good, the omnipotence of Law. With this there should come a growing and an abiding faith in your ability to use this Law.

Summary

The technique of spiritual mind healing is a process of thought, which stated in its simplest terms denies everything that ought not to be and affirms everything which ought to be. This technique is based on the theory that thoughts are creative because they operate in a Universal field of creativity which acts upon them.

The practitioner identifies his treatment with the person, place, condition, or thing he wishes to help, and because there is but one Mind Principle it reaches that person, place, condition, or thing.

We change the thought conditions but of course we do not change the Principle. We reverse our position in It.

We do not deny that people are sick, unhappy, or in unfortunate circumstances, for if they were not why would we be seeking to help them? What we do is affirm that wrong conditions can be changed, that good can overcome evil, love can dissipate hate, and peace rout confusion, while a consciousness of abundance will heal impoverishment.

The practitioner learns by experience. There are only certain things that can be taught him. The rest he must learn through applying the Principle to everyday needs.

In a certain sense everyone is hypnotized from the cradle to the grave, since the whole race consciousness operates in and through all people. To become freed from the race consciousness and to think back to God and consciously unite ourselves with pure Spirit is to be made whole.

Questions

Brief answers to these questions should be written out by the student after studying the lesson, and the answers compared with those which will be included in next week's lesson.

1. What is the process of spiritual mind healing?

2. What is the theory upon which the technique of spiritual mind healing is based?
3. Does the theory upon which the technique of spiritual mind healing is based also apply to prayer and faith?
4. Do we create or coerce the power of mind?
5. Does the fact that disease, discord, and unhappiness exist in human experience imply two ultimate powers?
6. How is it possible for an ignorant use of the Law of Freedom to create bondage?
7. If, in ignorance of the Law, our thought has produced bondage, how can we use this same Law to produce freedom?
8. In spiritual mind healing, what is meant by righteous judgment?
9. Do we deny that there is sickness, unhappiness, or poverty in the world?
10. In using the realization, *There is one Life, that Life is God*, why should we add, *That Life is my life now*?
11. What do we mean by race suggestion?
12. In what way does race suggestion affect us?
13. Is race belief necessarily evil or limiting?
14. What should be one's attitude toward race belief, carnal mind, karma, and the collective unconscious?
15. Why do we say that the more spiritual the thought, the more power it has?
16. In what way does spiritual thought differ from other thought?
17. What do we mean by saying that the Principle of Mind works creatively and mathematically?
18. What do we mean when we say that when we command, that which follows is automatic?
19. Explain the statement, *The first man to be healed is the practitioner*.
20. What would cause a practitioner to feel strain or fatigue in mental treatment?
21. Is spiritual mind healing magnetic, hypnotic, or mental suggestion?
22. How would one treat for proper physical circulation?

Answers to Questions on Lesson 23

1. When we say that the correct conclusion rather than the argument makes a treatment effective, we mean that it is the state of spiritual conviction which the mental argument produces that gives the treatment power.
2. It is possible to produce results without first arriving at an exalted state of spiritual realization, because any series of statements made in Mind and believed in will produce results.
3. By mental procedure in treatment being definite and conscious, we mean that when a person gives a treatment he is deliberately, specifically, and consciously using the Law of Mind for a definite purpose.
4. The office of the will in mental treatment is solely one of decision and direction.
5. The unifying mental action between a practitioner and his patient is: first, complete acceptance in the thought of the practitioner; and second, an equal acceptance, either consciously or unconsciously, in the thought of the patient.

6. We do not know just how the realization of the practitioner's thought rises into expression in his patient's experience; but we assume that it does so in mental law, just as water reaches its own level by its own weight in physical law.
7. We shall keep our thought free from that which contradicts the Truth of our being: first, by realizing what the Truth of our being is; next, by contradicting anything which opposes it; and finally, by affirming the presence of Good and of right action.
8. The steps Jesus used in demonstrating the Truth were realization, recognition of power; consciousness of unity; speaking with authority.
9. Passive mental activity does not mean mental inaction. It means mental activity of pure acceptance, free from confusion and resistance.
10. The fundamental supposition in the philosophy of Jesus was that all power was delivered unto him.
11. Our mental work should be based upon the premise of the power of Spirit, Its willingness to respond, and the necessity of the Law corresponding.
12. The mental practitioner takes for granted that the Law will work, believes that It is working, and believes in his own statement.
13. A demonstration is made when the word takes objective form.
14. The limit of our ability to demonstrate lies not in Principle but in our mental embodiment of our ideas. This embodiment can be increased.
15. Thought must transcend the condition it wishes to change, else it will be bound by the same mental images which produced the condition.
16. We say that treatment is independent of any situation or circumstance because mental treatment deals with the Power which is the cause of all situations and circumstances.
17. By *the* Absolute we mean unconditioned Spirit, Law, Cause. By *our* relative we mean our use of the Absolute, which constitutes our mental and physical experience.
18. By conscious belief becoming a subjective embodiment we mean that ideas entertained by the conscious mind must be subconsciously received and embodied before they can automatically externalize.
19. Our subjective state of thought is the automatic medium between the Absolute and our relative, because it is the center from which our habitual thought patterns continuously radiate.

Alcoholism

As An Escape Mechanism from the Viewpoint of Science of Mind

This discussion of alcoholism has been written especially for those whose addiction is a definite escape mechanism. While this class of addicts is in the majority, it is also recognized that there are many emotional reasons for alcoholism.

Alcoholic addiction, to a great extent, is the result of an emotional unbalance following an individual's inability to meet the situations that arise in his personal experience. This is largely unconscious; it is subjective, hidden, and therefore unknown to the conscious faculties.

When this maladjustment reaches a point where a person becomes an alcoholic, it is evident that in an unconscious manner he is seeking self-destruction. His attempt to avoid the realities of everyday life has reached a point where delusion alone compensates for that which he desires to become or to attain.

We all are familiar with the type of person who throws his finest opportunity to the wind and seeks oblivion through the loss of consciousness. The desire to lose oneself, even to destroy oneself, becomes stronger than the assurance that one can meet and handle any situation that arises.

This does not mean that everyone who drinks is seeking self-destruction. We are talking about those who become submerged in the habit, and unfortunately all too many drinkers are of this type.

In such cases the habit itself is not the real disease. It is an unconscious attempt to escape from the real disease. The disease itself is some inner emotional state of which the patient generally is not aware but from which he *unconsciously* shrinks. He is impelled to seek escape through the act of self-forgetting or self-destruction. If this is the case it follows that the habit will be healed only when its cause is destroyed. It is not alcoholism as though it were a thing in itself that should be attacked, but the hidden cause back of the addiction that needs to be eradicated.

If a cure is to become real and lasting it will be accomplished only by uprooting those hidden subjective causes which lie back of the actual disease; the elimination of unconscious frustrations, whether they occurred in early youth or in later life. Addiction is an unconscious attempt either to express what is felt but not consciously known—to escape from some subjective frustration—or by self-destruction to reach an imaginary oblivion.

This requires mental surgery, an expression which a few years ago might have caused amusement but which today is quite familiar among psychologists as well as mental and spiritual practitioners. Indeed, mental surgery is a reality in many cases, and the things that may be operated on mentally with hope of success outnumber those that may be operated upon physically with the same expectation.

The alcoholic is not necessarily a mental, spiritual, or moral weakling. Many of the best minds have experienced the flight into delusion, an unconscious attempt to escape from the real disease which is hidden.

Of course there are other causes for certain forms of alcoholism: the habit of the "pick me up," the bracer after a hard day's work; the social habit of the too occasional cocktail; the environment of childhood; the tendency to conform to the behavior of associates. Unfortunately there are those who think that to be a good drinker is to be manly and virile. Nothing can be further from the truth. Often virility lies in abstinence rather than in indulgence.

It is because the reasons for inebriety may be legion that one finds difficulty in uncovering them; perhaps a frustration in childhood, perhaps a faulty environment, possibly the result of a social habit, neglect and loneliness in childhood, a too indulgent father or mother, an immature attitude—but in most cases of alcoholism some subtle inferiority complex is indicated.

Such flights into the unconscious may be an attempt to turn back the stream of life into channels where there is no longer any self-discipline or self-restraint. The lack of self-confidence causes the person to feel that he must have release from the real issues and problems of living. Thus we see that the cause of much alcoholism is a seed of desire planted in the garden of emotional unfulfillment. It follows that to remove this inner conflict is to remove its objective effect. And what is this but a healing of the mind?

In psychology this is accomplished by bringing the compulsion to the surface to be self-seen and thereby dissipated. This is the mental surgery of psychology; the analysis of the soul, the taking apart and the reassembling of the psyche. The afflicted person has lost conscious command of himself. His mental faculties have weakened. His physical, mental, emotional and spiritual faculties are no longer in proper balance. He is unstable and can no longer meet the everyday issues of life.

In turning from reality the sufferer seeks the unreality of illusion. He temporarily feels himself supreme, the master of his destiny through fantasy rather than accomplishment. He is the make-believe person, the overgrown child impersonating his desires through a world of delusion. But in trying to express himself he is never himself.

The form which any individual habit takes is naturally conditioned by the temperament of the one seeking self-expression. There is really no single type of drinker. The cause of over-indulgence depends largely on the conditions surrounding the one who is afflicted, and as we are all individuals the cause must be handled in such a manner as to meet the individual need. This problem is always individual, as are all other problems.

The general theory underlying all such causes is that behind any habit where one seeks escape from reality—that is, from the normal contact with everyday life and its problems—there is a lack of true self-confidence; a dearth of self-realization; a lack of emotional balance.

This is shown by the fact that in nearly all such cases the patient is penitent, remorseful, discouraged, unhappy, nervous, irritable, dodges responsibility, and is filled with self-condemnation. He feels himself no good, not worthwhile; he is desperate, and as soon as possible must escape again into his dream world—into his world of illusion where he reigns supreme in his own imagination. He is now king, creator, conqueror, the master of his own destiny. He feels confident, happy, and temporarily self-sufficient. But he is soon deprived of his fleeting dream; the vision vanishes and the hard facts of reality again confront him.

After each flight into illusion he is less able to cope with the world of reality. More and more frequently he seeks his dream world, and finally he will do anything in his power to accomplish his purpose, which is to escape into a wilderness of self-deception.

And what of the cure, for cure there must be to every human ill?

The patient must be given back to himself. There are two methods through which this giving-back process may be accomplished. One way is in the field of psychiatry, unrelated to spiritual values but none the less scientific. The patient is helped to see for himself where the real cause of his trouble lies. He must start with a sincere desire to be healed; he must wish to be rid of his habit.

The object of the treatment is to give the patient back to himself, and in the new life which he is to vision, alcohol plays no part. The subtle cause of the habit which lies deep in the unconscious is to be uncovered and self-seen. This calls for the most complete cooperation between patient and psychiatrist.

The psychiatrist is understanding, patient, and gentle, but he remorselessly probes into the lower streams of consciousness until he uncovers the cause of the disease. Such a process is long and expensive. It is reasonable to suppose that for the average individual such treatment is out of the question.

What, then, is to become of the majority of cases who are unable to avail themselves of what is certainly a scientific and a most effective form of treatment?

In spiritual science we believe that there is a Mind Principle which is ever present. It is responsive to all demands made upon it, responding alike to all. The knowledge that this power of Mind is a reign of law available for all purposes is a dividing line between superstition and fear, and science and intelligence.

We believe that the issues of life are from within and not from without. The most powerful forces operating in and through man are invisible. This is why emotion has such power; why imagination takes form and becomes objectified in experience.

Now the only way that spiritual forces can operate for us is through the avenues of thought action. This is why thought action is creative, actually molding conditions from invisible but real causes. The world of causes is in Mind and Spirit; the world of effects is in conditions and things. Since the Spirit is never evil it follows that it is the use we make of the Life Principle which decides whether or not our lives shall be destructive or constructive.

The emotional craving for self-expression is not evil, and any belief that we must remove all desire before we can become spiritual is just so much nonsense. If we could remove all desire for self-expression we should no longer exist. An attempt to remove all desire is an unconscious impulsion toward self-oblivion which arises from a maladjustment to life.

All outward self-expression is the product of thought, whether or not the thought be conscious, for unconscious thought is thought action just as truly as is conscious thought.

Mental and emotional experiences are activities of the intelligence that is within us. The multiplication of ideas or the subtraction of ideas from the mental are actual activities. Where there are a given number of thought impulses there will be a corresponding physical reaction. Wherever there is a different arrangement of thought there will be a corresponding and a new reaction to life and to living. This is the secret of the cleansing process of thought which takes place as undesirable thought impulses are removed and transmuted or sublimated into other channels.

The mental and spiritual practitioner recognizes that the seat of the trouble lies in the unconscious realm of desire and unfulfillment. He knows that people actually hunger and thirst after self-expression. He also knows that when people hunger and thirst after righteousness (a constructive mode of living) they shall be filled.

In spiritual mind healing it is unnecessary for the practitioner or the patient to know just what caused the trouble. Wisdom, strength, courage, and all harmonious conditions are the direct result of spiritual power with which man is already equipped. All power is from within, and as the deep within of the patient is awakened, weakness, fear, and failure disappear. Loss is converted into gain and weakness into strength. The remedy for weakness is to develop power. Perfect love casts out fear, and joy transmutes sadness into song.

Faith, through imagination, has the power to heal. It can transmute depression into gladness. It can sublimate the energy of wrong emotional desire into constructive channels. Faith stirs at the roots of man's spiritual nature and quickens the flesh with its life-giving message of love.

The metaphysician recognizes the value of faith as a healing and a regenerating power for good. But faith must be in something deeper than the material self. The patient must come to feel himself rooted in the Infinite.

The success of the treatment depends upon the patient seeing for himself that his fears are ungrounded, for just as Truth known becomes demonstrated, so fear seen and understood vanishes.

Metaphysical or spiritual mind healing is based on the assumption that we live in a spiritual Universe *now*; that we are spiritual beings *now*; that the Kingdom of Heaven is at hand *now*; that spiritual man is perfect *now*; that the Mind of God and the Energy of the Universe are available *now*.

The field of metaphysics deals with a Universal Wholeness more than does the field of psychology. Nor need this seem less scientific, for anything is scientific that produces results through known and demonstrable laws. The Science of Mind is just as valid a science as is psychiatry. Indeed it is psychiatry plus, for without denying the known laws of psychiatry it becomes an extension of that field. It adds the Universal to the individual.

It proclaims the spiritual nature of man, and it removes fear by introducing love. It places man in the Mind of God as some part of the Eternal Wholeness, gives shelter to the soul, satisfies the natural hunger of the intellect for the larger life. It surrenders indecision for Divine guidance; for human fear it gives spiritual faith. This, psychiatry has not done, for while psychiatric practice may empty the subjective of its false impulses and desires, with what shall it refill this psychic void? This is its weakness.

If alcoholic addiction is an unconscious attempt at self-destruction; if it is a flight of fancy into oblivion, what would happen if the individual were to understand that there is no possible oblivion? What if he were to understand that the soul must be some part of God, sufficient unto itself in the great whole? If man is to be made whole in his own imagination, how will the desired result be obtained unless his wholeness is linked with a Cosmic Wholeness of which it is a part?

There seems no possible escape, and the newer psychology will have to wed itself to some form of religious emotion; not to any particular theology, not to superstition nor to a fear of God, but to a real fellowship with the Invisible. We come out of the Invisible. We live on, in, and by It. How can we be separated from It?

The metaphysician or the spiritual mind practitioner starts with the assumption that God is in all, over all, and through all. The impulse to express God is the very desire that lies back of the emotional craving for self-expression. It is the natural and inevitable necessity that the Spirit be expressed through us.

If alcoholics seek self-destruction through oblivion it is because they have not been acquainted with themselves or the true relationship to the Universe in which they live. They have not known that there is an inner completeness, a spiritual wholeness to their real natures. Surely it would not be amiss to tell them.

Why not allow the imagination to enter into the larger life, not through any flight of fancy but through a deep, inner conviction of man's spiritual nature? Spiritual experience is just as valid as any other experience. It need not be accompanied by any particular outward form of religious worship; no dogma has to attend it. All forms of superstition should be avoided, for superstition itself is a flight of the imagination into a world of fantasy.

But just what would a spiritual re-education of the mind mean? It would mean first of all the removal of fear. Of what is man afraid? He is afraid of the universe in which he lives; he is afraid of what happens to him in this universe. He is afraid of pain, suffering, misunderstanding, of social and economic insecurity. He is hurt by his contacts with life. It matters not whether this fear started when he first entered a cold world, or whether it is a result of some form of frustration early in life . . . it is always *fear*.

There are a thousand and one forms of fear. Fear may be old or just beginning, but it is always a feeling of some form of insecurity. Why not educate the mind into an understanding that the Divine Plan is perfect and that good must come, at last, alike to all?

This has been the power of all religions. They may have been crude, superstitious, and uncouth in many respects, but at least they have been effective. Regeneration, transmutation, and sublimation through faith have been a reality in the experience of countless thousands throughout the ages. Nor has the human mind so far found any other power of sublimation that can equal faith and a constructive spiritual program. Why not make use of the highest and best in human experience? Why discard that which has proved effective wherever it has been used?

What is God but Intelligent Life running through everything, sustaining and animating everything? The very imagination through which man seeks his flight of fantasy could as easily have been directed into constructive channels for self-expression. Emerson felt the presence of the Invisible peopling the lonely places with life, warmth, and beauty. This is not a flight of fancy from Reality, but the shadow of a rock in a weary place.

Where love is, fear cannot linger, for love dissipates the anguish of fear as light neutralizes the darkness. The human sense of aloneness becomes submerged in the larger vision of an overshadowing Presence. Who could think that Jesus was laboring under a delusion when he stated that the Kingdom of Heaven is within?

To train one's mind to believe in this inner Kingdom is not illusion but the very essence of Reality. And as the analyst carefully replaces fear with confidence in giving his patient back to himself, why not add the larger self, the greater hope, the deeper realization—the realization of the Self as an indestructible part of the Cosmos? Why not link this spiritual realization with the most trivial everyday occurrences, for the eternal day in which man is to live begins right here and now. To know of the immediate nowness of the Kingdom will produce not a flight of fancy away from reality but will have the reverse effect of causing the mind to enter into its inheritance now and here.

To feel a Presence guiding and directing will heal psychic confusion. We must come to understand that the Spirit Itself is guiding, controlling, and assisting. We must seek to link our minds with It. No psychic confusion can follow such mental action.

Just as the analyst leads his patient away from illusion and self-deception, so the spiritual mind practitioner must lead him into a new and better realization of his unity with the Cosmos. He points to spiritual truths which the patient must practice for himself.

Believing that there is one mind common to all individual men, the spiritual mind practitioner realizes that no matter where his patient is, he can be reached and helped. This is a process whereby he thinks within himself for his patient.

If asked to treat an alcoholic, the practitioner turns back to his premise of Perfect God, Perfect Man, Perfect Being. He fills his own consciousness with the truth about Spirit, Its completion, Its satisfaction, Its wholeness. He knows that this same Spirit is the life of his patient. He fills his own mind with the truth about the real Self of his patient; he knows that that Self is never depressed nor discouraged, that it is forever conscious of its unity with God, of its oneness with Spirit.

The practitioner uses whatever argument he finds necessary to bring his own mind to an acceptance of the truth about his patient. He mentally frees his patient from any belief that the habit of drink has any power over him. To the extent that he is able to recognize the complete freedom of his patient, this freedom will become objectified in the life of the addict.

The practitioner must have a calm, unfaltering trust in his ability to reveal the real man, and in so doing to free the physical man from the false belief. He must know that his patient is pure Spirit and is wholly satisfied within himself. The discouragement, the maladjustment, the inhibitions never existed in Spirit and can no longer appear to exist in or operate through the one whom he is healing.

Following is a suggested treatment for self-help. (If used for someone else, say “He is” instead of “I am.”)

> I know that the Spirit within me is God. I know that my life is God. I know that my mind and my imagination are filled with peace and with a sense of completeness. I am satisfied within myself.

There is nothing that I fear or that I am afraid to meet. I am not running away from anything nor am I afraid of anything. Being whole and complete within myself I need no stimulant to bolster my imagination, and I seek no escape from reality.

I am conscious of my ability to meet every situation in life with calmness and peace. There is nothing in my memory that causes me to feel uncertain or unable to cope with any situation that might arise in my experience. The belief that I need alcohol in any form is an illusion. For I do not need anything outside myself to make me happy. I am happy and fulfilled now.

Within me is that which is perfect, that which is complete, that which is divine; that which was never born and can never die; that which lives, the Eternal Reality. Within myself is peace, poise, power, wholeness, and happiness. I fear nothing. I am whole and completely satisfied within myself.

All the Power there is, all the Presence there is, and all the Life there is, is God—the Living Spirit Almighty, and this Divine and Living Spirit is within me now. It is Wholeness. It is never weary. It is Life. It is complete Peace and cannot be afraid, nor can It seek to escape from anything, for It is All.

My life is never confused. It is always peaceful and happy. I know that my Divine Self is not separated from my physical and mental self. This consciousness of Wholeness, this recognition of my true Self obliterates every belief that could cause me to wish for or desire any type of stimulant whatsoever. There is no memory of any such desire nor is there any expectation of any such desire. The truth about my real Self reveals to my mind complete freedom from any habit that could rob me of peace or of my rightful mentality.

Since there is no memory of ever having needed any false stimulant, and since there is no anticipation of ever needing to be bolstered up by anything but the Spirit, and since I know that I am Spirit, I know and realize my complete freedom now and forever.

Practical Suggestion for Mental Treatment

There Is But One Healer

The belief that we do not have the ability to heal arises out of the mistaken idea that *our* power does the healing, or that the intellect does the healing. All that the will and the intellect could do is to behold or watch the process. The mind fixes its gaze steadfastly upon the Principle and then declares that this Principle is operative in human affairs, and particularly in the affairs of the one being treated.

There is but One Healer. This is the Spirit of Truth. There is but One Life Principle. This is God in us. There is but one final Law. This is the Law of Good. There is but one ultimate Impulsion. This Impulsion is Love.

That which really does the healing can never fluctuate, can never change in Its nature. It is not more one day and less the next. It is at this moment absolutely all there is and It is ever available.

We must forever rid ourselves of the idea that it is the personal man who does the healing. We must know that it is not I *but the Father that dwelleth in me, He doeth the works*. Principle operates irrespective of personal opinion, and when through acquiescence we agree that It is operating, then It must operate.

It is not enough for the practitioner to know this or to state it as his belief, or to affirm it as a conviction. This is but the foundation upon which he builds his edifice of faith. These are the materials which he molds into the form of definite desire. He must not only know that God is all there is, but he must know that God exists right where the need is—not in the form of the need but in the form of an answer to the need.

The Divine Spirit is the only Actor, the true Savior, the All-in-All, and is now manifesting Itself. Being All-in-All, It has no opposition, competition, or otherness.

Song of the Creator

Introduction

We must not forget that there are other religions beside our own. In reading the many passages from the Bibles of the World you will have noticed the similarity running through all of them. They are but different ways of saying the same thing, which amounts to this: that God or an Original Creative Cause is all there is, all there ever was, and all there ever will be. The ancients said that that which is real has never changed, that which is unreal has never taken place.

Frequently in our Bible, particularly in the Old Testament, we find expressions similar to this: "Thus saith the Lord," or "God spake unto Moses (or some of the other prophets), saying thus and so." All religions have followed this same form and proclaimed what God has revealed to them, because revelation is the experience of someone concerning the nature of Reality which is God.

And so I am putting the following verses in this lesson, which I have called SONG OF THE CREATOR. The verses were inspired by reading Sir Edwin Arnold's translation of the *Bhagavad Gita*, called The Song Celestial.

What I want you to know is that just as our Bible says, "God spoke and said so and so" all the great inspired teachings have followed a similar method of saying "This is the way God thinks."

These verses are after the ancient Eastern method of explaining the thoughts and feelings of one who has learned to listen to the words of the Invisible.

I hope you will like them.

Song of the Creator

From sorrow, pain, disaster
This truth alone can set man free:

The self knowing, known and knower
Are ever one with Changeless Me.

It is I, the Truth Incarnate,
Light of everlasting day,
Who's supreme in every soul,
To each the life, the truth, the way.

Those who see Me as the all
Uncaught by separate desire,
Find light and flame of single life
Is lit by One Eternal Fire.

All signs are holy things to Me
When faith and love with them conspire
To bring each seeker of the way
To light of My celestial fire.

All paths of worship lead to Me,
All shrines to Me alone belong;
The hymns of praise through all the ages
Are parts of My celestial song.

I am the beginning and the end—
All that is, is one vast whole;
I am the Father and the Son;
I am—Spirit—Body—Mind and Soul.

Nature clothes My many forms
In plant and tree, in air and stone,
In iron, wood, in bird and beast,
In the sower and the sown.

Smaller than the smallest atom,
Larger than the greatest sea,
The moving force in each and all,
The pageant and the pageantry—

I am the source, the cause, the all;
Darkness of earth, light of star,
Radiance of the sun and moon;
I am here, there, close, and far.

All beings have their root in Me,
My Soul the primal cause of all—
The flowering of the seed of life,
Eternal spring, eternal fall.

I am the seed, the root, the branch,
The earth, the moon, the sun, the air;
I am present, past, and future,
I am here, there, and everywhere.

Though formless is My hidden life
I am the form of what is made;
I am the way, the truth, the life,
Substance, shadow, light, and shade.

I, the Eternal Word made flesh,
Am both namer and the name,
The creator and what's created,
The fire, the ashes, and the flame;

Splendor of light supernal,
Knower and known, wisdom of wise,
Giver, receiver, and keeper,
Heaven, hell, doom, and paradise;

Flame of uncaught cause in heaven,
Seed of what is born on earth,
Action, reaction, time, and timeless,
Infant, aged, death, and birth.

Hidden within all forms evolved,
In silence, beauty, wisdom, will,
Is that which makes the cycle move,
Unmoved, immovable, and still.

. . . Ernest Holmes

Made in United States
North Haven, CT
01 April 2023

34848837R00113